I0168765

DICTIONARY
THEME – BASED

British English Collection

ENGLISH-
NORWEGIAN

The most useful words
To expand your lexicon and sharpen
your language skills

9000 words

Theme-based dictionary British English-Norwegian - 9000 words
By Andrey Taranov

T&P Books vocabularies are intended for helping you learn, memorize and review foreign words. The dictionary is divided into themes, covering all major spheres of everyday activities, business, science, culture, etc.

The process of learning words using T&P Books' theme-based dictionaries gives you the following advantages:

- Correctly grouped source information predetermines success at subsequent stages of word memorization
- Availability of words derived from the same root allowing memorization of word units (rather than separate words)
- Small units of words facilitate the process of establishing associative links needed for consolidation of vocabulary
- Level of language knowledge can be estimated by the number of learned words

T&P Books Publishing
www.tpbooks.com

This book is also available in E-book formats.
Please visit www.tpbooks.com or the major online bookstores.

NORWEGIAN THEME-BASED DICTIONARY
British English collection

T&P Books vocabularies are intended to help you learn, memorize, and review foreign words. The vocabulary contains over 9000 commonly used words arranged thematically.

- Vocabulary contains the most commonly used words
- Recommended as an addition to any language course
- Meets the needs of beginners and advanced learners of foreign languages
- Convenient for daily use, revision sessions, and self-testing activities
- Allows you to assess your vocabulary

Special features of the vocabulary

- Words are organized according to their meaning, not alphabetically
- Words are presented in three columns to facilitate the reviewing and self-testing processes
- Words in groups are divided into small blocks to facilitate the learning process
- The vocabulary offers a convenient and simple transcription of each foreign word

The vocabulary has 256 topics including:

Basic Concepts, Numbers, Colors, Months, Seasons, Units of Measurement, Clothing & Accessories, Food & Nutrition, Restaurant, Family Members, Relatives, Character, Feelings, Emotions, Diseases, City, Town, Sightseeing, Shopping, Money, House, Home, Office, Working in the Office, Import & Export, Marketing, Job Search, Sports, Education, Computer, Internet, Tools, Nature, Countries, Nationalities and more ...

TABLE OF CONTENTS

PRONUNCIATION GUIDE

Letter	Norwegian example	T&P phonetic alphabet	English example
Aa	plass	[ɑ], [ɑ:]	bath, to pass
Bb	bøtte, albue	[b]	baby, book
Cc [1]	centimeter	[s]	city, boss
Cc [2]	Canada	[k]	clock, kiss
Dd	radius	[d]	day, doctor
Ee	rett	[e:]	longer than in bell
Ee [3]	begå	[ɛ]	man, bad
Ff	fattig	[f]	face, food
Gg [4]	golf	[g]	game, gold
Gg [5]	gyllen	[j]	yes, New York
Gg [6]	regnbue	[ŋ]	English, ring
Hh	hektar	[h]	humor
Ii	kilometer	[ı], [i]	tin, see
Kk	konge	[k]	clock, kiss
Kk [7]	kirke	[h]	humor
Jj	fjerde	[j]	yes, New York
kj	bikkje	[h]	humor
Ll	halvår	[l]	lace, people
Mm	middag	[m]	magic, milk
Nn	november	[n]	name, normal
ng	langt	[ŋ]	English, ring
Oo [8]	honning	[ɔ]	bottle, doctor
Oo [9]	fot, krone	[u]	book
Pp	plomme	[p]	pencil, private
Qq	sequoia	[k]	clock, kiss
Rr	sverge	[r]	rice, radio
Ss	appelsin	[s]	city, boss
sk [10]	skikk, skyte	[ʃ]	machine, shark
Tt	stør, torsk	[t]	tourist, trip
Uu	brudd	[y]	fuel, tuna
Vv	kraftverk	[v]	very, river
Ww	webside	[v]	very, river
Xx	mexicaner	[ks]	box, taxi
Yy	nytte	[ı], [i]	tin, see
Zz [11]	New Zealand	[s]	star, cats
Ææ	vær, stær	[æ]	chess, man
Øø	ørn, gjø	[ø]	eternal, church
Åå	gås, værhår	[o:]	fall, bomb

Comments

[1] before **e, i**
[2] elsewhere
[3] unstressed
[4] before **a, o, u, å**
[5] before **i** and **y**
[6] in combination **gn**
[7] before **i** and **y**
[8] before two consonants
[9] before one consonant
[10] before **i** and **y**
[11] in loanwords only

ABBREVIATIONS
used in the dictionary

English abbreviations

ab.	-	about
adj	-	adjective
adv	-	adverb
anim.	-	animate
as adj	-	attributive noun used as adjective
e.g.	-	for example
etc.	-	et cetera
fam.	-	familiar
fem.	-	feminine
form.	-	formal
inanim.	-	inanimate
masc.	-	masculine
math	-	mathematics
mil.	-	military
n	-	noun
pl	-	plural
pron.	-	pronoun
sb	-	somebody
sing.	-	singular
sth	-	something
v aux	-	auxiliary verb
vi	-	intransitive verb
vi, vt	-	intransitive, transitive verb
vt	-	transitive verb

Norwegian abbreviations

f	-	feminine noun
f pl	-	feminine plural
m	-	masculine noun
m pl	-	masculine plural
m/f	-	masculine, feminine
m/f pl	-	masculine/feminine plural
m/f/n	-	masculine/feminine/neuter
m/n	-	masculine, neuter
n	-	neuter
n pl	-	neuter plural
pl	-	plural

BASIC CONCEPTS

Basic concepts. Part 1

1. Pronouns

I, me	jeg	['jæj]
you	du	[dʉ]
he	han	['hɑn]
she	hun	['hʉn]
it	det, den	['de], ['den]
we	vi	['vi]
you (to a group)	dere	['derə]
they	de	['de]

2. Greetings. Salutations. Farewells

Hello! (fam.)	Hei!	['hæj]
Hello! (form.)	Hallo! God dag!	[hɑ'lʉ], [gʉ 'dɑ]
Good morning!	God morn!	[gʉ 'mɔ:n]
Good afternoon!	God dag!	[gʉ'dɑ]
Good evening!	God kveld!	[gʉ 'kvɛl]
to say hello	å hilse	[ɔ 'hilsə]
Hi! (hello)	Hei!	['hæj]
greeting (n)	hilsen (m)	['hilsən]
to greet (vt)	å hilse	[ɔ 'hilsə]
How are you? (form.)	Hvordan står det til?	['vʉ:dɑn sto:r de til]
How are you? (fam.)	Hvordan går det?	['vʉ:dɑn gor de]
What's new?	Hva nytt?	[vɑ 'nʏt]
Goodbye!	Ha det bra!	[hɑ de 'brɑ]
Bye!	Ha det!	[hɑ 'de]
See you soon!	Vi ses!	[vi sɛs]
Farewell!	Farvel!	[fɑr'vɛl]
to say goodbye	å si farvel	[ɔ 'si fɑr'vɛl]
Cheers!	Ha det!	[hɑ 'de]
Thank you! Cheers!	Takk!	['tɑk]
Thank you very much!	Tusen takk!	['tʉsən tɑk]
My pleasure!	Bare hyggelig	['bɑrə 'hʏgeli]
Don't mention it!	Ikke noe å takke for!	['ikə 'nʉe ɔ 'tɑkə fɔr]
It was nothing	Ingen årsak!	['iŋən 'o:ʂɑk]
Excuse me! (fam.)	Unnskyld, ...	['ʉn,ʂyl ...]
Excuse me! (form.)	Unnskyld meg, ...	['ʉn,ʂyl me ...]

to excuse (forgive)	å unnskylde	[ɔ 'ʉnˌsylə]
to apologize (vi)	å unnskylde seg	[ɔ 'ʉnˌsylə sæj]
My apologies	Jeg ber om unnskyldning	[jæj ber ɔm 'ʉnˌsyldnin]
I'm sorry!	Unnskyld!	['ʉnˌsyl]
to forgive (vt)	å tilgi	[ɔ 'tilˌji]
It's okay! (that's all right)	Ikke noe problem	['ikə 'nʉe prʉ'blem]
please (adv)	vær så snill	['vær ʂɔ 'snil]

Don't forget!	Ikke glem!	['ikə 'glem]
Certainly!	Selvfølgelig!	[sɛl'følgəli]
Of course not!	Selvfølgelig ikke!	[sɛl'følgəli 'ikə]
Okay! (I agree)	OK! Enig!	[ɔ'kɛj], ['ɛni]
That's enough!	Det er nok!	[de ær 'nɔk]

3. How to address

Excuse me, ...	Unnskyld, ...	['ʉnˌsyl ...]
mister, sir	Herr	['hær]
madam	Fru	['frʉ]
miss	Frøken	['frøkən]
young man	unge mann	['ʉnə ˌman]
young man (little boy)	guttunge	['gʉtˌʉnə]
miss (little girl)	frøken	['frøkən]

4. Cardinal numbers. Part 1

0 zero	null	['nʉl]
1 one	en	['en]
2 two	to	['tʉ]
3 three	tre	['tre]
4 four	fire	['fire]

5 five	fem	['fɛm]
6 six	seks	['sɛks]
7 seven	sju	['ʂʉ]
8 eight	åtte	['ɔtə]
9 nine	ni	['ni]

10 ten	ti	['ti]
11 eleven	elleve	['ɛlvə]
12 twelve	tolv	['tɔl]
13 thirteen	tretten	['trɛtən]
14 fourteen	fjorten	['fjɔ:tən]

15 fifteen	femten	['fɛmtən]
16 sixteen	seksten	['sæjstən]
17 seventeen	sytten	['sʏtən]
18 eighteen	atten	['atən]
19 nineteen	nitten	['nitən]

| 20 twenty | tjue | ['çʉe] |
| 21 twenty-one | tjueen | ['çʉe en] |

15

22 twenty-two	tjueto	['çʉe tʉ]
23 twenty-three	tjuetre	['çʉe tre]
30 thirty	tretti	['trɛti]
31 thirty-one	trettien	['trɛti en]
32 thirty-two	trettito	['trɛti tʉ]
33 thirty-three	trettitre	['trɛti tre]
40 forty	førti	['fœ:ʈi]
41 forty-one	førtien	['fœ:ʈi en]
42 forty-two	førtito	['fœ:ʈi tʉ]
43 forty-three	førtitre	['fœ:ʈi tre]
50 fifty	femti	['fɛmti]
51 fifty-one	femtien	['fɛmti en]
52 fifty-two	femtito	['fɛmti tʉ]
53 fifty-three	femtitre	['fɛmti tre]
60 sixty	seksti	['sɛksti]
61 sixty-one	sekstien	['sɛksti en]
62 sixty-two	sekstito	['sɛksti tʉ]
63 sixty-three	sekstitre	['sɛksti tre]
70 seventy	sytti	['sʏti]
71 seventy-one	syttien	['sʏti en]
72 seventy-two	syttito	['sʏti tʉ]
73 seventy-three	syttitre	['sʏti tre]
80 eighty	åtti	['ɔti]
81 eighty-one	åttien	['ɔti en]
82 eighty-two	åttito	['ɔti tʉ]
83 eighty-three	åttitre	['ɔti tre]
90 ninety	nitti	['niti]
91 ninety-one	nittien	['niti en]
92 ninety-two	nittito	['niti tʉ]
93 ninety-three	nittitre	['niti tre]

5. Cardinal numbers. Part 2

100 one hundred	hundre	['hʉndrə]
200 two hundred	to hundre	['tʉ ˌhʉndrə]
300 three hundred	tre hundre	['tre ˌhʉndrə]
400 four hundred	fire hundre	['fire ˌhʉndrə]
500 five hundred	fem hundre	['fɛm ˌhʉndrə]
600 six hundred	seks hundre	['sɛks ˌhʉndrə]
700 seven hundred	syv hundre	['syv ˌhʉndrə]
800 eight hundred	åtte hundre	['ɔtə ˌhʉndrə]
900 nine hundred	ni hundre	['ni ˌhʉndrə]
1000 one thousand	tusen	['tʉsən]
2000 two thousand	to tusen	['tʉ ˌtʉsən]
3000 three thousand	tre tusen	['tre ˌtʉsən]

10000 ten thousand	ti tusen	['ti ˌtʉsən]
one hundred thousand	hundre tusen	['hʉndrə ˌtʉsən]
million	million (m)	[mi'ljun]
billion	milliard (m)	[mi'lja:d]

6. Ordinal numbers

first (adj)	første	['fœ̞ʂtə]
second (adj)	annen	['anən]
third (adj)	tredje	['trɛdjə]
fourth (adj)	fjerde	['fjærə]
fifth (adj)	femte	['fɛmtə]

sixth (adj)	sjette	['ʂɛtə]
seventh (adj)	sjuende	['ʂʉenə]
eighth (adj)	åttende	['ɔtenə]
ninth (adj)	niende	['nienə]
tenth (adj)	tiende	['tienə]

7. Numbers. Fractions

fraction	brøk (m)	['brøk]
one half	en halv	[en 'hal]
one third	en tredjedel	[en 'trɛdjəˌdel]
one quarter	en fjerdedel	[en 'fjærəˌdel]

one eighth	en åttendedel	[en 'ɔtenəˌdel]
one tenth	en tiendedel	[en 'tienəˌdel]
two thirds	to tredjedeler	['tʉ 'trɛdjəˌdelər]
three quarters	tre fjerdedeler	['tre 'fjærˌdelər]

8. Numbers. Basic operations

subtraction	subtraksjon (m)	[sʉbtrak'ʂun]
to subtract (vi, vt)	å subtrahere	[ɔ 'sʉbtraˌherə]
division	divisjon (m)	[divi'ʂun]
to divide (vt)	å dividere	[ɔ divi'derə]

addition	addisjon (m)	[adi'ʂun]
to add up (vt)	å addere	[ɔ a'derə]
to add (vi)	å addere	[ɔ a'derə]
multiplication	multiplikasjon (m)	[mʉltiplika'ʂun]
to multiply (vt)	å multiplisere	[ɔ mʉltipli'serə]

9. Numbers. Miscellaneous

| digit, figure | siffer (n) | ['sifər] |
| number | tall (n) | ['tal] |

numeral	tallord (n)	['tɑlˌuːr]
minus sign	minus (n)	['minʉs]
plus sign	pluss (n)	['plʉs]
formula	formel (m)	['fɔrmǝl]

calculation	beregning (m/f)	[be'rɛjniŋ]
to count (vi, vt)	å telle	[ɔ 'tɛlǝ]
to count up	å telle opp	[ɔ 'tɛlǝ ɔp]
to compare (vt)	å sammenlikne	[ɔ 'samǝnˌliknǝ]

| How much? | Hvor mye? | [vʊr 'mye] |
| How many? | Hvor mange? | [vʊr 'maŋǝ] |

sum, total	sum (m)	['sʉm]
result	resultat (n)	[resʉl'tɑt]
remainder	rest (m)	['rɛst]

a few (e.g., ~ years ago)	noen	['nʊǝn]
few (I have ~ friends)	få, ikke mange	['fɔ], ['ikǝ ˌmaŋǝ]
a little (~ water)	lite	['litǝ]
the rest	rest (m)	['rɛst]
one and a half	halvannen	[hal'anǝn]
dozen	dusin (n)	[dʉ'sin]

in half (adv)	i 2 halvdeler	[i tʉ hal'delǝr]
equally (evenly)	jevnt	['jɛvnt]
half	halvdel (m)	['haldel]
time (three ~s)	gang (m)	['gaŋ]

10. The most important verbs. Part 1

to advise (vt)	å råde	[ɔ 'rɔːdǝ]
to agree (say yes)	å samtykke	[ɔ 'samˌtʏkǝ]
to answer (vi, vt)	å svare	[ɔ 'svarǝ]
to apologize (vi)	å unnskylde seg	[ɔ 'ʉnˌʂylǝ sæj]
to arrive (vi)	å ankomme	[ɔ 'anˌkɔmǝ]

to ask (~ oneself)	å spørre	[ɔ 'spørǝ]
to ask (~ sb to do sth)	å be	[ɔ 'be]
to be (vi)	å være	[ɔ 'værǝ]

to be afraid	å frykte	[ɔ 'frʏktǝ]
to be hungry	å være sulten	[ɔ 'værǝ 'sʉltǝn]
to be interested in ...	å interessere seg	[ɔ intǝre'serǝ sæj]
to be needed	å være behøv	[ɔ 'værǝ bǝ'høv]
to be surprised	å bli forundret	[ɔ 'bli fo'rʉndrǝt]

to be thirsty	å være tørst	[ɔ 'værǝ 'tœʂt]
to begin (vt)	å begynne	[ɔ be'jinǝ]
to belong to ...	å tilhøre ...	[ɔ 'tilˌhørǝ ...]
to boast (vi)	å prale	[ɔ 'pralǝ]
to break (split into pieces)	å bryte	[ɔ 'brytǝ]
to call (~ for help)	å tilkalle	[ɔ 'tilˌkalǝ]
can (v aux)	å kunne	[ɔ 'kʉnǝ]

to catch (vt)	å fange	[ɔ ˈfaŋə]
to change (vt)	å endre	[ɔ ˈɛndrə]
to choose (select)	å velge	[ɔ ˈvɛlgə]
to come down (the stairs)	å gå ned	[ɔ ˈgɔ ne]

to compare (vt)	å sammenlikne	[ɔ ˈsamən,liknə]
to complain (vi, vt)	å klage	[ɔ ˈklagə]
to confuse (mix up)	å forveksle	[ɔ forˈvɛkşlə]
to continue (vt)	å fortsette	[ɔ ˈfort,sɛtə]
to control (vt)	å kontrollere	[ɔ kuntrɔˈlerə]
to cook (dinner)	å lage	[ɔ ˈlagə]

to cost (vt)	å koste	[ɔ ˈkɔstə]
to count (add up)	å telle	[ɔ ˈtɛlə]
to count on ...	å regne med ...	[ɔ ˈrɛjnə me ...]
to create (vt)	å opprette	[ɔ ˈɔp,rɛtə]
to cry (weep)	å gråte	[ɔ ˈgroːtə]

11. The most important verbs. Part 2

to deceive (vi, vt)	å fuske	[ɔ ˈfʉskə]
to decorate (tree, street)	å pryde	[ɔ ˈprydə]
to defend (a country, etc.)	å forsvare	[ɔ foˈşvɑrə]
to demand (request firmly)	å kreve	[ɔ ˈkrevə]
to dig (vt)	å grave	[ɔ ˈgrɑvə]

to discuss (vt)	å diskutere	[ɔ diskʉˈterə]
to do (vt)	å gjøre	[ɔ ˈjørə]
to doubt (have doubts)	å tvile	[ɔ ˈtvilə]
to drop (let fall)	å tappe	[ɔ ˈtapə]
to enter (room, house, etc.)	å komme inn	[ɔ ˈkomə in]

to excuse (forgive)	å unnskylde	[ɔ ˈʉn,şylə]
to exist (vi)	å eksistere	[ɔ ɛksiˈsterə]
to expect (foresee)	å forutse	[ɔ ˈforʉt,se]
to explain (vt)	å forklare	[ɔ forˈklɑrə]
to fall (vi)	å falle	[ɔ ˈfalə]

to fancy (vt)	å like	[ɔ ˈlikə]
to find (vt)	å finne	[ɔ ˈfinə]
to finish (vt)	å slutte	[ɔ ˈşlʉtə]
to fly (vi)	å fly	[ɔ ˈfly]
to follow ... (come after)	å følge etter ...	[ɔ ˈfølə ˈɛtər ...]

to forget (vi, vt)	å glemme	[ɔ ˈglemə]
to forgive (vt)	å tilgi	[ɔ ˈtil,ji]
to give (vt)	å gi	[ɔ ˈji]
to give a hint	å gi et vink	[ɔ ˈji et ˈvink]
to go (on foot)	å gå	[ɔ ˈgɔ]

to go for a swim	å bade	[ɔ ˈbɑdə]
to go out (for dinner, etc.)	å gå ut	[ɔ ˈgɔ ʉt]
to guess (the answer)	å gjette	[ɔ ˈjɛtə]
to have (vt)	å ha	[ɔ ˈhɑ]

to have breakfast	å spise frokost	[ɔ 'spisə ˌfrʊkɔst]
to have dinner	å spise middag	[ɔ 'spisə 'miˌdɑ]
to have lunch	å spise lunsj	[ɔ 'spisə ˌlʉnʂ]
to hear (vt)	å høre	[ɔ 'hørə]

to help (vt)	å hjelpe	[ɔ 'jɛlpə]
to hide (vt)	å gjemme	[ɔ 'jɛmə]
to hope (vi, vt)	å håpe	[ɔ 'hoːpə]
to hunt (vi, vt)	å jage	[ɔ 'jagə]
to hurry (vi)	å skynde seg	[ɔ 'ʂynə sæj]

12. The most important verbs. Part 3

to inform (vt)	å informere	[ɔ infɔr'merə]
to insist (vi, vt)	å insistere	[ɔ insi'sterə]
to insult (vt)	å fornærme	[ɔ fɔ:'ŋærmə]
to invite (vt)	å innby, å invitere	[ɔ 'inby], [ɔ invi'terə]
to joke (vi)	å spøke	[ɔ 'spøkə]

to keep (vt)	å beholde	[ɔ be'hɔlə]
to keep silent, to hush	å tie	[ɔ 'tie]
to kill (vt)	å døde, å myrde	[ɔ 'dødə], [ɔ 'mʏːɖə]
to know (sb)	å kjenne	[ɔ 'çɛnə]
to know (sth)	å vite	[ɔ 'vitə]
to laugh (vi)	å le, å skratte	[ɔ 'le], [ɔ 'skrɑtə]

to liberate (city, etc.)	å befri	[ɔ be'fri]
to look for ... (search)	å søke ...	[ɔ 'søkə ...]
to love (sb)	å elske	[ɔ 'ɛlskə]
to make a mistake	å gjøre feil	[ɔ 'jørə ˌfæjl]
to manage, to run	å styre, å lede	[ɔ 'styrə], [ɔ 'ledə]

to mean (signify)	å bety	[ɔ 'bety]
to mention (talk about)	å omtale, å nevne	[ɔ 'ɔmˌtɑlə], [ɔ 'nɛvnə]
to miss (school, etc.)	å skulke	[ɔ 'skʉlkə]
to notice (see)	å bemerke	[ɔ be'mærkə]
to object (vi, vt)	å innvende	[ɔ 'inˌvɛnə]

to observe (see)	å observere	[ɔ ɔbsɛr'verə]
to open (vt)	å åpne	[ɔ 'ɔpnə]
to order (meal, etc.)	å bestille	[ɔ be'stilə]
to order (mil.)	å beordre	[ɔ be'ɔrdrə]
to own (possess)	å besidde, å eie	[ɔ bɛ'sidə], [ɔ 'æjə]

to participate (vi)	å delta	[ɔ 'dɛltɑ]
to pay (vi, vt)	å betale	[ɔ be'tɑlə]
to permit (vt)	å tillate	[ɔ 'tiˌlɑtə]
to plan (vt)	å planlegge	[ɔ 'plɑnˌlegə]
to play (children)	å leke	[ɔ 'lekə]

to pray (vi, vt)	å be	[ɔ 'be]
to prefer (vt)	å foretrekke	[ɔ 'fɔrəˌtrɛkə]
to promise (vt)	å love	[ɔ 'lovə]
to pronounce (vt)	å uttale	[ɔ 'ʉtˌtɑlə]

| to propose (vt) | å foreslå | [ɔ 'fɔrə‚slɔ] |
| to punish (vt) | å straffe | [ɔ 'strɑfə] |

13. The most important verbs. Part 4

to read (vi, vt)	å lese	[ɔ 'lesə]
to recommend (vt)	å anbefale	[ɔ 'ɑnbe‚fɑlə]
to refuse (vi, vt)	å vegre seg	[ɔ 'vɛgrə sæj]
to regret (be sorry)	å beklage	[ɔ be'klɑgə]
to rent (sth from sb)	å leie	[ɔ 'læjə]

to repeat (say again)	å gjenta	[ɔ 'jɛntɑ]
to reserve, to book	å reservere	[ɔ resɛr'verə]
to run (vi)	å løpe	[ɔ 'løpə]
to save (rescue)	å redde	[ɔ 'rɛdə]

to say (~ thank you)	å si	[ɔ 'si]
to scold (vt)	å skjelle	[ɔ 'ʂɛːlə]
to see (vt)	å se	[ɔ 'se]
to sell (vt)	å selge	[ɔ 'sɛlə]

to send (vt)	å sende	[ɔ 'sɛnə]
to shoot (vi)	å skyte	[ɔ 'ʂytə]
to shout (vi)	å skrike	[ɔ 'skrikə]
to show (vt)	å vise	[ɔ 'visə]
to sign (document)	å underskrive	[ɔ 'ʉnə‚skrivə]

to sit down (vi)	å sette seg	[ɔ 'sɛtə sæj]
to smile (vi)	å smile	[ɔ 'smilə]
to speak (vi, vt)	å tale	[ɔ 'tɑlə]
to steal (money, etc.)	å stjele	[ɔ 'stjelə]
to stop (for pause, etc.)	å stoppe	[ɔ 'stɔpə]

to stop (please ~ calling me)	å slutte	[ɔ 'ʂlutə]
to study (vt)	å studere	[ɔ stʉ'derə]
to swim (vi)	å svømme	[ɔ 'svœmə]
to take (vt)	å ta	[ɔ 'tɑ]
to think (vi, vt)	å tenke	[ɔ 'tɛnkə]

to threaten (vt)	å true	[ɔ 'trʉə]
to touch (with hands)	å røre	[ɔ 'rørə]
to translate (vt)	å oversette	[ɔ 'ɔve‚sɛtə]
to trust (vt)	å stole på	[ɔ 'stʉlə pɔ]
to try (attempt)	å prøve	[ɔ 'prøvə]

to turn (e.g., ~ left)	å svinge	[ɔ 'sviŋə]
to underestimate (vt)	å undervurdere	[ɔ 'ʉnərvʉː‚derə]
to understand (vt)	å forstå	[ɔ fɔ'ʂtɔ]
to unite (vt)	å forene	[ɔ fɔ'renə]
to wait (vt)	å vente	[ɔ 'vɛntə]

to want (wish, desire)	å ville	[ɔ 'vilə]
to warn (vt)	å varsle	[ɔ 'vaʂlə]
to work (vi)	å arbeide	[ɔ 'ar‚bæjdə]

to write (vt)	å skrive	[ɔ 'skrivə]
to write down	å skrive ned	[ɔ 'skrivə ne]

14. Colours

colour	farge (m)	['fɑrgə]
shade (tint)	nyanse (m)	[ny'ɑnse]
hue	fargetone (m)	['fɑrgə,tʉnə]
rainbow	regnbue (m)	['ræjn,bʉːə]

white (adj)	hvit	['vit]
black (adj)	svart	['svɑːţ]
grey (adj)	grå	['grɔ]

green (adj)	grønn	['grœn]
yellow (adj)	gul	['gʉl]
red (adj)	rød	['rø]

blue (adj)	blå	['blɔ]
light blue (adj)	lyseblå	['lysə,blɔ]
pink (adj)	rosa	['rɔsɑ]
orange (adj)	oransje	[ɔ'rɑnşɛ]
violet (adj)	fiolett	[fiʉ'lət]
brown (adj)	brun	['brʉn]

golden (adj)	gullgul	['gʉl]
silvery (adj)	sølv-	['søl-]

beige (adj)	beige	['bɛ:ş]
cream (adj)	kremfarget	['krɛm,fɑrgət]
turquoise (adj)	turkis	[tʉr'kis]
cherry red (adj)	kirsebærrød	['çişəbær,rød]
lilac (adj)	lilla	['lilɑ]
crimson (adj)	karminrød	['kɑrmʉ'sin,rød]

light (adj)	lys	['lys]
dark (adj)	mørk	['mœrk]
bright, vivid (adj)	klar	['klɑr]

coloured (pencils)	farge-	['fɑrgə-]
colour (e.g. ~ film)	farge-	['fɑrgə-]
black-and-white (adj)	svart-hvit	['svɑːţ vit]
plain (one-coloured)	ensfarget	['ɛns,fɑrgət]
multicoloured (adj)	mangefarget	['mɑŋə,fɑrgət]

15. Questions

Who?	Hvem?	['vɛm]
What?	Hva?	['vɑ]
Where? (at, in)	Hvor?	['vʉr]
Where (to)?	Hvorhen?	['vʉrhen]
From where?	Hvorfra?	['vʉrfrɑ]

When?	Når?	[nɔr]
Why? (What for?)	Hvorfor?	['vʊrfʊr]
Why? (~ are you crying?)	Hvorfor?	['vʊrfʊr]

What for?	Hvorfor?	['vʊrfʊr]
How? (in what way)	Hvordan?	['vʊːdɑn]
What? (What kind of ...?)	Hvilken?	['vilkən]
Which?	Hvilken?	['vilkən]

To whom?	Til hvem?	[til 'vɛm]
About whom?	Om hvem?	[ɔm 'vɛm]
About what?	Om hva?	[ɔm 'va]
With whom?	Med hvem?	[me 'vɛm]

How many?	Hvor mange?	[vʊr 'mɑŋə]
How much?	Hvor mye?	[vʊr 'mye]
Whose?	Hvis?	['vis]

16. Prepositions

with (accompanied by)	med	[me]
without	uten	['ʉtən]
to (indicating direction)	til	['til]
about (talking ~ ...)	om	['ɔm]
before (in time)	før	['før]
in front of ...	foran, framfor	['fɔrɑn], ['frɑmfɔr]

under (beneath, below)	under	['ʉnər]
above (over)	over	['ɔvər]
on (atop)	på	['pɔ]
from (off, out of)	fra	['frɑ]
of (made from)	av	[ɑː]

in (e.g. ~ ten minutes)	om	['ɔm]
over (across the top of)	over	['ɔvər]

17. Function words. Adverbs. Part 1

Where? (at, in)	Hvor?	['vʊr]
here (adv)	her	['hɛr]
there (adv)	der	['dɛr]

somewhere (to be)	et sted	[et 'sted]
nowhere (not in any place)	ingensteds	['iŋən,stɛts]

by (near, beside)	ved	['ve]
by the window	ved vinduet	[ve 'vindʉə]

Where (to)?	Hvorhen?	['vʊrhen]
here (e.g. come ~!)	hit	['hit]
there (e.g. to go ~)	dit	['dit]
from here (adv)	herfra	['hɛr,frɑ]

from there (adv)	derfra	['dɛr‚frɑ]
close (adv)	nær	['nær]
far (adv)	langt	['lɑŋt]

near (e.g. ~ Paris)	nær	['nær]
nearby (adv)	i nærheten	[i 'nær‚hetən]
not far (adv)	ikke langt	['ikə 'lɑŋt]

left (adj)	venstre	['vɛnstrə]
on the left	til venstre	[til 'vɛnstrə]
to the left	til venstre	[til 'vɛnstrə]

right (adj)	høyre	['højrə]
on the right	til høyre	[til 'højrə]
to the right	til høyre	[til 'højrə]

in front (adv)	foran	['fɔrɑn]
front (as adj)	fremre	['frɛmrə]
ahead (the kids ran ~)	fram	['frɑm]

behind (adv)	bakom	['bɑkɔm]
from behind	bakfra	['bɑk‚frɑ]
back (towards the rear)	tilbake	[til'bɑkə]

middle	midt (m)	['mit]
in the middle	i midten	[i 'mitən]

at the side	fra siden	[frɑ 'sidən]
everywhere (adv)	overalt	[ɔvər'alt]
around (in all directions)	rundt omkring	['rʉnt ɔm'kriŋ]

from inside	innefra	['inə‚frɑ]
somewhere (to go)	et sted	[et 'sted]
straight (directly)	rett, direkte	['rɛt], ['di'rɛktə]
back (e.g. come ~)	tilbake	[til'bɑkə]

from anywhere	et eller annet steds fra	[et 'elər ‚ɑːnt 'stɛts frɑ]
from somewhere	et eller annet steds fra	[et 'elər ‚ɑːnt 'stɛts frɑ]

firstly (adv)	for det første	[fɔr de 'fœʂtə]
secondly (adv)	for det annet	[fɔr de 'ɑːnt]
thirdly (adv)	for det tredje	[fɔr de 'trɛdje]

suddenly (adv)	plutselig	['plʉtseli]
at first (in the beginning)	i begynnelsen	[i be'jinəlsən]
for the first time	for første gang	[fɔr 'fœʂtə ‚gɑŋ]
long before ...	lenge før ...	['leŋə 'før ...]
anew (over again)	på nytt	[pɔ 'nʏt]
for good (adv)	for godt	[fɔr 'gɔt]

never (adv)	aldri	['ɑldri]
again (adv)	igjen	[i'jɛn]
now (at present)	nå	['nɔ]
often (adv)	ofte	['ɔftə]
then (adv)	da	['dɑ]
urgently (quickly)	omgående	['ɔm‚gɔːnə]

usually (adv)	vanligvis	['vɑnli‚vis]
by the way, ...	forresten, ...	[fɔ'rɛstən ...]
possibly	mulig, kanskje	['mʉli], ['kɑnʂə]
probably (adv)	sannsynligvis	[sɑn'sʏnli‚vis]
maybe (adv)	kanskje	['kɑnʂə]
besides ...	dessuten, ...	[des'ʉtən ...]
that's why ...	derfor ...	['dɛrfor ...]
in spite of ...	på tross av ...	['pɔ 'trɔs ɑ: ...]
thanks to ...	takket være ...	['tɑkət ‚værə ...]

what (pron.)	hva	['vɑ]
that (conj.)	at	[ɑt]
something	noe	['nʉe]
anything (something)	noe	['nʉe]
nothing	ingenting	['iŋəntiŋ]

who (pron.)	hvem	['vɛm]
someone	noen	['nʉən]
somebody	noen	['nʉən]

nobody	ingen	['iŋən]
nowhere (a voyage to ~)	ingensteds	['iŋən‚stɛts]
nobody's	ingens	['iŋəns]
somebody's	noens	['nʉəns]

so (I'm ~ glad)	så	['sɔ:]
also (as well)	også	['ɔsɔ]
too (as well)	også	['ɔsɔ]

18. Function words. Adverbs. Part 2

Why?	Hvorfor?	['vʉrfʉr]
for some reason	av en eller annen grunn	[ɑ: en elər 'ɑnən ‚grʉn]
because ...	fordi ‚‚‚	[fɔ'di ‚‚‚]
for some purpose	av en eller annen grunn	[ɑ: en elər 'ɑnən ‚grʉn]

and	og	['ɔ]
or	eller	['elər]
but	men	['men]
for (e.g. ~ me)	for, til	[fɔr], [til]

too (excessively)	for, altfor	['fɔr], ['altfɔr]
only (exclusively)	bare	['bɑrə]
exactly (adv)	presis, eksakt	[prɛ'sis], [ɛk'sɑkt]
about (more or less)	cirka	['sirkɑ]

approximately (adv)	omtrent	[ɔm'trɛnt]
approximate (adj)	omtrentlig	[ɔm'trɛntli]
almost (adv)	nesten	['nɛstən]
the rest	rest (m)	['rɛst]

the other (second)	den annen	[den 'ɑnən]
other (different)	andre	['ɑndrə]
each (adj)	hver	['vɛr]

any (no matter which)	hvilken som helst	['vilkən som 'hɛlst]
many, much (a lot of)	mye	['mye]
many people	mange	['maŋə]
all (everyone)	alle	['alə]

in return for ...	til gjengjeld for ...	[til 'jɛnjɛl for ...]
in exchange (adv)	istedenfor	[i'steden,for]
by hand (made)	for hånd	[for 'hon]
hardly (negative opinion)	neppe	['nepə]

probably (adv)	sannsynligvis	[san'synli,vis]
on purpose (intentionally)	med vilje	[me 'vilje]
by accident (adv)	tilfeldigvis	[til'fɛldivis]

very (adv)	meget	['megət]
for example (adv)	for eksempel	[for ɛk'sɛmpəl]
between	mellom	['mɛlom]
among	blant	['blant]
so much (such a lot)	så mye	['so: mye]
especially (adv)	særlig	['sæ:ļi]

Basic concepts. Part 2

19. Opposites

rich (adj)	rik	['rik]
poor (adj)	fattig	['fɑti]
ill, sick (adj)	syk	['syk]
well (not sick)	frisk	['frisk]
big (adj)	stor	['stʊr]
small (adj)	liten	['litən]
quickly (adv)	fort	['fʊːt]
slowly (adv)	langsomt	['lɑŋsɔmt]
fast (adj)	hurtig	['høːti]
slow (adj)	langsom	['lɑŋsɔm]
glad (adj)	glad	['glɑ]
sad (adj)	sørgmodig	[sør'mʊdi]
together (adv)	sammen	['samən]
separately (adv)	separat	[sepɑ'rat]
aloud (to read)	høyt	['højt]
silently (to oneself)	for seg selv	[fɔr sæj 'sɛl]
tall (adj)	høy	['høj]
low (adj)	lav	['lɑv]
deep (adj)	dyp	['dyp]
shallow (adj)	grunn	['grʉn]
yes	ja	['ja]
no	nei	['næj]
distant (in space)	fjern	['fjæːn]
nearby (adj)	nær	['nær]
far (adv)	langt	['lɑŋt]
nearby (adv)	i nærheten	[i 'nær‚hetən]
long (adj)	lang	['lɑŋ]
short (adj)	kort	['kʊːt]
good (kindhearted)	god	['gʊ]
evil (adj)	ond	['ʊn]

married (adj)	gift	['jift]
single (adj)	ugift	[ʉːˈjift]
to forbid (vt)	å forby	[ɔ forˈby]
to permit (vt)	å tillate	[ɔ ˈtiˌlɑtə]
end	slutt (m)	[ˈʂlʉt]
beginning	begynnelse (m)	[beˈjinəlsə]
left (adj)	venstre	[ˈvɛnstrə]
right (adj)	høyre	[ˈhøjrə]
first (adj)	første	[ˈfœʂtə]
last (adj)	sist	[ˈsist]
crime	forbrytelse (m)	[forˈbrytəlsə]
punishment	straff (m)	[ˈstrɑf]
to order (vt)	å beordre	[ɔ beˈɔrdrə]
to obey (vi, vt)	å underordne seg	[ɔ ˈʉnərˌɔrdnə sæj]
straight (adj)	rett	[ˈrɛt]
curved (adj)	kroket	[ˈkrɔkət]
paradise	paradis (n)	[ˈpɑrɑˌdis]
hell	helvete (n)	[ˈhɛlvetə]
to be born	å fødes	[ɔ ˈfødə]
to die (vi)	å dø	[ɔ ˈdø]
strong (adj)	sterk	[ˈstærk]
weak (adj)	svak	[ˈsvɑk]
old (adj)	gammel	[ˈgɑməl]
young (adj)	ung	[ˈʉŋ]
old (adj)	gammel	[ˈgɑməl]
new (adj)	ny	[ˈny]
hard (adj)	hard	[ˈhɑr]
soft (adj)	bløt	[ˈbløt]
warm (tepid)	varm	[ˈvɑrm]
cold (adj)	kald	[ˈkɑl]
fat (adj)	tykk	[ˈtʏk]
thin (adj)	tynn	[ˈtʏn]
narrow (adj)	smal	[ˈsmɑl]
wide (adj)	bred	[ˈbre]
good (adj)	bra	[ˈbrɑ]
bad (adj)	dårlig	[ˈdoː[i]
brave (adj)	tapper	[ˈtɑpər]
cowardly (adj)	feig	[ˈfæjg]

20. Weekdays

Monday	mandag (m)	['mɑnˌdɑ]
Tuesday	tirsdag (m)	['tiʂˌdɑ]
Wednesday	onsdag (m)	['ʊnsˌdɑ]
Thursday	torsdag (m)	['toʂˌdɑ]
Friday	fredag (m)	['frɛˌdɑ]
Saturday	lørdag (m)	['løɾˌdɑ]
Sunday	søndag (m)	['sønˌdɑ]

today (adv)	i dag	[i 'dɑ]
tomorrow (adv)	i morgen	[i 'mɔːən]
the day after tomorrow	i overmorgen	[i 'ɔvərˌmɔːən]
yesterday (adv)	i går	[i 'gɔr]
the day before yesterday	i forgårs	[i 'fɔrˌgɔʂ]

day	dag (m)	['dɑ]
working day	arbeidsdag (m)	['ɑrbæjdsˌdɑ]
public holiday	festdag (m)	['fɛstˌdɑ]
day off	fridag (m)	['friˌdɑ]
weekend	ukeslutt (m), helg (f)	['ʉkəˌslʉt], ['hɛlg]

all day long	hele dagen	['helə 'dɑgən]
the next day (adv)	neste dag	['nɛstə ˌdɑ]
two days ago	for to dager siden	[fɔr tʉ 'dɑgər ˌsidən]
the day before	dagen før	['dɑgən 'før]
daily (adj)	daglig	['dɑgli]
every day (adv)	hver dag	['vɛr dɑ]

week	uke (m/f)	['ʉkə]
last week (adv)	siste uke	['sistə 'ʉkə]
next week (adv)	i neste uke	[i 'nɛstə 'ʉkə]
weekly (adj)	ukentlig	['ʉkəntli]
every week (adv)	hver uke	['vɛr 'ʉkə]
twice a week	to ganger per uke	['tʉ 'gaŋər per 'ʉkə]
every Tuesday	hver tirsdag	['vɛr 'tiʂdɑ]

21. Hours. Day and night

morning	morgen (m)	['mɔːən]
in the morning	om morgenen	[ɔm 'mɔːenən]
noon, midday	middag (m)	['miˌdɑ]
in the afternoon	om ettermiddagen	[ɔm 'ɛtərˌmidagən]

evening	kveld (m)	['kvɛl]
in the evening	om kvelden	[ɔm 'kvɛlən]
night	natt (m/f)	['nat]
at night	om natta	[ɔm 'nata]
midnight	midnatt (m/f)	['midˌnat]

second	sekund (m/n)	[se'kʉn]
minute	minutt (n)	[mi'nʉt]
hour	time (m)	['timə]

half an hour	halvtime (m)	['hal͵timə]
a quarter-hour	kvarter (n)	[kvɑːʈer]
fifteen minutes	femten minutter	['fɛmtən mi'nʉtər]
24 hours	døgn (n)	['døjn]

sunrise	soloppgang (m)	['sʉlɔp͵gɑŋ]
dawn	daggry (n)	['dag͵gry]
early morning	tidlig morgen (m)	['tili 'mɔːən]
sunset	solnedgang (m)	['sʉlned͵gɑŋ]

early in the morning	tidlig om morgenen	['tili ɔm 'mɔːenən]
this morning	i morges	[i 'mɔrəs]
tomorrow morning	i morgen tidlig	[i 'mɔːən 'tili]

this afternoon	i formiddag	[i 'fɔrmi͵dɑ]
in the afternoon	om ettermiddagen	[ɔm 'ɛtər͵midɑgən]
tomorrow afternoon	i morgen ettermiddag	[i 'mɔːən 'ɛtər͵midɑ]

| tonight (this evening) | i kveld | [i 'kvɛl] |
| tomorrow night | i morgen kveld | [i 'mɔːən ͵kvɛl] |

at 3 o'clock sharp	presis klokka tre	[prɛ'sis 'klɔka tre]
about 4 o'clock	ved fire-tiden	[ve 'fire ͵tidən]
by 12 o'clock	innen klokken tolv	['inən 'klɔkən tɔl]

in 20 minutes	om tjue minutter	[ɔm 'çʉə mi'nʉtər]
in an hour	om en time	[ɔm en 'timə]
on time (adv)	i tide	[i 'tidə]

a quarter to ...	kvart på ...	['kvɑːʈ pɔ ...]
within an hour	innen en time	['inən en 'timə]
every 15 minutes	hvert kvarter	['vɛːʈ kvɑː'ʈer]
round the clock	døgnet rundt	['døjne ͵rʉnt]

22. Months. Seasons

January	januar (m)	['janʉ͵ɑr]
February	februar (m)	['febrʉ͵ɑr]
March	mars (m)	['mɑʂ]
April	april (m)	[ɑ'pril]
May	mai (m)	['mɑj]
June	juni (m)	['jʉni]

July	juli (m)	['jʉli]
August	august (m)	[aʉ'gʉst]
September	september (m)	[sep'tɛmbər]
October	oktober (m)	[ɔk'tʉbər]
November	november (m)	[nʉ'vɛmbər]
December	desember (m)	[de'sɛmbər]

spring	vår (m)	['vɔːr]
in spring	om våren	[ɔm 'voːrən]
spring (as adj)	vår-, vårlig	['vɔːr-], ['vɔːli]
summer	sommer (m)	['sɔmər]

| in summer | om sommeren | [ɔm 'sɔmerən] |
| summer (as adj) | sommer- | ['sɔmər-] |

autumn	høst (m)	['høst]
in autumn	om høsten	[ɔm 'høstən]
autumn (as adj)	høst-, høstlig	['høst-], ['høstli]

winter	vinter (m)	['vintər]
in winter	om vinteren	[ɔm 'vinterən]
winter (as adj)	vinter-	['vintər-]
month	måned (m)	['mo:nət]
this month	denne måneden	['dɛnə 'mo:nedən]
next month	neste måned	['nɛstə 'mo:nət]
last month	forrige måned	['fɔriə ˌmo:nət]

a month ago	for en måned siden	[fɔr en 'mo:nət ˌsidən]
in a month (a month later)	om en måned	[ɔm en 'mo:nət]
in 2 months (2 months later)	om to måneder	[ɔm 'tʉ 'mo:nedər]
the whole month	en hel måned	[en 'hel 'mo:nət]
all month long	hele måned	['helə 'mo:nət]

monthly (~ magazine)	månedlig	['mo:nədli]
monthly (adv)	månedligt	['mo:nedlət]
every month	hver måned	[ˌvɛr 'mo:nət]
twice a month	to ganger per måned	['tʉ 'gɑŋər per 'mo:nət]

year	år (n)	['ɔr]
this year	i år	[i 'o:r]
next year	neste år	['nɛstə ˌo:r]
last year	i fjor	[i 'fjɔr]
a year ago	for et år siden	[fɔr et 'o:r ˌsidən]
in a year	om et år	[ɔm et 'o:r]
in two years	om to år	[ɔm 'tʉ 'o:r]
the whole year	hele året	['helə 'o:re]
all year long	hele året	['helə 'o:re]

every year	hvert år	['vɛ:ʈ 'o:r]
annual (adj)	årlig	['o:li]
annually (adv)	årlig, hvert år	['o:li], ['vɛ:ʈ 'ɔr]
4 times a year	fire ganger per år	['fire 'gɑŋər per 'o:r]

date (e.g. today's ~)	dato (m)	['dɑtʉ]
date (e.g. ~ of birth)	dato (m)	['dɑtʉ]
calendar	kalender (m)	[kɑ'lendər]

half a year	halvår (n)	['hɑlˌo:r]
six months	halvår (n)	['hɑlˌo:r]
season (summer, etc.)	årstid (m/f)	['o:ʂˌtid]
century	århundre (n)	['ɔrˌhʉndrə]

23. Time. Miscellaneous

| time | tid (m/f) | ['tid] |
| moment | øyeblikk (n) | ['øjəˌblik] |

instant (n)	øyeblikk (n)	['øjə͵blik]
instant (adj)	øyeblikkelig	['øjə͵blikəli]
lapse (of time)	tidsavsnitt (n)	['tids͵afsnit]
life	liv (n)	['liv]
eternity	evighet (m)	['ɛvi͵het]

epoch	epoke (m)	[ɛ'pʊkə]
era	æra (m)	['ærɑ]
cycle	syklus (m)	['syklʉs]
period	periode (m)	[pæri'ʉdə]
term (short-~)	sikt (m)	['sikt]

the future	framtid (m/f)	['frɑm͵tid]
future (as adj)	framtidig, fremtidig	['frɑm͵tidi], ['frɛm͵tidi]
next time	neste gang	['nɛstə ͵gɑŋ]
the past	fortid (m/f)	['foː͵tid]
past (recent)	forrige	['foriə]
last time	siste gang	['sistə ͵gɑŋ]

later (adv)	senere	['senerə]
after (prep.)	etterpå	['ɛtər͵pɔ]
nowadays (adv)	for nærværende	[for 'nær͵værnə]
now (at this moment)	nå	['nɔ]
immediately (adv)	umiddelbart	['ʉmidel͵bɑːt]
soon (adv)	snart	['snɑːt]
in advance (beforehand)	på forhånd	[pɔ 'foːr͵hon]

a long time ago	for lenge siden	[for 'leŋə ͵sidən]
recently (adv)	nylig	['nyli]
destiny	skjebne (m)	['ʂɛbnə]
recollections	minner (n pl)	['minər]
archives	arkiv (n)	[ɑr'kiv]
during ...	under ...	['ʉnər ...]
long, a long time (adv)	lenge	['leŋə]
not long (adv)	ikke lenge	['ikə 'leŋə]
early (in the morning)	tidlig	['tili]
late (not early)	sent	['sɛnt]

forever (for good)	for alltid	[for 'ɑl͵tid]
to start (begin)	å begynne	[ɔ be'jinə]
to postpone (vt)	å utsette	[ɔ 'ʉt͵sɛtə]

at the same time	samtidig	['sɑm͵tidi]
permanently (adv)	alltid, stadig	['ɑl͵tid], ['stɑdi]
constant (noise, pain)	konstant	[kʊn'stɑnt]
temporary (adj)	midlertidig, temporær	['midlə͵tidi], ['tɛmpɔ͵rær]
sometimes (adv)	av og til	['ɑv ɔ ͵til]
rarely (adv)	sjelden	['ʂɛlən]
often (adv)	ofte	['ɔftə]

24. Lines and shapes

| square | kvadrat (n) | [kvɑ'drɑt] |
| square (as adj) | kvadratisk | [kvɑ'drɑtisk] |

circle	sirkel (m)	['sirkəl]
round (adj)	rund	['run]
triangle	trekant (m)	['tre͵kant]
triangular (adj)	trekantet	['tre͵kantət]

oval	oval (m)	[ʊ'val]
oval (as adj)	oval	[ʊ'val]
rectangle	rektangel (n)	['rɛk͵taŋəl]
rectangular (adj)	rettvinklet	['rɛt͵vinklət]

pyramid	pyramide (m)	[pyra'midə]
rhombus	rombe (m)	['rumbə]
trapezium	trapes (m/n)	[tra'pes]
cube	kube, terning (m)	['kubə], ['tæːni̥ŋ]
prism	prisme (n)	['prismə]

circumference	omkrets (m)	['ɔm͵krɛts]
sphere	sfære (m)	['sfærə]
ball (solid sphere)	kule (m/f)	['kuːlə]
diameter	diameter (m)	['dia͵metər]
radius	radius (m)	['radiʉs]
perimeter (circle's ~)	perimeter (n)	[peri'metər]
centre	midtpunkt (n)	['mit͵puŋkt]

horizontal (adj)	horisontal	[hʉrisɔn'tal]
vertical (adj)	loddrett, lodd-	['lɔd͵rɛt], ['lɔd-]
parallel (n)	parallell (m)	[para'lel]
parallel (as adj)	parallell	[para'lel]

line	linje (m)	['linjə]
stroke	strek (m)	['strek]
straight line	rett linje (m/f)	['rɛt 'linjə]
curve (curved line)	kurve (m)	['kurvə]
thin (line, etc.)	tynn	['tyn]
contour (outline)	kontur (m)	[kun'tur]

intersection	skjæringspunkt (n)	['ʂæriŋs͵puŋkt]
right angle	rett vinkel (m)	['rɛt 'vinkəl]
segment	segment (n)	[seg'mɛnt]
sector (circular ~)	sektor (m)	['sɛktur]
side (of a triangle)	side (m/f)	['sidə]
angle	vinkel (m)	['vinkəl]

25. Units of measurement

weight	vekt (m)	['vɛkt]
length	lengde (m/f)	['leŋdə]
width	bredde (m)	['brɛdə]
height	høyde (m)	['højdə]
depth	dybde (m)	['dybdə]
volume	volum (n)	[vɔ'lʉm]
area	areal (n)	[͵are'al]
gram	gram (n)	['gram]
milligram	milligram (n)	['mili͵gram]

kilogram	kilogram (n)	['çilu‚gram]
ton	tonn (m/n)	['tɔn]
pound	pund (n)	['pʉn]
ounce	unse (m)	['ʉnsə]

metre	meter (m)	['metər]
millimetre	millimeter (m)	['mili‚metər]
centimetre	centimeter (m)	['sɛnti‚metər]
kilometre	kilometer (m)	['çilu‚metər]
mile	mil (m/f)	['mil]

inch	tomme (m)	['tɔmə]
foot	fot (m)	['fʊt]
yard	yard (m)	['jaːrd]

square metre	kvadratmeter (m)	[kva'drat‚metər]
hectare	hektar (n)	['hɛktar]

litre	liter (m)	['litər]
degree	grad (m)	['grad]
volt	volt (m)	['vɔlt]
ampere	ampere (m)	[am'pɛr]
horsepower	hestekraft (m/f)	['hɛstə‚kraft]

quantity	mengde (m)	['mɛŋdə]
a little bit of ...	få ...	['fɔ ...]
half	halvdel (m)	['haldel]
dozen	dusin (n)	[dʉ'sin]
piece (item)	stykke (n)	['stʏkə]

size	størrelse (m)	['stœrəlsə]
scale (map ~)	målestokk (m)	['moːlə‚stɔk]

minimal (adj)	minimal	[mini'mal]
the smallest (adj)	minste	['minstə]
medium (adj)	middel-	['midəl-]
maximal (adj)	maksimal	[maksi'mal]
the largest (adj)	største	['stœʂtə]

26. Containers

canning jar (glass ~)	glaskrukke (m/f)	['glas‚krʉkə]
tin, can	boks (m)	['bɔks]
bucket	bøtte (m/f)	['bœtə]
barrel	tønne (m)	['tœnə]

wash basin (e.g., plastic ~)	vaskefat (n)	['vaskə‚fat]
tank (100L water ~)	tank (m)	['tank]
hip flask	lommelerke (m/f)	['lʉmə‚lærkə]
jerrycan	bensinkanne (m/f)	[bɛn'sin‚kanə]
tank (e.g., tank car)	tank (m)	['tank]

mug	krus (n)	['krʉs]
cup (of coffee, etc.)	kopp (m)	['kɔp]

saucer	tefat (n)	['te̞fɑt]
glass (tumbler)	glass (n)	['glɑs]
wine glass	vinglass (n)	['vin͵glɑs]
stock pot (soup pot)	gryte (m/f)	['grytə]

bottle (~ of wine)	flaske (m)	['flɑskə]
neck (of the bottle, etc.)	flaskehals (m)	['flɑskə͵hɑls]

carafe (decanter)	karaffel (m)	[kɑ'rɑfəl]
pitcher	mugge (m/f)	['mʉgə]
vessel (container)	beholder (m)	[be'hɔlər]
pot (crock, stoneware ~)	pott, potte (m)	['pɔt], ['pɔtə]
vase	vase (m)	['vɑsə]

flacon, bottle (perfume ~)	flakong (m)	[flɑ'kɔŋ]
vial, small bottle	flaske (m/f)	['flɑskə]
tube (of toothpaste)	tube (m)	['tʉbə]

sack (bag)	sekk (m)	['sɛk]
bag (paper ~, plastic ~)	pose (m)	['pʉsə]
packet (of cigarettes, etc.)	pakke (m/f)	['pɑkə]

box (e.g. shoebox)	eske (m/f)	['ɛskə]
crate	kasse (m/f)	['kɑsə]
basket	kurv (m)	['kʉrv]

27. Materials

material	materiale (n)	[mɑteri'ɑlə]
wood (n)	tre (n)	['trɛ]
wood-, wooden (adj)	tre-, av tre	['trɛ-], [ɑ: 'trɛ]

glass (n)	glass (n)	['glɑs]
glass (as adj)	glass-	['glɑs-]

stone (n)	stein (m)	['stæjn]
stone (as adj)	stein-	['stæjn-]

plastic (n)	plast (m)	['plɑst]
plastic (as adj)	plast-	['plɑst-]

rubber (n)	gummi (m)	['gʉmi]
rubber (as adj)	gummi-	['gʉmi-]

cloth, fabric (n)	tøy (n)	['tøj]
fabric (as adj)	tøy-	['tøj-]

paper (n)	papir (n)	[pɑ'pir]
paper (as adj)	papir-	[pɑ'pir-]

cardboard (n)	papp, kartong (m)	['pɑp], [kɑ:'tɔŋ]
cardboard (as adj)	papp-, kartong-	['pɑp-], [kɑ:'tɔŋ-]
polyethylene	polyetylen (n)	['pʉlyɛty͵len]
cellophane	cellofan (m)	[sɛlu'fɑn]

| linoleum | linoleum (m) | [li'nɔleum] |
| plywood | kryssfiner (m) | ['krʏsfiˌnɛr] |

porcelain (n)	porselen (n)	[pɔʂə'len]
porcelain (as adj)	porselens-	[pɔʂə'lens-]
clay (n)	leir (n)	['læjr]
clay (as adj)	leir-	['læjr-]
ceramic (n)	keramikk (m)	[çera'mik]
ceramic (as adj)	keramisk	[çe'ramisk]

28. Metals

metal (n)	metall (n)	[me'tal]
metal (as adj)	metall-	[me'tal-]
alloy (n)	legering (m/f)	[le'geriŋ]

gold (n)	gull (n)	['gʉl]
gold, golden (adj)	av gull, gull-	[ɑ: 'gʉl], ['gʉl-]
silver (n)	sølv (n)	['søl]
silver (as adj)	sølv-, av sølv	['søl-], [ɑ: 'søl]

iron (n)	jern (n)	['jæːɳ]
iron-, made of iron (adj)	jern-	['jæːɳ-]
steel (n)	stål (n)	['stɔl]
steel (as adj)	stål-	['stɔl-]
copper (n)	kobber (n)	['kɔbər]
copper (as adj)	kobber-	['kɔbər-]

aluminium (n)	aluminium (n)	[alu'minium]
aluminium (as adj)	aluminium-	[alu'minium-]
bronze (n)	bronse (m)	['brɔnsə]
bronze (as adj)	bronse-	['brɔnsə-]

brass	messing (m)	['mɛsiŋ]
nickel	nikkel (m)	['nikəl]
platinum	platina (m/n)	['platina]
mercury	kvikksølv (n)	['kvikˌsøl]
tin	tinn (n)	['tin]
lead	bly (n)	['bly]
zinc	sink (m/n)	['sink]

HUMAN BEING

Human being. The body

29. Humans. Basic concepts

human being	**menneske** (n)	['mɛnəskə]
man (adult male)	**mann** (m)	['man]
woman	**kvinne** (m/f)	['kvinə]
child	**barn** (n)	['bɑːɳ]
girl	**jente** (m/f)	['jɛntə]
boy	**gutt** (m)	['gʉt]
teenager	**tenåring** (m)	['tɛnoːriŋ]
old man	**eldre mann** (m)	['ɛldrə ˌman]
old woman	**eldre kvinne** (m/f)	['ɛldrə ˌkvinə]

30. Human anatomy

organism (body)	**organisme** (m)	[ɔrgɑ'nismə]
heart	**hjerte** (n)	['jæːʈə]
blood	**blod** (n)	['blʉ]
artery	**arterie** (m)	[ɑːˈʈeriə]
vein	**vene** (m)	['veːnə]
brain	**hjerne** (m)	['jæːɳə]
nerve	**nerve** (m)	['nærvə]
nerves	**nerver** (m pl)	['nærvər]
vertebra	**ryggvirvel** (m)	['rʏgˌvirvəl]
spine (backbone)	**ryggrad** (m)	['rʏgˌrad]
stomach (organ)	**magesekk** (m)	['mɑgəˌsɛk]
intestines, bowels	**innvoller, tarmer** (m pl)	['inˌvolər], ['tarmər]
intestine (e.g. large ~)	**tarm** (m)	['tarm]
liver	**lever** (m)	['levər]
kidney	**nyre** (m/n)	['nyrə]
bone	**bein** (n)	['bæjn]
skeleton	**skjelett** (n)	[seˈlet]
rib	**ribbein** (n)	['ribˌbæjn]
skull	**hodeskalle** (m)	['hʉdəˌskɑlə]
muscle	**muskel** (m)	['mʉskəl]
biceps	**biceps** (m)	['bisɛps]
triceps	**triceps** (m)	['trisɛps]
tendon	**sene** (m/f)	['seːnə]
joint	**ledd** (n)	['led]

lungs	lunger (m pl)	['lʉŋər]
genitals	kjønnsorganer (n pl)	['çœnsˌɔrˈɡanər]
skin	hud (m/f)	['hʉd]

31. Head

head	hode (n)	['hʉdə]
face	ansikt (n)	['ansikt]
nose	nese (m/f)	['nese]
mouth	munn (m)	['mʉn]

eye	øye (n)	['øjə]
eyes	øyne (n pl)	['øjnə]
pupil	pupill (m)	[pʉ'pil]
eyebrow	øyenbryn (n)	['øjənˌbryn]
eyelash	øyenvipp (m)	['øjənˌvip]
eyelid	øyelokk (m)	['øjəˌlɔk]

tongue	tunge (m/f)	['tʉŋə]
tooth	tann (m/f)	['tan]
lips	lepper (m/f pl)	['lepər]
cheekbones	kinnbein (n pl)	['çinˌbæjn]
gum	tannkjøtt (n)	['tanˌçœt]
palate	gane (m)	['ɡanə]

nostrils	nesebor (n pl)	['nesəˌbʉr]
chin	hake (m/f)	['hakə]
jaw	kjeve (m)	['çɛvə]
cheek	kinn (n)	['çin]

forehead	panne (m/f)	['panə]
temple	tinning (m)	['tiniŋ]
ear	øre (n)	['ørə]
back of the head	bakhode (n)	['bakˌhodə]
neck	hals (m)	['hals]
throat	strupe, hals (m)	['strʉpə], ['hals]

hair	hår (n pl)	['hɔr]
hairstyle	frisyre (m)	[fri'syrə]
haircut	hårfasong (m)	['hoːrfaˌsoŋ]
wig	parykk (m)	[pa'rʏk]

moustache	mustasje (m)	[mʉ'staʂə]
beard	skjegg (n)	['ʂɛɡ]
to have (a beard, etc.)	å ha	[ɔ 'ha]
plait	flette (m/f)	['fletə]
sideboards	bakkenbarter (pl)	['bakənˌbɑːʈər]

red-haired (adj)	rødhåret	['røˌhoːrət]
grey (hair)	grå	['ɡrɔ]
bald (adj)	skallet	['skalət]
bald patch	skallet flekk (m)	['skalət ˌflek]
ponytail	hestehale (m)	['hɛstəˌhalə]
fringe	pannelugg (m)	['panəˌlʉɡ]

32. Human body

| hand | hånd (m/f) | ['hɔn] |
| arm | arm (m) | ['ɑrm] |

finger	finger (m)	['fiŋər]
toe	tå (m/f)	['tɔ]
thumb	tommel (m)	['tɔməl]
little finger	lillefinger (m)	['lilə,fiŋər]
nail	negl (m)	['nɛjl]

fist	knyttneve (m)	['knʏt,nevə]
palm	håndflate (m/f)	['hɔn,flɑtə]
wrist	håndledd (n)	['hɔn,led]
forearm	underarm (m)	['ʉnər,ɑrm]
elbow	albue (m)	['ɑl,bʉə]
shoulder	skulder (m)	['skʉldər]

leg	bein (n)	['bæjn]
foot	fot (m)	['fʊt]
knee	kne (n)	['knɛ]
calf	legg (m)	['leg]
hip	hofte (m)	['hɔftə]
heel	hæl (m)	['hæl]

body	kropp (m)	['krɔp]
stomach	mage (m)	['mɑgə]
chest	bryst (n)	['brʏst]
breast	bryst (n)	['brʏst]
flank	side (m/f)	['sidə]
back	rygg (m)	['rʏg]
lower back	korsrygg (m)	['kɔːʂ,rʏg]
waist	liv (n), midje (m/f)	['liv], ['midjə]

navel (belly button)	navle (m)	['nɑvlə]
buttocks	rumpeballer (m pl)	['rʉmpə,bɑlər]
bottom	bak (m)	['bɑk]

beauty spot	føflekk (m)	['fø,flek]
birthmark (café au lait spot)	fødselsmerke (n)	['førsəls,mærke]
tattoo	tatovering (m/f)	[tɑtʉ'vɛriŋ]
scar	arr (n)	['ɑr]

Clothing & Accessories

33. Outerwear. Coats

clothes	klær (n)	['klær]
outerwear	yttertøy (n)	['ytə‚tøj]
winter clothing	vinterklær (n pl)	['vintər‚klær]
coat (overcoat)	frakk (m), kåpe (m/f)	['frɑk], ['koːpə]
fur coat	pels (m), pelskåpe (m/f)	['pɛls], ['pɛls‚koːpə]
fur jacket	pelsjakke (m/f)	['pɛls‚jakə]
down coat	dunjakke (m/f)	['dʉn‚jakə]
jacket (e.g. leather ~)	jakke (m/f)	['jakə]
raincoat (trenchcoat, etc.)	regnfrakk (m)	['ræjn‚frɑk]
waterproof (adj)	vanntett	['vɑn‚tɛt]

34. Men's & women's clothing

shirt (button shirt)	skjorte (m/f)	['ʂoeːʈə]
trousers	bukse (m)	['bʉksə]
jeans	jeans (m)	['dʒins]
suit jacket	dressjakke (m/f)	['drɛs‚jakə]
suit	dress (m)	['drɛs]
dress (frock)	kjole (m)	['çulə]
skirt	skjørt (n)	['ʂøːʈ]
blouse	bluse (m)	['blʉsə]
knitted jacket (cardigan, etc.)	strikket trøye (m/f)	['strikə 'trøjə]
jacket (of a woman's suit)	blazer (m)	['blæsər]
T-shirt	T-skjorte (m/f)	['te‚ʂoeːʈə]
shorts (short trousers)	shorts (m)	['ʂɔːʈs]
tracksuit	treningsdrakt (m/f)	['treniŋs‚drɑkt]
bathrobe	badekåpe (m/f)	['bɑdə‚koːpə]
pyjamas	pyjamas (m)	[py'ʂɑmɑs]
jumper (sweater)	sweater (m)	['svɛtər]
pullover	pullover (m)	[pʉ'lovər]
waistcoat	vest (m)	['vɛst]
tailcoat	livkjole (m)	['liv‚çulə]
dinner suit	smoking (m)	['smɔkiŋ]
uniform	uniform (m)	[ʉni'fɔrm]
workwear	arbeidsklær (n pl)	['ɑrbæjds‚klær]
boiler suit	kjeledress, overall (m)	['çelə‚drɛs], ['ovɛr‚ɔl]
coat (e.g. doctor's smock)	kittel (m)	['çitəl]

35. Clothing. Underwear

underwear	undertøy (n)	['ɵnəˌtøj]
pants	underbukse (m/f)	['ɵnərˌbɵksə]
panties	truse (m/f)	['trɵsə]
vest (singlet)	undertrøye (m/f)	['ɵnəˌtrøjə]
socks	sokker (m pl)	['sɔkər]
nightdress	nattkjole (m)	['natˌçulə]
bra	behå (m)	['beˌhɔ]
knee highs (knee-high socks)	knestrømper (m/f pl)	['knɛˌstrømpər]
tights	strømpebukse (m/f)	['strømpəˌbɵksə]
stockings (hold ups)	strømper (m/f pl)	['strømpər]
swimsuit, bikini	badedrakt (m/f)	['badəˌdrakt]

36. Headwear

hat	hatt (m)	['hat]
trilby hat	hatt (m)	['hat]
baseball cap	baseball cap (m)	['bɛjsbɔl kɛp]
flatcap	sikspens (m)	['sikspens]
beret	alpelue, baskerlue (m/f)	['alpəˌlɵə], ['baskəˌlɵə]
hood	hette (m/f)	['hɛtə]
panama hat	panamahatt (m)	['panamaˌhat]
knit cap (knitted hat)	strikket lue (m/f)	['strikəˌlɵə]
headscarf	skaut (n)	['skaʋt]
women's hat	hatt (m)	['hat]
hard hat	hjelm (m)	['jɛlm]
forage cap	båtlue (m/f)	['bɔtˌlɵə]
helmet	hjelm (m)	['jɛlm]
bowler	bowlerhatt, skalk (m)	['bɔulərˌhat], ['skalk]
top hat	flosshatt (m)	['flɔsˌhat]

37. Footwear

footwear	skotøy (n)	['skɵtøj]
shoes (men's shoes)	skor (m pl)	['skʋr]
shoes (women's shoes)	pumps (m pl)	['pɵmps]
boots (e.g., cowboy ~)	støvler (m pl)	['støvlər]
carpet slippers	tøfler (m pl)	['tøflər]
trainers	tennissko (m pl)	['tɛnisˌskʋ]
trainers	canvas sko (m pl)	['kanvas ˌskʋ]
sandals	sandaler (m pl)	[san'dalər]
cobbler (shoe repairer)	skomaker (m)	['skʋˌmakər]
heel	hæl (m)	['hæl]

pair (of shoes)	par (n)	['pɑr]
lace (shoelace)	skolisse (m/f)	['skuˌlisə]
to lace up (vt)	å snøre	[ɔ 'snørə]
shoehorn	skohorn (n)	['skuˌhuːn]
shoe polish	skokrem (m)	['skuˌkrɛm]

38. Textile. Fabrics

cotton (n)	bomull (m/f)	['buˌmʉl]
cotton (as adj)	bomulls-	['buˌmʉls-]
flax (n)	lin (n)	['lin]
flax (as adj)	lin-	['lin-]

silk (n)	silke (m)	['silkə]
silk (as adj)	silke-	['silkə-]
wool (n)	ull (m/f)	['ʉl]
wool (as adj)	ull-, av ull	['ʉl-], ['ɑː ʉl]

velvet	fløyel (m)	['fløjəl]
suede	semsket skinn (n)	['sɛmsket ˌʂin]
corduroy	kordfløyel (m/n)	['kɔːd̪fløjəl]

nylon (n)	nylon (n)	['nyˌlɔn]
nylon (as adj)	nylon-	['nyˌlɔn-]
polyester (n)	polyester (m)	[pʉly'ɛstər]
polyester (as adj)	polyester-	[pʉly'ɛstər-]

leather (n)	lær, skinn (n)	['lær], ['ʂin]
leather (as adj)	lær-, av lær	['lær-], ['ɑː lær]
fur (n)	pels (m)	['pɛls]
fur (e.g. ~ coat)	pels-	['pɛls-]

39. Personal accessories

gloves	hansker (m pl)	['hɑnskər]
mittens	votter (m pl)	['vɔtər]
scarf (muffler)	skjerf (n)	['ʂærf]

glasses	briller (m pl)	['brilər]
frame (eyeglass ~)	innfatning (m/f)	['inˌfatniŋ]
umbrella	paraply (m)	[parɑ'ply]
walking stick	stokk (m)	['stɔk]
hairbrush	hårbørste (m)	['hɔrˌbœʂtə]
fan	vifte (m/f)	['viftə]

tie (necktie)	slips (n)	['slips]
bow tie	sløyfe (m/f)	['ʂløjfə]
braces	bukseseler (m pl)	['bʉksə'selər]
handkerchief	lommetørkle (n)	['lʉməˌtœrklə]

| comb | kam (m) | ['kam] |
| hair slide | hårspenne (m/f/n) | ['hoːrˌspɛnə] |

hairpin	hårnål (m/f)	['ho:r,nol]
buckle	spenne (m/f/n)	['spɛnə]

belt	belte (m)	['bɛltə]
shoulder strap	skulderreim, rem (m/f)	['skʉldə,ræjm], ['rem]

bag (handbag)	veske (m/f)	['vɛskə]
handbag	håndveske (m/f)	['hɔn,vɛskə]
rucksack	ryggsekk (m)	['rʏg,sɛk]

40. Clothing. Miscellaneous

fashion	mote (m)	['mʉtə]
in vogue (adj)	moteriktig	['mʉtə,rikti]
fashion designer	moteskaper (m)	['mʉtə,skɑpər]

collar	krage (m)	['krɑgə]
pocket	lomme (m/f)	['lʊmə]
pocket (as adj)	lomme-	['lʊmə-]
sleeve	erme (n)	['ærmə]
hanging loop	hempe (m)	['hɛmpə]
flies (on trousers)	gylf, buksesmekk (m)	['gylf], ['bʉksə,smɛk]

zip (fastener)	glidelås (m/n)	['glidə,lɔs]
fastener	hekte (m/f), knepping (m)	['hɛktə], ['knɛpiŋ]
button	knapp (m)	['knɑp]
buttonhole	klapphull (n)	['klɑp,hʉl]
to come off (ab. button)	å falle av	[ɔ 'falə ɑ:]

to sew (vi, vt)	å sy	[ɔ 'sy]
to embroider (vi, vt)	å brodere	[ɔ brʉ'derə]
embroidery	broderi (n)	[brʉde'ri]
sewing needle	synål (m/f)	['sy,nɔl]
thread	tråd (m)	['trɔ]
seam	søm (m)	['søm]

to get dirty (vi)	å skitne seg til	[ɔ 'ʂitnə sæj til]
stain (mark, spot)	flekk (m)	['flek]
to crease, to crumple	å bli skrukkete	[ɔ 'bli 'skrʉketə]
to tear, to rip (vt)	å rive	[ɔ 'rivə]
clothes moth	møll (m/n)	['møl]

41. Personal care. Cosmetics

toothpaste	tannpasta (m)	['tɑn,pɑstɑ]
toothbrush	tannbørste (m)	['tɑn,bœʂtə]
to clean one's teeth	å pusse tennene	[ɔ 'pʉsə 'tɛnənə]

razor	høvel (m)	['høvəl]
shaving cream	barberkrem (m)	[bɑr'bɛr,krɛm]
to shave (vi)	å barbere seg	[ɔ bɑr'berə sæj]
soap	såpe (m/f)	['so:pə]

shampoo	sjampo (m)	['ʂɑmˌpu]
scissors	saks (m/f)	['sɑks]
nail file	neglefil (m/f)	['nɛjləˌfil]
nail clippers	negleklipper (m)	['nɛjləˌklipər]
tweezers	pinsett (m)	[pin'sɛt]

cosmetics	kosmetikk (m)	[kʊsme'tik]
face mask	ansiktsmaske (m/f)	['ɑnsiktsˌmɑskə]
manicure	manikyr (m)	[mɑni'kyr]
to have a manicure	å få manikyr	[ɔ 'fɔ mɑni'kyr]
pedicure	pedikyr (m)	[pedi'kyr]

make-up bag	sminkeveske (m/f)	['sminkəˌvɛskə]
face powder	pudder (n)	['pʉdər]
powder compact	pudderdåse (m)	['pʉdərˌdo:sə]
blusher	rouge (m)	['ru:ʂ]

perfume (bottled)	parfyme (m)	[pɑr'fymə]
toilet water (lotion)	eau de toilette (m)	['ɔ: də twɑ'let]
lotion	lotion (m)	['loʉʂɛn]
cologne	eau de cologne (m)	['ɔ: də kɔ'lɔɲ]

eyeshadow	øyeskygge (m)	['øjəˌʂygə]
eyeliner	eyeliner (m)	['ɑ:jˌlɑjnər]
mascara	maskara (m)	[mɑ'skɑrɑ]

lipstick	leppestift (m)	['lepəˌstift]
nail polish	neglelakk (m)	['nɛjləˌlɑk]
hair spray	hårlakk (m)	['ho:rˌlɑk]
deodorant	deodorant (m)	[deudʊ'rɑnt]

cream	krem (m)	['krɛm]
face cream	ansiktskrem (m)	['ɑnsiktsˌkrɛm]
hand cream	håndkrem (m)	['honˌkrɛm]
anti-wrinkle cream	antirynkekrem (m)	[ɑnti'rʏnkəˌkrɛm]
day cream	dagkrem (m)	['dɑgˌkrɛm]
night cream	nattkrem (m)	['nɑtˌkrɛm]
day (as adj)	dag-	['dɑg-]
night (as adj)	natt-	['nɑt-]

tampon	tampong (m)	[tɑm'pɔŋ]
toilet paper (toilet roll)	toalettpapir (n)	[tʊɑ'let pɑ'pir]
hair dryer	hårføner (m)	['ho:rˌfønər]

42. Jewellery

jewellery, jewels	smykker (n pl)	['smʏkər]
precious (e.g. ~ stone)	edel-	['ɛdəl-]
hallmark stamp	stempel (n)	['stɛmpəl]

ring	ring (m)	['riŋ]
wedding ring	giftering (m)	['jiftəˌriŋ]
bracelet	armbånd (n)	['armˌbɔn]
earrings	øreringer (m pl)	['ørəˌriŋər]

necklace (~ of pearls)	halssmykke (n)	['hals,smʏkə]
crown	krone (m/f)	['krʊnə]
bead necklace	perlekjede (m/n)	['pærlə,çɛ:də]

diamond	diamant (m)	[dia'mant]
emerald	smaragd (m)	[sma'ragd]
ruby	rubin (m)	[rʉ'bin]
sapphire	safir (m)	[sa'fir]
pearl	perler (m pl)	['pærlər]
amber	rav (n)	['rav]

43. Watches. Clocks

watch (wristwatch)	armbåndsur (n)	['armbɔns,ʉr]
dial	urskive (m/f)	['ʉ:,șivə]
hand (clock, watch)	viser (m)	['visər]
metal bracelet	armbånd (n)	['arm,bɔn]
watch strap	rem (m/f)	['rem]

battery	batteri (n)	[batɛ'ri]
to be flat (battery)	å bli utladet	[ɔ 'bli 'ʉt,ladət]
to change a battery	å skifte batteriene	[ɔ 'șiftə batɛ'riene]
to run fast	å gå for fort	[ɔ 'gɔ fɔ 'fɔ:t]
to run slow	å gå for sakte	[ɔ 'gɔ fɔ 'saktə]

wall clock	veggur (n)	['vɛg,ʉr]
hourglass	timeglass (n)	['timə,glas]
sundial	solur (n)	['sʊl,ʉr]
alarm clock	vekkerklokka (m/f)	['vɛkər,klɔka]
watchmaker	urmaker (m)	['ʉr,makər]
to repair (vt)	å reparere	[ɔ repa'rerə]

45

Food. Nutricion

44. Food

English	Norwegian	Pronunciation
meat	kjøtt (n)	['çœt]
chicken	høne (m/f)	['høne]
poussin	kylling (m)	['çyliŋ]
duck	and (m/f)	['an]
goose	gås (m/f)	['gɔs]
game	vilt (n)	['vilt]
turkey	kalkun (m)	[kɑl'kʉn]
pork	svinekjøtt (n)	['svine‚çœt]
veal	kalvekjøtt (n)	['kalve‚çœt]
lamb	fårekjøtt (n)	['foːre‚çœt]
beef	oksekjøtt (n)	['ɔkse‚çœt]
rabbit	kanin (m)	[kɑ'nin]
sausage (bologna, etc.)	pølse (m/f)	['pølse]
vienna sausage (frankfurter)	wienerpølse (m/f)	['viner‚pølse]
bacon	bacon (n)	['bɛjken]
ham	skinke (m)	['ʂinke]
gammon	skinke (m)	['ʂinke]
pâté	pate, paté (m)	[pɑ'te]
liver	lever (m)	['lever]
mince (minced meat)	kjøttfarse (m)	['çœt‚farʂe]
tongue	tunge (m/f)	['tʉŋe]
egg	egg (n)	['ɛg]
eggs	egg (n pl)	['ɛg]
egg white	eggehvite (m)	['ɛge‚vite]
egg yolk	plomme (m/f)	['plʉme]
fish	fisk (m)	['fisk]
seafood	sjømat (m)	['ʂø‚mat]
crustaceans	krepsdyr (n pl)	['krɛps‚dyr]
caviar	kaviar (m)	['kɑvi‚ɑr]
crab	krabbe (m)	['krɑbe]
prawn	reke (m/f)	['reke]
oyster	østers (m)	['østeʂ]
spiny lobster	langust (m)	[lɑŋ'gʉst]
octopus	blekksprut (m)	['blek‚sprʉt]
squid	blekksprut (m)	['blek‚sprʉt]
sturgeon	stør (m)	['stør]
salmon	laks (m)	['lɑks]
halibut	kveite (m/f)	['kvæjte]
cod	torsk (m)	['tɔʂk]

mackerel	makrell (m)	[mɑ'krɛl]
tuna	tunfisk (m)	['tʉnˌfisk]
eel	ål (m)	['ɔl]

trout	ørret (m)	['øret]
sardine	sardin (m)	[sɑ:'din]
pike	gjedde (m/f)	['jɛdə]
herring	sild (m/f)	['sil]

bread	brød (n)	['brø]
cheese	ost (m)	['ʊst]
sugar	sukker (n)	['sʉkər]
salt	salt (n)	['sɑlt]

rice	ris (m)	['ris]
pasta (macaroni)	pasta, makaroni (m)	['pɑstɑ], [mɑkɑ'rʉni]
noodles	nudler (m pl)	['nʉdlər]

butter	smør (n)	['smør]
vegetable oil	vegetabilsk olje (m)	[vegetɑ'bilsk ˌɔljə]
sunflower oil	solsikkeolje (m)	['sʉlsikəˌɔlje]
margarine	margarin (m)	[mɑrgɑ'rin]

| olives | olivener (m pl) | [ʊ'livenər] |
| olive oil | olivenolje (m) | [ʊ'livənˌɔljə] |

milk	melk (m/f)	['mɛlk]
condensed milk	kondensert melk (m/f)	[kʊndən'se:t ˌmɛlk]
yogurt	jogurt (m)	['jɔgʉ:t]
soured cream	rømme, syrnet fløte (m)	['rœmə], ['sy:ɳet 'fløtə]
cream (of milk)	fløte (m)	['fløtə]

| mayonnaise | majones (m) | [mɑjɔ'nɛs] |
| buttercream | krem (m) | ['krɛm] |

groats (barley ~, etc.)	gryn (n)	['gryn]
flour	mel (n)	['mel]
tinned food	hermetikk (m)	[hɛrme'tik]

cornflakes	cornflakes (m)	['kɔ:ɳˌflejks]
honey	honning (m)	['hɔniŋ]
jam	syltetøy (n)	['syltəˌtøj]
chewing gum	tyggegummi (m)	['tygəˌgʉmi]

45. Drinks

water	vann (n)	['vɑn]
drinking water	drikkevann (n)	['drikəˌvɑn]
mineral water	mineralvann (n)	[minə'rɑlˌvɑn]

still (adj)	uten kullsyre	['ʉtən kʉl'syrə]
carbonated (adj)	kullsyret	[kʉl'syrət]
sparkling (adj)	med kullsyre	[me kʉl'syrə]
ice	is (m)	['is]

with ice	med is	[me 'is]
non-alcoholic (adj)	alkoholfri	['alkʊhʊlˌfri]
soft drink	alkoholfri drikk (m)	['alkʊhʊlˌfri drik]
refreshing drink	leskedrikk (m)	['leskəˌdrik]
lemonade	limonade (m)	[limɔ'nadə]

spirits	rusdrikker (m pl)	['rʉsˌdrikər]
wine	vin (m)	['vin]
white wine	hvitvin (m)	['vitˌvin]
red wine	rødvin (m)	['røˌvin]

liqueur	likør (m)	[li'kør]
champagne	champagne (m)	[ṣam'panjə]
vermouth	vermut (m)	['værmʉt]

whisky	whisky (m)	['viski]
vodka	vodka (m)	['vɔdka]
gin	gin (m)	['dʒin]
cognac	konjakk (m)	['kʊnjak]
rum	rom (m)	['rʊm]

coffee	kaffe (m)	['kafə]
black coffee	svart kaffe (m)	['svaːʈ 'kafə]
white coffee	kaffe (m) med melk	['kafə me 'mɛlk]
cappuccino	cappuccino (m)	[kapʊ'ʧinɔ]
instant coffee	pulverkaffe (m)	['pʉlvərˌkafə]

milk	melk (m/f)	['mɛlk]
cocktail	cocktail (m)	['kɔkˌtɛjl]
milkshake	milkshake (m)	['milkˌṣɛjk]

juice	jus, juice (m)	['dʒʉs]
tomato juice	tomatjuice (m)	[tʉ'matˌdʒʉs]
orange juice	appelsinjuice (m)	[apel'sinˌdʒʉs]
freshly squeezed juice	nypresset juice (m)	['nyˌprɛsə 'dʒʉs]

beer	øl (m/n)	['øl]
lager	lettøl (n)	['letˌøl]
bitter	mørkt øl (n)	['mœrktˌøl]

tea	te (m)	['te]
black tea	svart te (m)	['svaːʈ ˌte]
green tea	grønn te (m)	['grœn ˌte]

46. Vegetables

| vegetables | grønnsaker (m pl) | ['grœnˌsakər] |
| greens | grønnsaker (m pl) | ['grœnˌsakər] |

tomato	tomat (m)	[tʉ'mat]
cucumber	agurk (m)	[a'gʉrk]
carrot	gulrot (m/f)	['gʉlˌrʊt]
potato	potet (m/f)	[pʉ'tet]
onion	løk (m)	['løk]

garlic	hvitløk (m)	['vit,løk]
cabbage	kål (m)	['kɔl]
cauliflower	blomkål (m)	['blɔm,kɔl]
Brussels sprouts	rosenkål (m)	['rʉsən,kɔl]
broccoli	brokkoli (m)	['brɔkɔli]

beetroot	rødbete (m/f)	['rø,betə]
aubergine	aubergine (m)	[ɔbɛr'şin]
courgette	squash (m)	['skvɔş]
pumpkin	gresskar (n)	['grɛskar]
turnip	nepe (m/f)	['nepə]

parsley	persille (m/f)	[pæ'şilə]
dill	dill (m)	['dil]
lettuce	salat (m)	[sɑ'lɑt]
celery	selleri (m/n)	[sɛle,ri]
asparagus	asparges (m)	[ɑ'sparşəs]
spinach	spinat (m)	[spi'nɑt]

pea	erter (m pl)	['æ:tər]
beans	bønner (m/f pl)	['bœnər]
maize	mais (m)	['mɑis]
kidney bean	bønne (m/f)	['bœnə]

sweet paper	pepper (m)	['pɛpər]
radish	reddik (m)	['rɛdik]
artichoke	artisjokk (m)	[,ɑ:ţi'şɔk]

47. Fruits. Nuts

fruit	frukt (m/f)	['frʉkt]
apple	eple (n)	['ɛplə]
pear	pære (m/f)	['pærə]
lemon	sitron (m)	[si'trʉn]
orange	appelsin (m)	[ɑpel'sin]
strawberry (garden ~)	jordbær (n)	['ju:r,bær]

tangerine	mandarin (m)	[mɑndɑ'rin]
plum	plomme (m/f)	['plʉmə]
peach	fersken (m)	['fæşkən]
apricot	aprikos (m)	[ɑpri'kʉs]
raspberry	bringebær (n)	['briŋə,bær]
pineapple	ananas (m)	['ɑnɑnɑs]

banana	banan (m)	[bɑ'nɑn]
watermelon	vannmelon (m)	['vɑnme,lʉn]
grape	drue (m)	['drʉə]
sour cherry	kirsebær (n)	['çişə,bær]
sweet cherry	morell (m)	[mʉ'rɛl]
melon	melon (m)	[me'lun]

grapefruit	grapefrukt (m/f)	['grɛjp,frʉkt]
avocado	avokado (m)	[avɔ'kadɔ]
papaya	papaya (m)	[pɑ'pɑjɑ]

| mango | mango (m) | ['maŋu] |
| pomegranate | granateple (n) | [gra'nat‚εplə] |

redcurrant	rips (m)	['rips]
blackcurrant	solbær (n)	['sʊl‚bær]
gooseberry	stikkelsbær (n)	['stikəls‚bær]
bilberry	blåbær (n)	['blɔ‚bær]
blackberry	bjørnebær (m)	['bjœ:ŋə‚bær]

raisin	rosin (m)	[rʊ'sin]
fig	fiken (m)	['fikən]
date	daddel (m)	['dadəl]

peanut	jordnøtt (m)	['ju:r‚nœt]
almond	mandel (m)	['mandəl]
walnut	valnøtt (m/f)	['val‚nœt]
hazelnut	hasselnøtt (m/f)	['hasəl‚nœt]
coconut	kokosnøtt (m/f)	['kʊkʊs‚nœt]
pistachios	pistasier (m pl)	[pi'staşiər]

48. Bread. Sweets

bakers' confectionery (pastry)	bakevarer (m/f pl)	['bakə‚varər]
bread	brød (n)	['brø]
biscuits	kjeks (m)	['çεks]

chocolate (n)	sjokolade (m)	[şʊkʊ'ladə]
chocolate (as adj)	sjokolade-	[şʊkʊ'ladə-]
candy (wrapped)	sukkertøy (n), karamell (m)	['sɵkə:‚tøj], [kara'mεl]
cake (e.g. cupcake)	kake (m/f)	['kakə]
cake (e.g. birthday ~)	bløtkake (m/f)	['bløt‚kakə]

| pie (e.g. apple ~) | pai (m) | ['paj] |
| filling (for cake, pie) | fyll (m/n) | ['fʏl] |

jam (whole fruit jam)	syltetøy (n)	['syltə‚tøj]
marmalade	marmelade (m)	[marme'ladə]
wafers	vaffel (m)	['vafəl]
ice-cream	iskrem (m)	['iskrεm]
pudding (Christmas ~)	pudding (m)	['pɵdiŋ]

49. Cooked dishes

course, dish	rett (m)	['rεt]
cuisine	kjøkken (n)	['çœkən]
recipe	oppskrift (m)	['ɔp‚skrift]
portion	porsjon (m)	[pɔ'şʊn]

salad	salat (m)	[sa'lat]
soup	suppe (m/f)	['sɵpə]
clear soup (broth)	buljong (m)	[bu'ljɔŋ]
sandwich (bread)	smørbrød (n)	['smør‚brø]

fried eggs	speilegg (n)	['spæjl‚ɛg]
hamburger (beefburger)	hamburger (m)	['hambʊrgər]
beefsteak	biff (m)	['bif]

side dish	tilbehør (n)	['tilbə‚hør]
spaghetti	spagetti (m)	[spa'gɛti]
mash	potetmos (m)	[pʊ'tet‚mʊs]
pizza	pizza (m)	['pitsa]
porridge (oatmeal, etc.)	grøt (m)	['grøt]
omelette	omelett (m)	[ɔmə'let]

boiled (e.g. ~ beef)	kokt	['kʊkt]
smoked (adj)	røkt	['røkt]
fried (adj)	stekt	['stɛkt]
dried (adj)	tørket	['tœrkət]
frozen (adj)	frossen, dypfryst	['frɔsən], ['dyp‚frʏst]
pickled (adj)	syltet	['sʏltət]

sweet (sugary)	søt	['søt]
salty (adj)	salt	['salt]
cold (adj)	kald	['kal]
hot (adj)	het, varm	['het], ['varm]
bitter (adj)	bitter	['bitər]
tasty (adj)	lekker	['lekər]

to cook in boiling water	å koke	[ɔ 'kʊkə]
to cook (dinner)	å lage	[ɔ 'lagə]
to fry (vt)	å steke	[ɔ 'stekə]
to heat up (food)	å varme opp	[ɔ 'varmə ɔp]

to salt (vt)	å salte	[ɔ 'saltə]
to pepper (vt)	å pepre	[ɔ 'pɛprə]
to grate (vt)	å rive	[ɔ 'rivə]
peel (n)	skall (n)	['skal]
to peel (vt)	å skrelle	[ɔ 'skrɛlə]

50. Spices

salt	salt (n)	['salt]
salty (adj)	salt	['salt]
to salt (vt)	å salte	[ɔ 'saltə]

black pepper	svart pepper (m)	['svɑːʈ 'pɛpər]
red pepper (milled ~)	rød pepper (m)	['rø 'pɛpər]
mustard	sennep (m)	['sɛnəp]
horseradish	pepperrot (m/f)	['pɛpər‚rʊt]

condiment	krydder (n)	['krʏdər]
spice	krydder (n)	['krʏdər]
sauce	saus (m)	['saʊs]
vinegar	eddik (m)	['ɛdik]

anise	anis (m)	['anis]
basil	basilik (m)	[basi'lik]

cloves	nellik (m)	['nɛlik]
ginger	ingefær (m)	['iŋəˌfær]
coriander	koriander (m)	[kʊri'andər]
cinnamon	kanel (m)	[ka'nel]

sesame	sesam (m)	['sesam]
bay leaf	laurbærblad (n)	['laʊrbærˌblɑ]
paprika	paprika (m)	['paprika]
caraway	karve, kummin (m)	['karvə], ['kʉmin]
saffron	safran (m)	[sa'fran]

51. Meals

| food | mat (m) | ['mɑt] |
| to eat (vi, vt) | å spise | [ɔ 'spisə] |

breakfast	frokost (m)	['frʊkɔst]
to have breakfast	å spise frokost	[ɔ 'spisə ˌfrʊkɔst]
lunch	lunsj, lunch (m)	['lʉnʂ]
to have lunch	å spise lunsj	[ɔ 'spisə ˌlʉnʂ]
dinner	middag (m)	['miˌda]
to have dinner	å spise middag	[ɔ 'spisə 'miˌda]

| appetite | appetitt (m) | [ape'tit] |
| Enjoy your meal! | God appetitt! | ['gʊ ape'tit] |

to open (~ a bottle)	å åpne	[ɔ 'ɔpnə]
to spill (liquid)	å spille	[ɔ 'spilə]
to spill out (vi)	å bli spilt	[ɔ 'bli 'spilt]

to boil (vi)	å koke	[ɔ 'kʊkə]
to boil (vt)	å koke	[ɔ 'kʊkə]
boiled (~ water)	kokt	['kʊkt]

| to chill, cool down (vt) | å svalne | [ɔ 'svalnə] |
| to chill (vi) | å avkjøles | [ɔ 'avˌçœləs] |

| taste, flavour | smak (m) | ['smak] |
| aftertaste | bismak (m) | ['bismak] |

to slim down (lose weight)	å være på diet	[ɔ 'værə pɔ di'et]
diet	diett (m)	[di'et]
vitamin	vitamin (n)	[vita'min]
calorie	kalori (m)	[kalʊ'ri]

| vegetarian (n) | vegetarianer (m) | [vegetari'anər] |
| vegetarian (adj) | vegetarisk | [vege'tarisk] |

fats (nutrient)	fett (n)	['fɛt]
proteins	proteiner (n pl)	[prɔte'inər]
carbohydrates	kullhydrater (n pl)	['kʉlhyˌdratər]
slice (of lemon, ham)	skive (m/f)	['ʂivə]
piece (of cake, pie)	stykke (n)	['stʏkə]
crumb (of bread, cake, etc.)	smule (m)	['smʉlə]

52. Table setting

spoon	skje (m)	['şe]
knife	kniv (m)	['kniv]
fork	gaffel (m)	['gafəl]

cup (e.g., coffee ~)	kopp (m)	['kɔp]
plate (dinner ~)	tallerken (m)	[ta'lærkən]
saucer	tefat (n)	['te͵fat]
serviette	serviett (m)	[sɛrvi'ɛt]
toothpick	tannpirker (m)	['tan͵pirkər]

53. Restaurant

restaurant	restaurant (m)	[rɛstu'raŋ]
coffee bar	kafé, kaffebar (m)	[ka'fe], ['kafə͵bar]
pub, bar	bar (m)	['bar]
tearoom	tesalong (m)	['tesɑ͵lɔŋ]

waiter	servitør (m)	['særvi'tør]
waitress	servitrise (m/f)	[særvi'trisə]
barman	bartender (m)	['bɑː͵tɛndər]

menu	meny (m)	[me'ny]
wine list	vinkart (n)	['vin͵kɑːt]
to book a table	å reservere bord	[ɔ resɛr'verə 'bur]

course, dish	rett (m)	['rɛt]
to order (meal)	å bestille	[ɔ be'stilə]
to make an order	å bestille	[ɔ be'stilə]

aperitif	aperitiff (m)	[aperi'tif]
starter	forrett (m)	['fɔrɛt]
dessert, pudding	dessert (m)	[de'sɛːr]

bill	regning (m/f)	['rɛjniŋ]
to pay the bill	å betale regningen	[ɔ be'talə 'rɛjniŋən]
to give change	å gi tilbake veksel	[ɔ ji til'bɑkə 'vɛksəl]
tip	driks (m)	['driks]

Family, relatives and friends

54. Personal information. Forms

name (first name)	**navn** (n)	['nɑvn]
surname (last name)	**etternavn** (n)	['ɛtə‚ŋɑvn]
date of birth	**fødselsdato** (m)	['føtsəls‚dɑtʉ]
place of birth	**fødested** (n)	['fødə‚sted]
nationality	**nasjonalitet** (m)	[naʂʉnɑli'tet]
place of residence	**bosted** (n)	['bʉ‚sted]
country	**land** (n)	['lɑn]
profession (occupation)	**yrke** (n), **profesjon** (m)	['yrkə], [prʉfe'ʂʉn]
gender, sex	**kjønn** (n)	['çœn]
height	**høyde** (m)	['højdə]
weight	**vekt** (m)	['vɛkt]

55. Family members. Relatives

mother	**mor** (m/f)	['mʉr]
father	**far** (m)	['fɑr]
son	**sønn** (m)	['sœn]
daughter	**datter** (m/f)	['dɑtər]
younger daughter	**yngste datter** (m/f)	['yŋstə 'dɑtər]
younger son	**yngste sønn** (m)	['yŋstə 'sœn]
eldest daughter	**eldste datter** (m/f)	['ɛlstə 'dɑtər]
eldest son	**eldste sønn** (m)	['ɛlstə 'sœn]
brother	**bror** (m)	['brʉr]
elder brother	**eldre bror** (m)	['ɛldrə ‚brʉr]
younger brother	**lillebror** (m)	['lilə‚brʉr]
sister	**søster** (m/f)	['søstər]
elder sister	**eldre søster** (m/f)	['ɛldrə ‚søstər]
younger sister	**lillesøster** (m/f)	['lilə‚søstər]
cousin (masc.)	**fetter** (m/f)	['fɛtər]
cousin (fem.)	**kusine** (m)	[kʉ'sinə]
mummy	**mamma** (m)	['mɑmɑ]
dad, daddy	**pappa** (m)	['pɑpɑ]
parents	**foreldre** (pl)	[for'ɛldrə]
child	**barn** (n)	['bɑːɳ]
children	**barn** (n pl)	['bɑːɳ]
grandmother	**bestemor** (m)	['bɛstə‚mʉr]
grandfather	**bestefar** (m)	['bɛstə‚fɑr]
grandson	**barnebarn** (n)	['bɑːɳə‚bɑːɳ]

| granddaughter | barnebarn (n) | ['bɑ:ŋə,bɑ:ŋ] |
| grandchildren | barnebarn (n pl) | ['bɑ:ŋə,bɑ:ŋ] |

uncle	onkel (m)	['ʊnkəl]
aunt	tante (m/f)	['tɑntə]
nephew	nevø (m)	[ne'vø]
niece	niese (m/f)	[ni'esə]

mother-in-law (wife's mother)	svigermor (m/f)	['svigər,mʊr]
father-in-law (husband's father)	svigerfar (m)	['svigər,fɑr]
son-in-law (daughter's husband)	svigersønn (m)	['svigər,sœn]
stepmother	stemor (m/f)	['ste,mʊr]
stepfather	stefar (m)	['ste,fɑr]

infant	brystbarn (n)	['brʏst,bɑ:ŋ]
baby (infant)	spedbarn (n)	['spe,bɑ:ŋ]
little boy, kid	lite barn (n)	['litə 'bɑ:ŋ]

wife	kone (m/f)	['kʊnə]
husband	mann (m)	['mɑn]
spouse (husband)	ektemann (m)	['ɛktə,mɑn]
spouse (wife)	hustru (m)	['hʊstrʉ]

married (masc.)	gift	['jift]
married (fem.)	gift	['jift]
single (unmarried)	ugift	[ʉ:'jift]
bachelor	ungkar (m)	['ʉŋ,kɑr]
divorced (masc.)	fraskilt	['frɑ,ʂilt]
widow	enke (m)	['ɛnkə]
widower	enkemann (m)	['ɛnkə,mɑn]

relative	slektning (m)	['ʂlektniŋ]
close relative	nær slektning (m)	['nær 'slektniŋ]
distant relative	fjern slektning (m)	['fjæ:ɳ 'slektniŋ]
relatives	slektninger (m pl)	['ʂlektniŋər]

orphan (boy or girl)	foreldreløst barn (n)	[for'ɛldrəløst ,bɑ:ŋ]
guardian (of a minor)	formynder (m)	['for,mʏnər]
to adopt (a boy)	å adoptere	[ɔ adɔp'terə]
to adopt (a girl)	å adoptere	[ɔ adɔp'terə]

56. Friends. Colleagues

friend (masc.)	venn (m)	['vɛn]
friend (fem.)	venninne (m/f)	[vɛ'ninə]
friendship	vennskap (n)	['vɛn,skɑp]
to be friends	å være venner	[ɔ 'værə 'vɛnər]

pal (masc.)	venn (m)	['vɛn]
pal (fem.)	venninne (m/f)	[vɛ'ninə]
partner	partner (m)	['pɑ:ʈnər]

chief (boss)	sjef (m)	['ʂɛf]
superior (n)	overordnet (m)	['ɔvərˌɔrdnet]
owner, proprietor	eier (m)	['æjər]
subordinate (n)	underordnet (m)	['ʉnərˌɔrdnet]
colleague	kollega (m)	[kʉ'lega]

acquaintance (person)	bekjent (m)	[be'çɛnt]
fellow traveller	medpassasjer (m)	['meˌpasa'ʂɛr]
classmate	klassekamerat (m)	['klasəˌkamə'raːt]

neighbour (masc.)	nabo (m)	['nabʉ]
neighbour (fem.)	nabo (m)	['nabʉ]
neighbours	naboer (m pl)	['nabʉər]

57. Man. Woman

woman	kvinne (m/f)	['kvinə]
girl (young woman)	jente (m/f)	['jɛntə]
bride	brud (m/f)	['brʉd]

beautiful (adj)	vakker	['vakər]
tall (adj)	høy	['høj]
slender (adj)	slank	['ʂlank]
short (adj)	liten av vekst	['litən aː 'vɛkst]

blonde (n)	blondine (m)	[blɔn'dinə]
brunette (n)	brunette (m)	[brʉ'nɛtə]

ladies' (adj)	dame-	['damə-]
virgin (girl)	jomfru (m/f)	['ʉmfrʉ]
pregnant (adj)	gravid	[gra'vid]
man (adult male)	mann (m)	['man]
blonde haired man	blond mann (m)	['blɔn ˌman]
dark haired man	mørkhåret mann (m)	['mœrkˌhoːret man]
tall (adj)	høy	['høj]
short (adj)	liten av vekst	['litən aː 'vɛkst]

rude (rough)	grov	['grɔv]
stocky (adj)	undersetsig	['ʉnəˌsɛtsi]
robust (adj)	robust	[rʉ'bʉst]
strong (adj)	sterk	['stærk]
strength	kraft, styrke (m)	['kraft], ['styrkə]

plump, fat (adj)	tykk	['tʏk]
swarthy (dark-skinned)	mørkhudet	['mœrkˌhʉdet]
slender (well-built)	slank	['ʂlank]
elegant (adj)	elegant	[ɛle'gant]

58. Age

age	alder (m)	['aldər]
youth (young age)	ungdom (m)	['ʉŋˌdɔm]

young (adj)	ung	['ʉŋ]
younger (adj)	yngre	['yŋrə]
older (adj)	eldre	['ɛldrə]

young man	unge mann (m)	['ʉŋə ˌman]
teenager	tenåring (m)	['tɛnoːriŋ]
guy, fellow	kar (m)	['kar]

| old man | gammel mann (m) | ['gaməl ˌman] |
| old woman | gammel kvinne (m/f) | ['gaməl ˌkvinə] |

adult (adj)	voksen	['vɔksən]
middle-aged (adj)	middelaldrende	['midəlˌaldrɛnə]
elderly (adj)	eldre	['ɛldrə]
old (adj)	gammel	['gaməl]

retirement	pensjon (m)	[pan'ʂʉn]
to retire (from job)	å gå av med pensjon	[ɔ 'gɔ ɑː me pan'ʂʉn]
retiree, pensioner	pensjonist (m)	[panʂu'nist]

59. Children

child	barn (n)	['baːɳ]
children	barn (n pl)	['baːɳ]
twins	tvillinger (m pl)	['tviliŋər]

cradle	vogge (m/f)	['vɔgə]
rattle	rangle (m/f)	['raŋlə]
nappy	bleie (m/f)	['blæjə]

dummy, comforter	smokk (m)	['smʉk]
pram	barnevogn (m/f)	['baːɳəˌvɔŋn]
nursery	barnehage (m)	['baːɳəˌhagə]
babysitter	babysitter (m)	['bɛbyˌsitər]

childhood	barndom (m)	['baːɳˌdɔm]
doll	dukke (m/f)	['dʉkə]
toy	leketøy (n)	['lekəˌtøj]
construction set (toy)	byggesett (n)	['bʏgəˌsɛt]
well-bred (adj)	veloppdragen	['velˌɔp'dragən]
ill-bred (adj)	uoppdragen	[ʉop'dragən]
spoilt (adj)	bortskjemt	['bʉːˌʈʂɛmt]

to be naughty	å være stygg	[ɔ 'værə 'stʏg]
mischievous (adj)	skøyeraktig	['skøjəˌrakti]
mischievousness	skøyeraktighet (m)	['skøjəˌraktihet]
mischievous child	skøyer (m)	['skøjər]

| obedient (adj) | lydig | ['lydi] |
| disobedient (adj) | ulydig | [ʉ'lydi] |

docile (adj)	føyelig	['føjli]
clever (intelligent)	klok	['klʉk]
child prodigy	vidunderbarn (n)	['vidˌʉndərˌbaːɳ]

60. Married couples. Family life

to kiss (vt)	å kysse	[ɔ 'çysə]
to kiss (vi)	å kysse hverandre	[ɔ 'çysə ˌverandrə]
family (n)	familie (m)	[faˈmiliə]
family (as adj)	familie-	[faˈmiliə-]
couple	par (n)	['par]
marriage (state)	ekteskap (n)	['ɛktəˌskap]
hearth (home)	hjemmets arne (m)	['jɛmɛts 'aːŋə]
dynasty	dynasti (n)	[dinasˈti]
date	stevnemøte (n)	['stɛvnəˌmøtə]
kiss	kyss (n)	['çys]
love (for sb)	kjærlighet (m)	['çæːⱡiˌhet]
to love (sb)	å elske	[ɔ 'ɛlskə]
beloved	elskling	['ɛlskliŋ]
tenderness	ømhet (m)	['ømˌhet]
tender (affectionate)	øm	['øm]
faithfulness	troskap (m)	['truˌskap]
faithful (adj)	trofast	['trʊfast]
care (attention)	omsorg (m)	['ɔmˌsɔrg]
caring (~ father)	omsorgsfull	['ɔmˌsɔrgsfʉl]
newlyweds	nygifte (n)	['nyˌjiftə]
honeymoon	hvetebrødsdager (m pl)	['vetɛbrøsˌdagər]
to get married (ab. woman)	å gifte seg	[ɔ 'jiftə sæj]
to get married (ab. man)	å gifte seg	[ɔ 'jiftə sæj]
wedding	bryllup (n)	['brʏlʉp]
golden wedding	gullbryllup (n)	['gʉlˌbrʏlʉp]
anniversary	årsdag (m)	['oːʂˌda]
lover (masc.)	elsker (m)	['ɛlskər]
mistress (lover)	elskerinne (m/f)	['ɛlskəˌrinə]
adultery	utroskap (m)	['ʉˌtrɔskap]
to cheat on ... (commit adultery)	å være utro	[ɔ 'værə 'ʉˌtrʊ]
jealous (adj)	sjalu	[ʂaˈlʉː]
to be jealous	å være sjalu	[ɔ 'værə ʂaˈlʉː]
divorce	skilsmisse (m)	['ʂilsˌmisə]
to divorce (vi)	å skille seg	[ɔ 'ʂilə sæj]
to quarrel (vi)	å krangle	[ɔ 'kraŋlə]
to be reconciled (after an argument)	å forsone seg	[ɔ fɔˈʂʉnə sæj]
together (adv)	sammen	['samən]
sex	sex (m)	['sɛks]
happiness	lykke (m/f)	['lʏkə]
happy (adj)	lykkelig	['lʏkəli]
misfortune (accident)	ulykke (m/f)	['ʉˌlʏkə]
unhappy (adj)	ulykkelig	['ʉˌlʏkəli]

Character. Feelings. Emotions

61. Feelings. Emotions

feeling (emotion)	følelse (m)	['følelsə]
feelings	følelser (m pl)	['følelsər]
to feel (vt)	å kjenne	[ɔ 'çɛnə]
hunger	sult (m)	['sʉlt]
to be hungry	å være sulten	[ɔ 'værə 'sʉltən]
thirst	tørst (m)	['tœʂt]
to be thirsty	å være tørst	[ɔ 'værə 'tœʂt]
sleepiness	søvnighet (m)	['sœvni,het]
to feel sleepy	å være søvnig	[ɔ 'værə 'sœvni]
tiredness	tretthet (m)	['trɛt,het]
tired (adj)	trett	['trɛt]
to get tired	å bli trett	[ɔ 'bli 'trɛt]
mood (humour)	humør (n)	[hʉ'mør]
boredom	kjedsomhet (m/f)	['çɛdsɔm,het]
to be bored	å kjede seg	[ɔ 'çedə sæj]
seclusion	avsondrethet (m/f)	['afsɔndrɛt,het]
to seclude oneself	å isolere seg	[ɔ isʉ'lerə sæj]
to worry (make anxious)	å bekymre, å uroe	[ɔ be'çymrə], [ɔ 'ʉ:rʊə]
to be worried	å bekymre seg	[ɔ be'çymrə sæj]
worrying (n)	bekymring (m/f)	[be'çymriŋ]
anxiety	uro (m/f)	['ʉrʊ]
preoccupied (adj)	bekymret	[be'çymrət]
to be nervous	å være nervøs	[ɔ 'værə nær'vøs]
to panic (vi)	å få panikk	[ɔ 'fɔ pa'nik]
hope	håp (n)	['hɔp]
to hope (vi, vt)	å håpe	[ɔ 'ho:pə]
certainty	sikkerhet (m/f)	['sikər,het]
certain, sure (adj)	sikker	['sikər]
uncertainty	usikkerhet (m)	['ʉsikər,het]
uncertain (adj)	usikker	['ʉ,sikər]
drunk (adj)	beruset, full	[be'rʉsət], ['fʉl]
sober (adj)	edru	['ɛdrʉ]
weak (adj)	svak	['svɑk]
happy (adj)	lykkelig	['lʏkəli]
to scare (vt)	å skremme	[ɔ 'skrɛmə]
fury (madness)	raseri (n)	[rɑsɛ'ri]
rage (fury)	raseri (n)	[rɑsɛ'ri]
depression	depresjon (m)	[dɛpre'ʂʊn]
discomfort (unease)	ubehag (n)	['ʉbe,hɑg]

comfort	komfort (m)	[kʊm'fɔːr]
to regret (be sorry)	å beklage	[ɔ be'klɑgə]
regret	beklagelse (m)	[be'klɑgəlsə]
bad luck	uhell (n)	['ʉˌhɛl]
sadness	sorg (m/f)	['sɔr]

shame (remorse)	skam (m/f)	['skɑm]
gladness	glede (m/f)	['glede]
enthusiasm, zeal	entusiasme (m)	[ɛntʉsi'ɑsme]
enthusiast	entusiast (m)	[ɛntʉsi'ɑst]
to show enthusiasm	å vise entusiasme	[ɔ 'vise ɛntʉsi'ɑsme]

62. Character. Personality

character	karakter (m)	[kɑrɑk'ter]
character flaw	karakterbrist (m/f)	[kɑrɑk'terˌbrist]
mind	sinn (n)	['sin]
reason	forstand (m)	[fɔ'ʂtɑn]

conscience	samvittighet (m)	[sɑm'vitiˌhet]
habit (custom)	vane (m)	['vɑne]
ability (talent)	evne (m/f)	['ɛvne]
can (e.g. ~ swim)	å kunne	[ɔ 'kʉne]

patient (adj)	tålmodig	[tɔl'mʊdi]
impatient (adj)	utålmodig	['ʉtɔlˌmʊdi]
curious (inquisitive)	nysgjerrig	['nɣˌsæri]
curiosity	nysgjerrighet (m)	['nɣˌsæriˌhet]

modesty	beskjedenhet (m)	[be'ʂedenˌhet]
modest (adj)	beskjeden	[be'ʂeden]
immodest (adj)	ubeskjeden	['ʉbeˌʂeden]

laziness	lathet (m)	['lɑtˌhet]
lazy (adj)	doven	['dʊven]
lazy person (masc.)	dovendyr (n)	['dʊvenˌdyr]

cunning (n)	list (m/f)	['list]
cunning (as adj)	listig	['listi]
distrust	mistro (m/f)	['misˌtrɔ]
distrustful (adj)	mistroende	['misˌtrʉene]

generosity	gavmildhet (m)	['gɑvmilˌhet]
generous (adj)	generøs	[ʂene'røs]
talented (adj)	talentfull	[tɑ'lentˌfʉl]
talent	talent (n)	[tɑ'lent]

courageous (adj)	modig	['mʊdi]
courage	mot (n)	['mʊt]
honest (adj)	ærlig	['æːˌli]
honesty	ærlighet (m)	['æːˌliˌhet]

| careful (cautious) | forsiktig | [fɔ'ʂikti] |
| brave (courageous) | modig | ['mʊdi] |

serious (adj)	alvorlig	[al'vɔ:[i]
strict (severe, stern)	streng	['strɛŋ]
decisive (adj)	besluttsom	[be'şlʉt,sɔm]
indecisive (adj)	ubesluttsom	[ʉbe'şlʉt,sɔm]
shy, timid (adj)	forsagt	['fɔ,şakt]
shyness, timidity	forsagthet (m)	['fɔşakt,het]
confidence (trust)	tillit (m)	['tilit]
to believe (trust)	å tro	[ɔ 'trʉ]
trusting (credulous)	tillitsfull	['tilits,fʉl]
sincerely (adv)	oppriktig	[ɔp'rikti]
sincere (adj)	oppriktig	[ɔp'rikti]
sincerity	oppriktighet (m)	[ɔp'rikti,het]
open (person)	åpen	['ɔpən]
calm (adj)	stille	['stilə]
frank (sincere)	oppriktig	[ɔp'rikti]
naïve (adj)	naiv	[na'iv]
absent-minded (adj)	forstrødd	['fʉ,ştrød]
funny (odd)	morsom	['mʉşɔm]
greed, stinginess	grådighet (m)	['gro:di,het]
greedy, stingy (adj)	grådig	['gro:di]
stingy (adj)	gjerrig	['jæri]
evil (adj)	ond	['ʊn]
stubborn (adj)	hårdnakket	['hɔ:r,nakət]
unpleasant (adj)	ubehagelig	[ʉbe'hageli]
selfish person (masc.)	egoist (m)	[ɛgʊ'ist]
selfish (adj)	egoistisk	[ɛgʊ'istisk]
coward	feiging (m)	['fæjgiŋ]
cowardly (adj)	feig	['fæjg]

63. Sleep. Dreams

to sleep (vi)	å sove	[ɔ 'sɔvə]
sleep, sleeping	søvn (m)	['sœvn]
dream	drøm (m)	['drøm]
to dream (in sleep)	å drømme	[ɔ 'drœmə]
sleepy (adj)	søvnig	['sœvni]
bed	seng (m/f)	['sɛŋ]
mattress	madrass (m)	[ma'dras]
blanket (eiderdown)	dyne (m/f)	['dynə]
pillow	pute (m/f)	['pʉtə]
sheet	laken (n)	['lakən]
insomnia	søvnløshet (m)	['sœvnløs,het]
sleepless (adj)	søvnløs	['sœvn,løs]
sleeping pill	sovetablett (n)	['sɔve,tab'let]
to take a sleeping pill	å ta en sovetablett	[ɔ 'ta en 'sɔve,tab'let]
to feel sleepy	å være søvnig	[ɔ 'værə 'sœvni]

61

to yawn (vi)	å gjespe	[ɔ 'jɛspə]
to go to bed	å gå til sengs	[ɔ 'gɔ til 'sɛŋs]
to make up the bed	å re opp sengen	[ɔ 're ɔp 'sɛŋən]
to fall asleep	å falle i søvn	[ɔ 'falə i 'sœvn]
nightmare	mareritt (n)	['marə,rit]
snore, snoring	snork (m)	['snɔrk]
to snore (vi)	å snorke	[ɔ 'snɔrkə]
alarm clock	vekkerklokka (m/f)	['vɛkər,klɔka]
to wake (vt)	å vekke	[ɔ 'vɛkə]
to wake up	å våkne	[ɔ 'vɔknə]
to get up (vi)	å stå opp	[ɔ 'stɔː ɔp]
to have a wash	å vaske seg	[ɔ 'vaskə sæj]

64. Humour. Laughter. Gladness

humour (wit, fun)	humor (m/n)	['hʉmʊr]
sense of humour	sans (m) for humor	['sans fɔr 'hʉmʊr]
to enjoy oneself	å more seg	[ɔ 'mʊrə sæj]
cheerful (merry)	glad, munter	['gla], ['mʉntər]
merriment (gaiety)	munterhet (m)	['mʉntər,het]
smile	smil (m/n)	['smil]
to smile (vi)	å smile	[ɔ 'smilə]
to start laughing	å begynne å skratte	[ɔ be'jinə ɔ 'skratə]
to laugh (vi)	å le, å skratte	[ɔ 'le], [ɔ 'skratə]
laugh, laughter	latter (m), skratt (m/n)	['latər], ['skrat]
anecdote	anekdote (m)	[anek'dotə]
funny (anecdote, etc.)	morsom	['mʉʂɔm]
funny (odd)	morsom	['mʉʂɔm]
to joke (vi)	å spøke	[ɔ 'spøkə]
joke (verbal)	skjemt, spøk (m)	['ʂɛmt], ['spøk]
joy (emotion)	glede (m/f)	['gledə]
to rejoice (vi)	å glede seg	[ɔ 'gledə sæj]
joyful (adj)	glad	['gla]

65. Discussion, conversation. Part 1

communication	kommunikasjon (m)	[kʊmʉnika'ʂʉn]
to communicate	å kommunisere	[ɔ kʊmʉni'serə]
conversation	samtale (m)	['sam,talə]
dialogue	dialog (m)	[dia'lɔg]
discussion (discourse)	diskusjon (m)	[diskʉ'ʂʉn]
dispute (debate)	debatt (m)	[de'bat]
to dispute, to debate	å diskutere	[ɔ diskʉ'terə]
interlocutor	samtalepartner (m)	['sam,talə 'paːʈnər]
topic (theme)	emne (n)	['ɛmnə]

point of view	synspunkt (n)	['syns‚pʉnt]
opinion (point of view)	mening (m/f)	['meniŋ]
speech (talk)	tale (m)	['tɑlə]

discussion (of a report, etc.)	diskusjon (m)	[diskʉ'ʂʉn]
to discuss (vt)	å drøfte, å diskutere	[ɔ 'drœftə], [ɔ diskʉ'terə]
talk (conversation)	samtale (m)	['sam‚talə]
to talk (to chat)	å snakke, å samtale	[ɔ 'snakə], [ɔ 'sam‚talə]
meeting (encounter)	møte (n)	['møtə]
to meet (vi, vt)	å møtes	[ɔ 'møtəs]

proverb	ordspråk (n)	['uːr‚sprɔk]
saying	ordstev (n)	['uːr‚stev]
riddle (poser)	gåte (m)	['goːtə]
to pose a riddle	å utgjøre en gåte	[ɔ ʉt'jørə en 'goːtə]
password	passord (n)	['pɑs‚uːr]
secret	hemmelighet (m/f)	['hɛməli‚het]

oath (vow)	ed (m)	['ɛd]
to swear (an oath)	å sverge	[ɔ 'sværgə]
promise	løfte (n), loven (m)	['lœftə], ['lɔvən]
to promise (vt)	å love	[ɔ 'lɔvə]

advice (counsel)	råd (n)	['rɔd]
to advise (vt)	å råde	[ɔ 'roːdə]
to follow one's advice	å følge råd	[ɔ 'følə 'roːd]
to listen to … (obey)	å adlyde	[ɔ 'ad‚lydə]

news	nyhet (m)	['nyhet]
sensation (news)	sensasjon (m)	[sɛnsɑ'ʂʉn]
information (report)	opplysninger (m/f pl)	['ɔp‚lysniŋər]
conclusion (decision)	slutning (m)	['ʂlʉtniŋ]
voice	røst (m/f), stemme (m)	['røst], ['stɛmə]
compliment	kompliment (m)	[kʉmpli'maŋ]
kind (nice)	elskverdig	[ɛlsk'værdi]

word	ord (n)	['uːr]
phrase	frase (m)	['frɑsə]
answer	svar (n)	['svar]

| truth | sannhet (m) | ['san‚het] |
| lie | løgn (m/f) | ['løjn] |

thought	tanke (m)	['tɑnkə]
idea (inspiration)	ide (m)	[i'de]
fantasy	fantasi (m)	[fantɑ'si]

66. Discussion, conversation. Part 2

respected (adj)	respektert	[rɛspɛk'tɛːt]
to respect (vt)	å respektere	[ɔ rɛspɛk'terə]
respect	respekt (m)	[rɛ'spɛkt]
Dear … (letter)	Kjære …	['çærə …]
to introduce (sb to sb)	å introdusere	[ɔ introdʉ'serə]

to make acquaintance	å stifte bekjentskap med ...	[ɔ 'stiftə be'çɛnˌskɑp me ...]
intention	hensikt (m)	['hɛnˌsikt]
to intend (have in mind)	å ha til hensikt	[ɔ 'hɑ til 'hɛnˌsikt]
wish	ønske (n)	['ønskə]
to wish (~ good luck)	å ønske	[ɔ 'ønskə]

surprise (astonishment)	overraskelse (m/f)	['ɔvəˌrɑskəlsə]
to surprise (amaze)	å forundre	[ɔ fɔ'rʉndrə]
to be surprised	å bli forundret	[ɔ 'bli fɔ'rʉndrət]

to give (vt)	å gi	[ɔ 'ji]
to take (get hold of)	å ta	[ɔ 'tɑ]
to give back	å gi tilbake	[ɔ 'ji til'bɑkə]
to return (give back)	å returnere	[ɔ retʉr'nerə]

to apologize (vi)	å unnskylde seg	[ɔ 'ʉnˌsylə sæj]
apology	unnskyldning (m/f)	['ʉnˌsyldniŋ]
to forgive (vt)	å tilgi	[ɔ 'tilˌji]

to talk (speak)	å tale	[ɔ 'tɑlə]
to listen (vi)	å lye, å lytte	[ɔ 'lye], [ɔ 'lʏtə]
to hear out	å høre på	[ɔ 'hørə pɔ]
to understand (vt)	å forstå	[ɔ fɔ'ʂtɔ]

to show (to display)	å vise	[ɔ 'visə]
to look at ...	å se på ...	[ɔ 'se pɔ ...]
to call (yell for sb)	å kalle	[ɔ 'kɑlə]
to distract (disturb)	å distrahere	[ɔ distrɑ'erə]
to disturb (vt)	å forstyrre	[ɔ fɔ'ʂtʏrə]
to pass (to hand sth)	å rekke	[ɔ 'rɛkə]

demand (request)	begjæring (m/f)	[be'jæriŋ]
to request (ask)	å be, å bede	[ɔ 'be], [ɔ 'bedə]
demand (firm request)	krav (n)	['krɑv]
to demand (request firmly)	å kreve	[ɔ 'krevə]

to tease (call names)	å erte	[ɔ 'ɛːʈə]
to mock (make fun of)	å håne	[ɔ 'hoːnə]
mockery, derision	hån (m)	['hɔn]
nickname	kallenavn, tilnavn (n)	['kɑləˌnɑvn], ['tilˌnɑvn]

insinuation	insinuasjon (m)	[insinʉɑ'ʂun]
to insinuate (imply)	å insinuere	[ɔ insinu'erə]
to mean (vt)	å bety	[ɔ 'bety]

description	beskrivelse (m)	[be'skrivəlsə]
to describe (vt)	å beskrive	[ɔ be'skrivə]
praise (compliments)	ros (m)	['rʉs]
to praise (vt)	å rose, å berømme	[ɔ 'rʉsə], [ɔ be'rœmə]

disappointment	skuffelse (m)	['skʉfəlsə]
to disappoint (vt)	å skuffe	[ɔ 'skʉfə]
to be disappointed	å bli skuffet	[ɔ 'bli 'skʉfət]

| supposition | antagelse (m) | [an'tɑgəlsə] |
| to suppose (assume) | å anta, å formode | [ɔ 'anˌtɑ], [ɔ fɔr'mʉdə] |

| warning (caution) | advarsel (m) | ['ad,vaʂəl] |
| to warn (vt) | å advare | [ɔ 'ad,varə] |

67. Discussion, conversation. Part 3

| to talk into (convince) | å overtale | [ɔ 'ovə,talə] |
| to calm down (vt) | å berolige | [ɔ be'rʉliə] |

silence (~ is golden)	taushet (m)	['taʊs,het]
to be silent (not speaking)	å tie	[ɔ 'tie]
to whisper (vi, vt)	å hviske	[ɔ 'viskə]
whisper	hvisking (m/f)	['viskiŋ]

| frankly, sincerely (adv) | oppriktig | [ɔp'rikti] |
| in my opinion ... | etter min mening ... | ['ɛtər min 'meniŋ ...] |

detail (of the story)	detalj (m)	[de'talj]
detailed (adj)	detaljert	[deta'ljɛ:t]
in detail (adv)	i detaljer	[i de'taljer]

| hint, clue | vink (n) | ['vink] |
| to give a hint | å gi et vink | [ɔ 'ji et 'vink] |

look (glance)	blikk (n)	['blik]
to have a look	å kaste et blikk	[ɔ 'kastə et 'blik]
fixed (look)	stiv	['stiv]
to blink (vi)	å blinke	[ɔ 'blinkə]
to wink (vi)	å blinke	[ɔ 'blinkə]
to nod (in assent)	å nikke	[ɔ 'nikə]

sigh	sukk (n)	['sʉk]
to sigh (vi)	å sukke	[ɔ 'sʉkə]
to shudder (vi)	å gyse	[ɔ 'jisə]
gesture	gest (m)	['gɛst]
to touch (one's arm, etc.)	å røre	[ɔ 'rørə]
to seize (e.g., ~ by the arm)	å gripe	[ɔ 'gripə]
to tap (on the shoulder)	å klappe	[ɔ 'klapə]

Look out!	Pass på!	['pas 'pɔ]
Really?	Virkelig?	['virkəli]
Are you sure?	Er du sikker?	[ɛr dʉ 'sikər]
Good luck!	Lykke til!	['lʏkə til]
I see!	Jeg forstår!	['jæ fɔ'sto:r]
What a pity!	Det var synd!	[de var 'sʏn]

68. Agreement. Refusal

consent	samtykke (n)	['sam,tʏkə]
to consent (vi)	å samtykke	[ɔ 'sam,tʏkə]
approval	godkjennelse (m)	['gʊ,çɛnəlsə]
to approve (vt)	å godkjenne	[ɔ 'gʊ,çɛnə]
refusal	avslag (n)	['af,slag]

to refuse (vi, vt)	å vegre seg	[ɔ 'vɛgrə sæj]
Great!	Det er fint!	['de ær 'fint]
All right!	Godt!	['gɔt]
Okay! (I agree)	OK! Enig!	[ɔ'kɛj], ['ɛni]

forbidden (adj)	forbudt	[fɔr'bʉt]
it's forbidden	det er forbudt	[de ær fɔr'bʉt]
it's impossible	det er umulig	[de ær ʉ'mʉli]
incorrect (adj)	uriktig, ikke riktig	['ʉˌrikti], ['ikə ˌrikti]

to reject (~ a demand)	å avslå	[ɔ 'afˌslɔ]
to support (cause, idea)	å støtte	[ɔ 'stœtə]
to accept (~ an apology)	å akseptere	[ɔ aksɛp'terə]

to confirm (vt)	å bekrefte	[ɔ be'krɛftə]
confirmation	bekreftelse (m)	[be'krɛftəlsə]
permission	tillatelse (m)	['tiˌlatəlsə]
to permit (vt)	å tillate	[ɔ 'tiˌlatə]
decision	beslutning (m)	[be'ʂlʉtniŋ]
to say nothing	å tie	[ɔ 'tie]
(hold one's tongue)		

condition (term)	betingelse (m)	[be'tiŋəlsə]
excuse (pretext)	foregivende (n)	['fɔrəˌjivnə]
praise (compliments)	ros (m)	['rus]
to praise (vt)	å rose, å berømme	[ɔ 'rusə], [ɔ be'rœmə]

69. Success. Good luck. Failure

success	suksess (m)	[sʉk'sɛ]
successfully (adv)	med suksess	[me sʉk'sɛ]
successful (adj)	vellykket	['velˌlʏkət]

luck (good luck)	hell (n), lykke (m/f)	['hɛl], ['lʏkə]
Good luck!	Lykke til!	['lʏkə til]
lucky (e.g. ~ day)	heldig, lykkelig	['hɛldi], ['lʏkəli]
lucky (fortunate)	heldig	['hɛldi]

failure	mislykkelse, fiasko (m)	['misˌlʏkəlsə], [fi'askʉ]
misfortune	uhell (n), utur (m)	['ʉˌhɛl], ['ʉˌtʉr]
bad luck	uhell (n)	['ʉˌhɛl]
unsuccessful (adj)	mislykket	['misˌlʏkət]
catastrophe	katastrofe (m)	[kata'strɔfə]

pride	stolthet (m)	['stɔltˌhet]
proud (adj)	stolt	['stɔlt]
to be proud	å være stolt	[ɔ 'værə 'stɔlt]

winner	seierherre (m)	['sæjərˌhɛrə]
to win (vi)	å seire, å vinne	[ɔ 'sæjrə], [ɔ 'vinə]
to lose (not win)	å tape	[ɔ 'tapə]
try	forsøk (n)	['fɔ'søk]
to try (vi)	å prøve, å forsøke	[ɔ 'prøvə], [ɔ fɔ'søkə]
chance (opportunity)	sjanse (m)	['ʂansə]

70. Quarrels. Negative emotions

shout (scream)	skrik (n)	['skrik]
to shout (vi)	å skrike	[ɔ 'skrikə]
to start to cry out	å begynne å skrike	[ɔ be'jinə ɔ 'skrikə]
quarrel	krangel (m)	['kraŋəl]
to quarrel (vi)	å krangle	[ɔ 'kraŋlə]
fight (squabble)	skandale (m)	[skan'dalə]
to make a scene	å gjøre skandale	[ɔ 'jørə skan'dalə]
conflict	konflikt (m)	[kʊn'flikt]
misunderstanding	misforståelse (m)	[misfɔ'stɔəlsə]
insult	fornærmelse (m)	[fɔ:'ŋærməlsə]
to insult (vt)	å fornærme	[ɔ fɔ:'ŋærmə]
insulted (adj)	fornærmet	[fɔ:'ŋærmət]
resentment	fornærmelse (m)	[fɔ:'ŋærməlsə]
to offend (vt)	å fornærme	[ɔ fɔ:'ŋærmə]
to take offence	å bli fornærmet	[ɔ 'bli fɔ:'ŋærmət]
indignation	forargelse (m)	[fɔ'rargəlsə]
to be indignant	å bli indignert	[ɔ 'bli indi'gnɛ:t]
complaint	klage (m)	['klagə]
to complain (vi, vt)	å klage	[ɔ 'klagə]
apology	unnskyldning (m/f)	['ʉnˌsyldniŋ]
to apologize (vi)	å unnskylde seg	[ɔ 'ʉnˌsylə sæj]
to beg pardon	å be om forlatelse	[ɔ 'be ɔm fɔ:'latəlsə]
criticism	kritikk (m)	[kri'tik]
to criticize (vt)	å kritisere	[ɔ kriti'serə]
accusation (charge)	anklagelse (m)	['anˌklagəlsə]
to accuse (vt)	å anklage	[ɔ 'anˌklagə]
revenge	hevn (m)	['hɛvn]
to avenge (get revenge)	å hevne	[ɔ 'hɛvnə]
to pay back	å hevne	[ɔ 'hɛvnə]
disdain	forakt (m)	[fɔ'rakt]
to despise (vt)	å forakte	[ɔ fɔ'raktə]
hatred, hate	hat (n)	['hat]
to hate (vt)	å hate	[ɔ 'hatə]
nervous (adj)	nervøs	[nær'vøs]
to be nervous	å være nervøs	[ɔ 'værə nær'vøs]
angry (mad)	vred, sint	['vred], ['sint]
to make angry	å gjøre sint	[ɔ 'jørə ˌsint]
humiliation	ydmykelse (m)	['ydˌmykəlsə]
to humiliate (vt)	å ydmyke	[ɔ 'ydˌmykə]
to humiliate oneself	å ydmyke seg	[ɔ 'ydˌmykə sæj]
shock	sjokk (n)	['ʂɔk]
to shock (vt)	å sjokkere	[ɔ ʂɔ'kerə]
trouble (e.g. serious ~)	knipe (m/f)	['knipə]

unpleasant (adj)	ubehagelig	[ɵbeˈhɑgeli]
fear (dread)	redsel, frykt (m)	[ˈrɛtsəl], [ˈfrʏkt]
terrible (storm, heat)	fryktelig	[ˈfrʏkteli]
scary (e.g. ~ story)	uhyggelig, skremmende	[ˈɵhʏgəli], [ˈskrɛmənə]
horror	redsel (m)	[ˈrɛtsəl]
awful (crime, news)	forferdelig	[fɔrˈfærdəli]

to begin to tremble	å begynne å ryste	[ɔ beˈjinə ɔ ˈrystə]
to cry (weep)	å gråte	[ɔ ˈgroːtə]
to start crying	å begynne å gråte	[ɔ beˈjinə ɔ ˈgroːtə]
tear	tåre (m/f)	[ˈtoːrə]

fault	skyld (m/f)	[ˈsyl]
guilt (feeling)	skyldfølelse (m)	[ˈsylˌføləlsə]
dishonor (disgrace)	skam, vanære (m/f)	[ˈskɑm], [ˈvɑnærə]
protest	protest (m)	[prɵˈtɛst]
stress	stress (m/n)	[ˈstrɛs]

to disturb (vt)	å forstyrre	[ɔ fɔˈʂtʏrə]
to be furious	å være sint	[ɔ ˈværə ˌsint]
angry (adj)	vred, sint	[ˈvred], [ˈsint]
to end (~ a relationship)	å avbryte	[ɔ ˈɑvˌbrytə]
to swear (at sb)	å sverge	[ɔ ˈsværgə]

to scare (become afraid)	å bli skremt	[ɔ ˈbli ˈskrɛmt]
to hit (strike with hand)	å slå	[ɔ ˈʂlɔ]
to fight (street fight, etc.)	å slåss	[ɔ ˈʂlɔs]

to settle (a conflict)	å løse	[ɔ ˈløsə]
discontented (adj)	misfornøyd, utilfreds	[ˈmisˌfɔːˈnøjd], [ˈɵtilˌfrɛds]
furious (adj)	rasende	[ˈrɑsenə]

It's not good!	Det er ikke bra!	[de ær ikə ˈbrɑ]
It's bad!	Det er dårlig!	[de ær ˈdoːli]

Medicine

illness	**sykdom** (m)	['sʏkˌdɔm]
to be ill	**å være syk**	[ɔ 'væːrə 'syk]
health	**helse** (m/f)	['hɛlsə]
runny nose (coryza)	**snue** (m)	['snʉə]
tonsillitis	**angina** (m)	[anˈgina]
cold (illness)	**forkjølelse** (m)	[fɔrˈçœləlsə]
to catch a cold	**å forkjøle seg**	[ɔ fɔrˈçœlə sæj]
bronchitis	**bronkitt** (m)	[brɔnˈkit]
pneumonia	**lungebetennelse** (m)	['lʉŋə beˈtɛnəlsə]
flu, influenza	**influensa** (m)	[inflʉˈɛnsa]
shortsighted (adj)	**nærsynt**	['næˌsʏnt]
longsighted (adj)	**langsynt**	['laŋsʏnt]
strabismus (crossed eyes)	**skjeløydhet** (m)	['ʂɛløjdˌhet]
squint-eyed (adj)	**skjeløyd**	['ʂɛlˌøjd]
cataract	**grå stær, katarakt** (m)	['grɔ ˌstær], [kataˈrakt]
glaucoma	**glaukom** (n)	[glaʊˈkɔm]
stroke	**hjerneslag** (n)	['jæːˌŋəˌslag]
heart attack	**infarkt** (n)	[inˈfarkt]
myocardial infarction	**myokardieinfarkt** (n)	['miɔˈkardiə inˈfarkt]
paralysis	**paralyse, lammelse** (m)	['paraˈlyse], ['laməlsə]
to paralyse (vt)	**å lamme**	[ɔ 'lamə]
allergy	**allergi** (m)	[alæːˈgi]
asthma	**astma** (m)	['astma]
diabetes	**diabetes** (m)	[diaˈbetəs]
toothache	**tannpine** (m/f)	['tanˌpine]
caries	**karies** (m)	['karies]
diarrhoea	**diaré** (m)	[diaˈrɛ]
constipation	**forstoppelse** (m)	[fɔˈʂtɔpəlsə]
stomach upset	**magebesvær** (m)	['magəˌbeˈsvær]
food poisoning	**matforgiftning** (m/f)	['matˌforˈjiftniŋ]
to get food poisoning	**å få matforgiftning**	[ɔ 'fɔ matˌforˈjiftniŋ]
arthritis	**artritt** (m)	[aːʈˈrit]
rickets	**rakitt** (m)	[raˈkit]
rheumatism	**revmatisme** (m)	[revmaˈtismə]
atherosclerosis	**arteriosklerose** (m)	[aːˈʈeriʊsklerˌrʊsə]
gastritis	**magekatarr, gastritt** (m)	['magəkaˌtar], [ˌgaˈstrit]
appendicitis	**appendisitt** (m)	[apɛndiˈsit]

cholecystitis	galleblærebetennelse (m)	['galə,blærə be'tɛnəlse]
ulcer	magesår (n)	['magə,sɔr]

measles	meslinger (m pl)	['mɛs,liŋər]
rubella (German measles)	røde hunder (m pl)	['rødə 'hʉnər]
jaundice	gulsott (m/f)	['gʉl,sʉt]
hepatitis	hepatitt (m)	[hepa'tit]

schizophrenia	schizofreni (m)	[ṣisʉfre'ni]
rabies (hydrophobia)	rabies (m)	['rabiəs]
neurosis	nevrose (m)	[nev'rʉsə]
concussion	hjernerystelse (m)	['jæːŋə,rʏstəlsə]

cancer	kreft, cancer (m)	['krɛft], ['kansər]
sclerosis	sklerose (m)	[skle'rʉsə]
multiple sclerosis	multippel sklerose (m)	[mʉl'tipəl skle'rʉsə]

alcoholism	alkoholisme (m)	[alkʉhʉ'lismə]
alcoholic (n)	alkoholiker (m)	[alkʉ'hʉlikər]
syphilis	syfilis (m)	['syfilis]
AIDS	AIDS, aids (m)	['ɛjds]

tumour	svulst, tumor (m)	['svʉlst], [tʉ'mʉr]
malignant (adj)	ondartet, malign	['ʉn,aːʈət], [ma'lign]
benign (adj)	godartet	['gʉ,aːʈət]

fever	feber (m)	['febər]
malaria	malaria (m)	[ma'laria]
gangrene	koldbrann (m)	['kɔlbran]
seasickness	sjøsyke (m)	['ṣø,syke]
epilepsy	epilepsi (m)	[ɛpilep'si]

epidemic	epidemi (m)	[ɛpide'mi]
typhus	tyfus (m)	['tyfʉs]
tuberculosis	tuberkulose (m)	[tubærkʉ'lɔsə]
cholera	kolera (m)	['kʉlera]
plague (bubonic ~)	pest (m)	['pɛst]

72. Symptoms. Treatments. Part 1

symptom	symptom (n)	[sʏmp'tʉm]
temperature	temperatur (m)	[tɛmpəra'tʉr]
high temperature (fever)	høy temperatur (m)	['høj tɛmpəra'tʉr]
pulse (heartbeat)	puls (m)	['pʉls]

dizziness (vertigo)	svimmelhet (m)	['sviməl,het]
hot (adj)	varm	['varm]
shivering	skjelving (m/f)	['ṣɛlviŋ]
pale (e.g. ~ face)	blek	['blek]

cough	hoste (m)	['hʉstə]
to cough (vi)	å hoste	[ɔ 'hʉstə]
to sneeze (vi)	å nyse	[ɔ 'nysə]
faint	besvimelse (m)	[bɛ'sviməlsə]

to faint (vi)	å besvime	[ɔ be'svimə]
bruise (hématome)	blåmerke (n)	['blɔˌmærkə]
bump (lump)	bule (m)	['bʉlə]
to bang (bump)	å slå seg	[ɔ 'ʂlɔ sæj]
contusion (bruise)	blåmerke (n)	['blɔˌmærkə]
to get a bruise	å slå seg	[ɔ 'ʂlɔ sæj]

to limp (vi)	å halte	[ɔ 'haltə]
dislocation	forvridning (m)	[fɔr'vridniŋ]
to dislocate (vt)	å forvri	[ɔ fɔr'vri]
fracture	brudd (n), fraktur (m)	['brʉd], [frɑk'tʉr]
to have a fracture	å få brudd	[ɔ 'fɔ 'brʉd]

cut (e.g. paper ~)	skjæresår (n)	['ʂæːrəˌsɔr]
to cut oneself	å skjære seg	[ɔ 'ʂæːrə sæj]
bleeding	blødning (m/f)	['blødniŋ]

burn (injury)	brannsår (n)	['brɑnˌsɔr]
to get burned	å brenne seg	[ɔ 'brɛnə sæj]

to prick (vt)	å stikke	[ɔ 'stikə]
to prick oneself	å stikke seg	[ɔ 'stikə sæj]
to injure (vt)	å skade	[ɔ 'skɑdə]
injury	skade (n)	['skɑdə]
wound	sår (n)	['sɔr]
trauma	traume (m)	['trɑʊmə]

to be delirious	å snakke i villelse	[ɔ 'snɑkə i 'viləlsə]
to stutter (vi)	å stamme	[ɔ 'stɑmə]
sunstroke	solstikk (n)	['sʉlˌstik]

73. Symptoms. Treatments. Part 2

pain, ache	smerte (m)	['smæːʈə]
splinter (in foot, etc.)	flis (m/f)	['flis]

sweat (perspiration)	svette (m)	['svɛtə]
to sweat (perspire)	å svette	[ɔ 'svɛtə]
vomiting	oppkast (n)	['ɔpˌkɑst]
convulsions	kramper (m pl)	['krɑmpər]

pregnant (adj)	gravid	[grɑ'vid]
to be born	å fødes	[ɔ 'fødə]
delivery, labour	fødsel (m)	['føtsəl]
to deliver (~ a baby)	å føde	[ɔ 'fødə]
abortion	abort (m)	[ɑ'bɔːʈ]

breathing, respiration	åndedrett (n)	['ɔŋdəˌdrɛt]
in-breath (inhalation)	innånding (m/f)	['inˌɔniŋ]
out-breath (exhalation)	utånding (m/f)	['ʉtˌɔndiŋ]
to exhale (breathe out)	å puste ut	[ɔ 'pʉstə ʉt]
to inhale (vi)	å ånde inn	[ɔ 'ɔŋdə ˌin]
disabled person	handikappet person (m)	['hɑndiˌkɑpet pæ'ʂʉn]
cripple	krøpling (m)	['krøpliŋ]

drug addict	narkoman (m)	[nɑrkʊ'mɑn]
deaf (adj)	døv	['døv]
mute (adj)	stum	['stʉm]
deaf mute (adj)	døvstum	['døf‚stʉm]

mad, insane (adj)	gal	['gɑl]
madman	gal mann (m)	['gɑl ‚mɑn]
(demented person)		
madwoman	gal kvinne (m/f)	['gɑl ‚kvinə]
to go insane	å bli sinnssyk	[ɔ 'bli 'sin‚syk]

gene	gen (m)	['gen]
immunity	immunitet (m)	[imʉni'tet]
hereditary (adj)	arvelig	['ɑrvəli]
congenital (adj)	medfødt	['me:‚føt]

virus	virus (m)	['virʉs]
microbe	mikrobe (m)	[mi'krʊbə]
bacterium	bakterie (m)	[bak'teriə]
infection	infeksjon (m)	[infɛk'ʂʊn]

74. Symptoms. Treatments. Part 3

| hospital | sykehus (n) | ['sykə‚hʉs] |
| patient | pasient (m) | [pɑsi'ɛnt] |

diagnosis	diagnose (m)	[diɑ'gnʉsə]
cure	kur (m)	['kʉr]
medical treatment	behandling (m/f)	[be'hɑndliŋ]
to get treatment	å bli behandlet	[ɔ 'bli be'hɑndlət]
to treat (~ a patient)	å behandle	[ɔ be'hɑndlə]
to nurse (look after)	å skjøtte	[ɔ 'ʂøtə]
care (nursing ~)	sykepleie (m/f)	['sykə‚plæjə]

operation, surgery	operasjon (m)	[ɔpərɑ'ʂʊn]
to bandage (head, limb)	å forbinde	[ɔ fɔr'binə]
bandaging	forbinding (m)	[fɔr'biniŋ]

vaccination	vaksinering (m/f)	[vɑksi'neriŋ]
to vaccinate (vt)	å vaksinere	[ɔ vɑksi'nerə]
injection	injeksjon (m), sprøyte (m/f)	[injɛk'ʂʊn], ['sprøjtə]
to give an injection	å gi en sprøyte	[ɔ 'ji en 'sprøjtə]

attack	anfall (n)	['ɑn‚fɑl]
amputation	amputasjon (m)	[ɑmpʉtɑ'ʂʊn]
to amputate (vt)	å amputere	[ɔ ɑmpʉ'terə]
coma	koma (m)	['kʊmɑ]
to be in a coma	å ligge i koma	[ɔ 'ligə i 'kʊmɑ]
intensive care	intensivavdeling (m/f)	['inten‚siv 'ɑv‚deliŋ]

to recover (~ from flu)	å bli frisk	[ɔ 'bli 'frisk]
condition (patient's ~)	tilstand (m)	['til‚stɑn]
consciousness	bevissthet (m)	[be'vist‚het]
memory (faculty)	minne (n), hukommelse (m)	['minə], [hʉ'kɔməlsə]

to pull out (tooth)	å trekke ut	[ɔ 'trɛkə ʉt]
filling	fylling (m/f)	['fʏliŋ]
to fill (a tooth)	å plombere	[ɔ plʊm'berə]

hypnosis	hypnose (m)	[hʏp'nʊsə]
to hypnotize (vt)	å hypnotisere	[ɔ hʏpnʊti'serə]

75. Doctors

doctor	lege (m)	['legə]
nurse	sykepleierske (m/f)	['sykə‚plæjeˌʂkə]
personal doctor	personlig lege (m)	[pæ'ʂʊnli 'legə]

dentist	tannlege (m)	['tɑnˌlegə]
optician	øyelege (m)	['øjəˌlegə]
general practitioner	terapeut (m)	[tera'pɛut]
surgeon	kirurg (m)	[çi'rʉrg]

psychiatrist	psykiater (m)	[syki'atər]
paediatrician	barnelege (m)	['bɑːɳəˌlegə]
psychologist	psykolog (m)	[sykʊ'lɔg]
gynaecologist	gynekolog (m)	[gynekʊ'lɔg]
cardiologist	kardiolog (m)	[kɑːdjʊ'lɔg]

76. Medicine. Drugs. Accessories

medicine, drug	medisin (m)	[medi'sin]
remedy	middel (n)	['midəl]
to prescribe (vt)	å ordinere	[ɔ ɔrdi'nerə]
prescription	resept (m)	[re'sɛpt]

tablet, pill	tablett (m)	[tɑb'let]
ointment	salve (m/f)	['sɑlvə]
ampoule	ampulle (m)	[am'pʉlə]
mixture, solution	mikstur (m)	[miks'tʉr]
syrup	sirup (m)	['sirʉp]
capsule	pille (m/f)	['pilə]
powder	pulver (n)	['pʉlvər]

gauze bandage	gasbind (n)	['gɑsˌbin]
cotton wool	vatt (m/n)	['vɑt]
iodine	jod (m/n)	['ʉd]

plaster	plaster (n)	['plɑstər]
eyedropper	pipette (m)	[pi'pɛtə]
thermometer	termometer (n)	[tɛrmʊ'metər]
syringe	sprøyte (m/f)	['sprøjtə]

wheelchair	rullestol (m)	['rʉləˌstʊl]
crutches	krykker (m/f pl)	['krʏkər]
painkiller	smertestillende middel (n)	['smæːʈəˌstilenə 'midəl]
laxative	laksativ (n)	[lɑksa'tiv]

spirits (ethanol)	sprit (m)	['sprit]
medicinal herbs	legeurter (m/f pl)	['legəˌʉːʈər]
herbal (~ tea)	urte-	['ʉːʈə-]

77. Smoking. Tobacco products

tobacco	tobakk (m)	[tʉ'bɑk]
cigarette	sigarett (m)	[sigɑ'rɛt]
cigar	sigar (m)	[si'gɑr]
pipe	pipe (m/f)	['piːpə]
packet (of cigarettes)	pakke (m/f)	['pɑkə]

matches	fyrstikker (m/f pl)	['fyˌʂtikər]
matchbox	fyrstikkeske (m)	['fyʂtikˌɛskə]
lighter	tenner (m)	['tɛnər]
ashtray	askebeger (n)	['ɑskəˌbegər]
cigarette case	sigarettetui (n)	[sigɑ'rɛt ɛtʉ'i]

| cigarette holder | munnstykke (n) | ['mʉnˌstʏkə] |
| filter (cigarette tip) | filter (n) | ['filtər] |

to smoke (vi, vt)	å røyke	[ɔ 'røjkə]
to light a cigarette	å tenne en sigarett	[ɔ 'tɛnə en sigɑ'rɛt]
smoking	røyking, røkning (m)	['røjkiŋ], ['røkniŋ]
smoker	røyker (m)	['røjkər]

cigarette end	stump (m)	['stʉmp]
smoke, fumes	røyk (m)	['røjk]
ash	aske (m/f)	['ɑskə]

HUMAN HABITAT

City

city, town	by (m)	['by]
capital city	hovedstad (m)	['huvəd‚stad]
village	landsby (m)	['lans‚by]

city map	bykart (n)	['by‚kɑːt]
city centre	sentrum (n)	['sɛntrum]
suburb	forstad (m)	['fɔ‚stad]
suburban (adj)	forstads-	['fɔ‚stads-]

outskirts	utkant (m)	['ʉt‚kant]
environs (suburbs)	omegner (m pl)	['ɔm‚æejnər]
city block	kvarter (n)	[kvɑːtɛr]
residential block (area)	boligkvarter (n)	['bʉli‚kvɑː'ʈer]

traffic	trafikk (m)	[trɑ'fik]
traffic lights	trafikklys (n)	[trɑ'fik‚lys]
public transport	offentlig transport (m)	['ɔfɛntli trɑns'pɔːʈ]
crossroads	veikryss (n)	['væejkrʏs]

zebra crossing	fotgjengerovergang (m)	['fʉtjɛŋər 'ɔvər‚gɑŋ]
pedestrian subway	undergang (m)	['ʉnər‚gɑŋ]
to cross (~ the street)	å gå over	[ɔ 'gɔ 'ɔvər]
pedestrian	fotgjenger (m)	['fʉtjɛŋər]
pavement	fortau (n)	['fɔː‚ʈaʉ]

bridge	bro (m/f)	['brʉ]
embankment (river walk)	kai (m/f)	['kaj]
fountain	fontene (m)	['fʉntnə]

allée (garden walkway)	allé (m)	[ɑ'leː]
park	park (m)	['pɑrk]
boulevard	bulevard (m)	[bule'vɑr]
square	torg (n)	['tɔr]
avenue (wide street)	aveny (m)	[ave'ny]
street	gate (m/f)	['gɑtə]
side street	sidegate (m/f)	['sidə‚gɑtə]
dead end	blindgate (m/f)	['blin‚gɑtə]

house	hus (n)	['hʉs]
building	bygning (m/f)	['bʏgniŋ]
skyscraper	skyskraper (m)	['şy‚skrɑpər]
facade	fasade (m)	[fɑ'sɑdə]
roof	tak (n)	['tɑk]

window	vindu (n)	['vindʉ]
arch	bue (m)	['bʉ:ə]
column	søyle (m)	['søjlə]
corner	hjørne (n)	['jœ:nə]

shop window	utstillingsvindu (n)	['ʉt‚stiliŋs 'vindʉ]
signboard (store sign, etc.)	skilt (n)	['ʂilt]
poster (e.g., playbill)	plakat (m)	[pla'kat]
advertising poster	reklameplakat (m)	[rɛ'klamə‚pla'kat]
hoarding	reklametavle (m/f)	[rɛ'klamə‚tavlə]

rubbish	søppel (m/f/n), avfall (n)	['sœpəl], ['av‚fal]
rubbish bin	søppelkasse (m/f)	['sœpəl‚kasə]
to litter (vi)	å kaste søppel	[ɔ 'kastə 'sœpəl]
rubbish dump	søppelfylling (m/f), deponi (n)	['sœpəl‚fʏliŋ], [‚depɔ'ni]

telephone box	telefonboks (m)	[tele'fʉn‚bɔks]
lamppost	lyktestolpe (m)	['lʏktə‚stɔlpə]
bench (park ~)	benk (m)	['bɛŋk]

police officer	politi (m)	[pʉli'ti]
police	politi (n)	[pʉli'ti]
beggar	tigger (m)	['tigər]
homeless (n)	hjemløs	['jɛm‚løs]

79. Urban institutions

shop	forretning, butikk (m)	[fɔ'rɛtniŋ], [bʉ'tik]
chemist, pharmacy	apotek (n)	[apʉ'tek]
optician (spectacles shop)	optikk (m)	[ɔp'tik]
shopping centre	kjøpesenter (n)	['çœpə‚sɛntər]
supermarket	supermarked (n)	['sʉpə‚market]

bakery	bakeri (n)	[bake'ri]
baker	baker (m)	['bakər]
cake shop	konditori (n)	[kʉnditɔ'ri]
grocery shop	matbutikk (m)	['matbʉ‚tik]
butcher shop	slakterbutikk (m)	['ʂlaktəbʉ‚tik]

greengrocer	grønnsaksbutikk (m)	['grœn‚saks bʉ'tik]
market	marked (n)	['markəd]

coffee bar	kafé, kaffebar (m)	[ka'fe], ['kafə‚bar]
restaurant	restaurant (m)	[rɛstʉ'raŋ]
pub, bar	pub (m)	['pʉb]
pizzeria	pizzeria (m)	[pitsə'ria]

hairdresser	frisørsalong (m)	[fri'sør sa‚lɔŋ]
post office	post (m)	['pɔst]
dry cleaners	renseri (n)	[rɛnse'ri]
photo studio	fotostudio (n)	['fɔtɔ‚stʉdiɔ]

shoe shop	skobutikk (m)	['skʉ‚bʉ'tik]
bookshop	bokhandel (m)	['bʉk‚handəl]

sports shop	idrettsbutikk (m)	['idrɛts bʉ'tik]
clothes repair shop	reparasjon (m) av klær	[repɑrɑ'ʂʉn ɑː ˌklær]
formal wear hire	leie (m/f) av klær	['læjə ɑː ˌklær]
video rental shop	filmutleie (m/f)	['filmˌʉt'læje]

circus	sirkus (m/n)	['sirkʉs]
zoo	zoo, dyrepark (m)	['sʉː], [dyrə'pɑrk]
cinema	kino (m)	['çinʉ]
museum	museum (n)	[mʉ'seum]
library	bibliotek (n)	[bibliʉ'tek]

theatre	teater (n)	[te'atər]
opera (opera house)	opera (m)	['ʉperɑ]
nightclub	nattklubb (m)	['natˌklʉb]
casino	kasino (n)	[kɑ'sinʉ]

mosque	moské (m)	[mʉ'ske]
synagogue	synagoge (m)	[synɑ'gʉgə]
cathedral	katedral (m)	[kate'drɑl]
temple	tempel (n)	['tɛmpəl]
church	kirke (m/f)	['çirkə]

college	institutt (n)	[insti'tʉt]
university	universitet (n)	[ʉnivæʂi'tet]
school	skole (m/f)	['skʉlə]

prefecture	prefektur (n)	[prɛfɛk'tʉr]
town hall	rådhus (n)	['rodˌhʉs]
hotel	hotell (n)	[hʉ'tɛl]
bank	bank (m)	['bɑnk]

embassy	ambassade (m)	[ɑmbɑ'sɑdə]
travel agency	reisebyrå (n)	['ræjsə byˌro]
information office	opplysningskontor (n)	[ɔp'lʏsniŋs kʉn'tʉr]
currency exchange	vekslingskontor (n)	['vɛkʂliŋs kʉn'tʉr]

| underground, tube | tunnelbane, T-bane (m) | ['tʉnəlˌbanə], ['tɛːˌbanə] |
| hospital | sykehus (n) | ['sykəˌhʉs] |

| petrol station | bensinstasjon (m) | [bɛn'sinˌstɑ'ʂʉn] |
| car park | parkeringsplass (m) | [pɑr'keriŋsˌplɑs] |

80. Signs

signboard (store sign, etc.)	skilt (n)	['ʂilt]
notice (door sign, etc.)	innskrift (m/f)	['inˌskrift]
poster	plakat, poster (m)	['plɑˌkɑt], ['pɔstər]
direction sign	veiviser (m)	['væjˌvisər]
arrow (sign)	pil (m/f)	['pil]

caution	advarsel (m)	['adˌvɑʂəl]
warning sign	varselskilt (n)	['vɑʂəlˌʂilt]
to warn (vt)	å varsle	[ɔ 'vɑʂlə]
rest day (weekly ~)	fridag (m)	['friˌdɑ]

| timetable (schedule) | rutetabell (m) | ['rʉtəˌtɑ'bɛl] |
| opening hours | åpningstider (m/f pl) | ['ɔpniŋsˌtidər] |

WELCOME!	VELKOMMEN!	['vɛlˌkɔmən]
ENTRANCE	INNGANG	['inˌgɑŋ]
WAY OUT	UTGANG	['ʉtˌgɑŋ]

PUSH	SKYV	['ʂyv]
PULL	TREKK	['trɛk]
OPEN	ÅPENT	['ɔpənt]
CLOSED	STENGT	['stɛŋt]

| WOMEN | DAMER | ['dɑmər] |
| MEN | HERRER | ['hæːrər] |

DISCOUNTS	RABATT	[rɑ'bɑt]
SALE	SALG	['sɑlg]
NEW!	NYTT!	['nʏt]
FREE	GRATIS	['grɑtis]

ATTENTION!	FORSIKTIG!	[fʊ'ʂiktə]
NO VACANCIES	INGEN LEDIGE ROM	['iŋən 'lediə rʉm]
RESERVED	RESERVERT	[resɛr'vɛːt]

| ADMINISTRATION | ADMINISTRASJON | [administrɑ'ʂʉn] |
| STAFF ONLY | KUN FOR ANSATTE | ['kʉn for ɑn'sɑtə] |

BEWARE OF THE DOG!	VOKT DEM FOR HUNDEN	['vɔkt dem fɔ 'hʉnən]
NO SMOKING	RØYKING FORBUDT	['røjkiŋ for'bʉt]
DO NOT TOUCH!	IKKE RØR!	['ikə 'rør]

DANGEROUS	FARLIG	['fɑːli]
DANGER	FARE	['fɑrə]
HIGH VOLTAGE	HØYSPENNING	['højˌspɛniŋ]
NO SWIMMING!	BADING FORBUDT	['bɑdiŋ for'bʉt]
OUT OF ORDER	I USTAND	[i 'ʉˌstɑn]

FLAMMABLE	BRANNFARLIG	['brɑnˌfɑːli]
FORBIDDEN	FORBUDT	[for'bʉt]
NO TRESPASSING!	INGEN INNKJØRING	['iŋən 'inˌçœriŋ]
WET PAINT	NYMALT	['nyˌmɑlt]

81. Urban transport

bus, coach	buss (m)	['bʉs]
tram	trikk (m)	['trik]
trolleybus	trolleybuss (m)	['trɔliˌbʉs]
route (bus ~)	rute (m/f)	['rʉtə]
number (e.g. bus ~)	nummer (n)	['nʉmər]

to go by ...	å kjøre med ...	[ɔ 'çœːrə me ...]
to get on (~ the bus)	å gå på ...	[ɔ 'gɔ pɔ ...]
to get off ...	å gå av ...	[ɔ 'gɔ ɑ: ...]
stop (e.g. bus ~)	holdeplass (m)	['hɔləˌplɑs]

next stop	neste holdeplass (m)	['nɛstə 'hɔləˌplɑs]
terminus	endestasjon (m)	['ɛnəˌstɑ'ʂʊn]
timetable	rutetabell (m)	['rʉtəˌtɑ'bɛl]
to wait (vt)	å vente	[ɔ 'vɛntə]

ticket	billett (m)	[bi'let]
fare	billettpris (m)	[bi'letˌpris]

cashier (ticket seller)	kasserer (m)	[kɑ'serər]
ticket inspection	billettkontroll (m)	[bi'let kʊnˌtrɔl]
ticket inspector	billett inspektør (m)	[bi'let inspɛk'tør]

to be late (for ...)	å komme for sent	[ɔ 'kɔmə fɔ'ʂɛnt]
to miss (~ the train, etc.)	å komme for sent til ...	[ɔ 'kɔmə fɔ'ʂɛnt til ...]
to be in a hurry	å skynde seg	[ɔ 'ʂynə sæj]

taxi, cab	drosje (m/f), taxi (m)	['drɔʂɛ], ['tɑksi]
taxi driver	taxisjåfør (m)	['tɑksi ʂɔ'før]
by taxi	med taxi	[me 'tɑksi]
taxi rank	taxiholdeplass (m)	['tɑksi 'hɔləˌplɑs]
to call a taxi	å taxi bestellen	[ɔ 'tɑksi be'stɛlən]
to take a taxi	å ta taxi	[ɔ 'tɑ ˌtɑksi]

traffic	trafikk (m)	[trɑ'fik]
traffic jam	trafikkork (m)	[trɑ'fikˌkɔrk]
rush hour	rushtid (m/f)	['rʉʂˌtid]
to park (vi)	å parkere	[ɔ pɑr'kerə]
to park (vt)	å parkere	[ɔ pɑr'kerə]
car park	parkeringsplass (m)	[pɑr'keriŋsˌplɑs]

underground, tube	tunnelbane, T-bane (m)	['tʉnəlˌbɑnə], ['tɛːˌbɑnə]
station	stasjon (m)	[stɑ'ʂʊn]
to take the tube	å kjøre med T-bane	[ɔ 'çœːrə me 'tɛːˌbɑnə]
train	tog (n)	['tɔg]
train station	togstasjon (m)	['tɔgˌstɑ'ʂʊn]

82. Sightseeing

monument	monument (n)	[mɔnʉ'mɛnt]
fortress	festning (m/f)	['fɛstniŋ]
palace	palass (n)	[pɑ'lɑs]
castle	borg (m)	['bɔrg]
tower	tårn (n)	['tɔːɳ]
mausoleum	mausoleum (n)	[mɑʊsʊ'leum]

architecture	arkitektur (m)	[ɑrkitɛk'tʉr]
medieval (adj)	middelalderlig	['midəlˌɑldeːˌi]
ancient (adj)	gammel	['gɑməl]
national (adj)	nasjonal	[nɑʂʊ'nɑl]
famous (monument, etc.)	kjent	['çɛnt]

tourist	turist (m)	[tʉ'rist]
guide (person)	guide (m)	['gɑjd]
excursion, sightseeing tour	utflukt (m/f)	['ʉtˌflʉkt]

| to show (vt) | å vise | [ɔ 'visə] |
| to tell (vt) | å fortelle | [ɔ fɔ:'tɛlə] |

to find (vt)	å finne	[ɔ 'finə]
to get lost (lose one's way)	å gå seg bort	[ɔ 'gɔ sæj 'bʊ:t]
map (e.g. underground ~)	kart, linjekart (n)	['ka:t], ['linjə'ka:t]
map (e.g. city ~)	kart (n)	['ka:t]

souvenir, gift	suvenir (m)	[sʉve'nir]
gift shop	suvenirbutikk (m)	[sʉve'nir bʉ'tik]
to take pictures	å fotografere	[ɔ fɔtɔgra'ferə]
to have one's picture taken	å bli fotografert	[ɔ 'bli fɔtɔgra'fɛ:t]

83. Shopping

to buy (purchase)	å kjøpe	[ɔ 'çœ:pə]
shopping	innkjøp (n)	['in,çœp]
to go shopping	å gå shopping	[ɔ 'gɔ ˌʂɔpiŋ]
shopping	shopping (m)	['ʂɔpiŋ]

| to be open (ab. shop) | å være åpen | [ɔ 'værə 'ɔpən] |
| to be closed | å være stengt | [ɔ 'værə 'stɛŋt] |

footwear, shoes	skotøy (n)	['skʊtøj]
clothes, clothing	klær (n)	['klær]
cosmetics	kosmetikk (m)	[kʊsme'tik]
food products	matvarer (m/f pl)	['mat,varər]
gift, present	gave (m/f)	['gavə]

| shop assistant (masc.) | forselger (m) | [fɔ'ʂɛlər] |
| shop assistant (fem.) | forselger (m) | [fɔ'ʂɛlər] |

cash desk	kasse (m/f)	['kasə]
mirror	speil (n)	['spæjl]
counter (shop ~)	disk (m)	['disk]
fitting room	prøverom (n)	['prøvə,rʊm]

to try on	å prøve	[ɔ 'prøvə]
to fit (ab. dress, etc.)	å passe	[ɔ 'pasə]
to fancy (vt)	å like	[ɔ 'likə]

price	pris (m)	['pris]
price tag	prislapp (m)	['pris,lap]
to cost (vt)	å koste	[ɔ 'kɔstə]
How much?	Hvor mye?	[vʊr 'mye]
discount	rabatt (m)	[ra'bat]

inexpensive (adj)	billig	['bili]
cheap (adj)	billig	['bili]
expensive (adj)	dyr	['dyr]
It's expensive	Det er dyrt	[de ær 'dy:t]

| hire (n) | utleie (m/f) | ['ʉt,læje] |
| to hire (~ a dinner jacket) | å leie | [ɔ 'læjə] |

| credit (trade credit) | kreditt (m) | [krɛ'dit] |
| on credit (adv) | på kreditt | [pɔ krɛ'dit] |

84. Money

money	penger (m pl)	['pɛŋər]
currency exchange	veksling (m/f)	['vɛkʂliŋ]
exchange rate	kurs (m)	['kuʂ]
cashpoint	minibank (m)	['mini,bank]
coin	mynt (m)	['mʏnt]

| dollar | dollar (m) | ['dɔlar] |
| euro | euro (m) | ['ɛʉrʊ] |

lira	lira (m)	['lire]
Deutschmark	mark (m/f)	['mark]
franc	franc (m)	['fran]
pound sterling	pund sterling (m)	['pʉn stɛ:'liŋ]
yen	yen (m)	['jɛn]

debt	skyld (m/f), gjeld (m)	['ʂyl], ['jɛl]
debtor	skyldner (m)	['ʂylnər]
to lend (money)	å låne ut	[ɔ 'lo:nə ʉt]
to borrow (vi, vt)	å låne	[ɔ 'lo:nə]

bank	bank (m)	['bank]
account	konto (m)	['kɔntʊ]
to deposit (vt)	å sette inn	[ɔ 'sɛtə in]
to deposit into the account	å sette inn på kontoen	[ɔ 'sɛtə in pɔ 'kɔntʊən]
to withdraw (vt)	å ta ut fra kontoen	[ɔ 'ta ʉt fra 'kɔntʊən]

credit card	kredittkort (n)	[krɛ'dit,kɔ:t]
cash	kontanter (m pl)	[kʊn'tantər]
cheque	sjekk (m)	['ʂɛk]
to write a cheque	å skrive en sjekk	[ɔ 'skrivə en 'ʂɛk]
chequebook	sjekkbok (m/f)	['ʂɛk,bʊk]

wallet	lommebok (m)	['lʊmə,bʊk]
purse	pung (m)	['pʉŋ]
safe	safe, seif (m)	['sɛjf]

heir	arving (m)	['arviŋ]
inheritance	arv (m)	['arv]
fortune (wealth)	formue (m)	['fɔr,mʉə]

lease	leie (m)	['læjə]
rent (money)	husleie (m/f)	['hʉs,læjə]
to rent (sth from sb)	å leie	[ɔ 'læjə]

price	pris (m)	['pris]
cost	kostnad (m)	['kɔstnad]
sum	sum (m)	['sʉm]
to spend (vt)	å bruke	[ɔ 'brʉkə]
expenses	utgifter (m/f pl)	['ʉt,jiftər]

| to economize (vi, vt) | å spare | [ɔ 'spɑrə] |
| economical | sparsom | ['spɑʂɔm] |

to pay (vi, vt)	å betale	[ɔ be'tɑlə]
payment	betaling (m/f)	[be'tɑliŋ]
change (give the ~)	vekslepenger (pl)	['vɛkʂlə,pɛŋər]

tax	skatt (m)	['skɑt]
fine	bot (m/f)	['bʊt]
to fine (vt)	å bøtelegge	[ɔ 'bøtə,legə]

85. Post. Postal service

post office	post (m)	['pɔst]
post (letters, etc.)	post (m)	['pɔst]
postman	postbud (n)	['pɔst,bʉd]
opening hours	åpningstider (m/f pl)	['ɔpniŋs,tidər]

letter	brev (n)	['brev]
registered letter	rekommandert brev (n)	[rekʉmɑn'dɛːt ,brev]
postcard	postkort (n)	['pɔst,kɔːt]
telegram	telegram (n)	[tele'grɑm]
parcel	postpakke (m/f)	['pɔst,pɑkə]
money transfer	pengeoverføring (m/f)	['pɛŋə 'ɔvər,føriŋ]

to receive (vt)	å motta	[ɔ 'mɔtɑ]
to send (vt)	å sende	[ɔ 'sɛnə]
sending	avsending (m)	['ɑf,sɛniŋ]

address	adresse (m)	[ɑ'drɛsə]
postcode	postnummer (n)	['pɔst,nʉmər]
sender	avsender (m)	['ɑf,sɛnər]
receiver	mottaker (m)	['mɔt,tɑkər]

| name (first name) | fornavn (n) | ['fɔr,nɑvn] |
| surname (last name) | etternavn (n) | ['ɛtə,ŋɑvn] |

postage rate	tariff (m)	[tɑ'rif]
standard (adj)	vanlig	['vɑnli]
economical (adj)	økonomisk	[økʉ'nɔmisk]

weight	vekt (m)	['vɛkt]
to weigh (~ letters)	å veie	[ɔ 'væje]
envelope	konvolutt (m)	[kʉnvʉ'lʉt]
postage stamp	frimerke (n)	['fri,mærkə]
to stamp an envelope	å sette på frimerke	[ɔ 'sɛtə pɔ 'fri,mærkə]

Dwelling. House. Home

86. House. Dwelling

house	hus (n)	['hʉs]
at home (adv)	hjemme	['jɛmə]
yard	gård (m)	['gɔːr]
fence (iron ~)	gjerde (n)	['jærə]

brick (n)	tegl (n), murstein (m)	['tæjl], ['mʉˌstæjn]
brick (as adj)	tegl-	['tæjl-]
stone (n)	stein (m)	['stæjn]
stone (as adj)	stein-	['stæjn-]
concrete (n)	betong (m)	[be'tɔŋ]
concrete (as adj)	betong-	[be'tɔŋ-]

new (new-built)	ny	['ny]
old (adj)	gammel	['gaməl]
decrepit (house)	falleferdig	['faləˌfæːɖi]
modern (adj)	moderne	[mʉ'dɛːɳə]
multistorey (adj)	fleretasjes-	['flerɛˌtaʂɛs-]
tall (~ building)	høy	['høj]

floor, storey	etasje (m)	[ɛ'taʂə]
single-storey (adj)	enetasjes	['ɛnɛˌtaʂɛs]

ground floor	første etasje (m)	['fœʂtə ɛ'taʂə]
top floor	øverste etasje (m)	['øvəʂtə ɛ'taʂə]

roof	tak (n)	['tɑk]
chimney	skorstein (m/f)	['skɔˌstæjn]

roof tiles	takstein (m)	['tɑkˌstæjn]
tiled (adj)	taksteins-	['tɑkˌstæjns-]
loft (attic)	loft (n)	['lɔft]

window	vindu (n)	['vindʉ]
glass	glass (n)	['glɑs]

window ledge	vinduskarm (m)	['vindʉsˌkɑrm]
shutters	vinduslemmer (m pl)	['vindʉsˌlemər]

wall	mur, vegg (m)	['mʉr], ['vɛg]
balcony	balkong (m)	[bɑl'kɔŋ]
downpipe	nedløpsrør (n)	['nedløpsˌrør]

upstairs (to be ~)	oppe	['ɔpə]
to go upstairs	å gå ovenpå	[ɔ 'gɔ 'ɔvənˌpɔ]
to come down (the stairs)	å gå ned	[ɔ 'gɔ ne]
to move (to new premises)	å flytte	[ɔ 'flʏtə]

87. House. Entrance. Lift

entrance	inngang (m)	['in,gɑŋ]
stairs (stairway)	trapp (m/f)	['trɑp]
steps	trinn (n pl)	['trin]
banisters	gelender (n)	[geˈlendər]
lobby (hotel ~)	hall, lobby (m)	['hɑl], ['lɔbi]

postbox	postkasse (m/f)	['pɔst,kɑsə]
waste bin	søppelkasse (m/f)	['sœpəl,kɑsə]
refuse chute	søppelsjakt (m/f)	['sœpəl,ʃɑkt]

lift	heis (m)	['hæjs]
goods lift	lasteheis (m)	['lɑstəˈhæjs]
lift cage	heiskorg (m/f)	['hæjs,kɔrg]
to take the lift	å ta heisen	[ɔ 'tɑ ,hæjsən]

flat	leilighet (m/f)	['læjli,het]
residents (~ of a building)	beboere (m pl)	[beˈbʉerə]
neighbour (masc.)	nabo (m)	['nɑbʉ]
neighbour (fem.)	nabo (m)	['nɑbʉ]
neighbours	naboer (m pl)	['nɑbʉər]

88. House. Electricity

electricity	elektrisitet (m)	[ɛlektrisiˈtet]
light bulb	lyspære (m/f)	['lys,pærə]
switch	strømbryter (m)	['strøm,brytər]
fuse (plug fuse)	sikring (m)	['sikriŋ]

cable, wire (electric ~)	ledning (m)	['ledniŋ]
wiring	ledningsnett (n)	['ledniŋs,nɛt]
electricity meter	elmåler (m)	['ɛl,molər]
readings	avlesninger (m/f pl)	['ɑv,lesniŋər]

89. House. Doors. Locks

door	dør (m/f)	['dœr]
gate (vehicle ~)	grind (m/f), port (m)	['grin], ['pɔːt]
handle, doorknob	dørhåndtak (n)	['dœr,hɔntɑk]
to unlock (unbolt)	å låse opp	[ɔ 'loːsə ɔp]
to open (vt)	å åpne	[ɔ 'ɔpnə]
to close (vt)	å lukke	[ɔ 'lʉkə]

key	nøkkel (m)	['nøkəl]
bunch (of keys)	knippe (n)	['knipə]
to creak (door, etc.)	å knirke	[ɔ 'knirkə]
creak	knirk (m/n)	['knirk]
hinge (door ~)	hengsel (m/n)	['hɛŋsel]
doormat	dørmatte (m/f)	['dœr,mɑtə]
door lock	dørlås (m/n)	['dœr,lɔs]

keyhole	nøkkelhull (n)	['nøkəlˌhʉl]
crossbar (sliding bar)	slå (m/f)	['ʂlɔ]
door latch	slå (m/f)	['ʂlɔ]
padlock	hengelås (m/n)	['hɛŋeˌlɔs]

to ring (~ the door bell)	å ringe	[ɔ 'riŋə]
ringing (sound)	ringing (m/f)	['riŋiŋ]
doorbell	ringeklokke (m/f)	['riŋeˌklɔkə]
doorbell button	ringeklokke knapp (m)	['riŋeˌklɔkə 'knap]
knock (at the door)	kakking (m/f)	['kakiŋ]
to knock (vi)	å kakke	[ɔ 'kakə]

code	kode (m)	['kʉdə]
combination lock	kodelås (m/n)	['kʉdəˌlɔs]
intercom	dørtelefon (m)	['dœrˌtele'fʉn]
number (on the door)	nummer (n)	['nʉmər]
doorplate	dørskilt (n)	['dœˌʂilt]
peephole	kikhull (n)	['çikˌhʉl]

90. Country house

village	landsby (m)	['lansˌby]
vegetable garden	kjøkkenhage (m)	['çœkənˌhagə]
fence	gjerde (n)	['jæərə]
picket fence	stakitt (m/n)	[sta'kit]
wicket gate	port, stakittport (m)	['pɔːt], [sta'kitˌpɔːt]

granary	kornlåve (m)	['kʉː̩ˌn̩ lo:və]
cellar	jordkjeller (m)	['juːrˌçɛlər]
shed (garden ~)	skur, skjul (n)	['skʉr], ['ʂʉl]
water well	brønn (m)	['brœn]

stove (wood-fired ~)	ovn (m)	['ɔvn]
to stoke the stove	å fyre	[ɔ 'fyrə]
firewood	ved (m)	['ve]
log (firewood)	vedstykke (n), vedskie (f)	['vɛdˌstʏkə], ['vɛˌʂiə]

veranda	veranda (m)	[væ'randa]
deck (terrace)	terrasse (m)	[tɛ'rasə]
stoop (front steps)	yttertrapp (m/f)	['ʏtəˌtrap]
swing (hanging seat)	gynge (m/f)	['jiŋə]

91. Villa. Mansion

country house	fritidshus (n)	['fritidsˌhʉs]
country-villa	villa (m)	['vila]
wing (~ of a building)	fløy (m)	['fløj]

garden	hage (m)	['hagə]
park	park (m)	['park]
conservatory (greenhouse)	drivhus (n)	['drivˌhʉs]
to look after (garden, etc.)	å ta vare	[ɔ 'ta ˌvarə]

swimming pool	svømmebasseng (n)	['svœmə‚ba'sɛŋ]
gym (home gym)	gym (m)	['dʒym]
tennis court	tennisbane (m)	['tɛnis‚banə]
home theater (room)	hjemmekino (m)	['jɛmə‚çinʉ]
garage	garasje (m)	[ga'raʂə]

| private property | privateiendom (m) | [pri'vat 'æjəndɔm] |
| private land | privat terreng (n) | [pri'vat tɛ'rɛŋ] |

| warning (caution) | advarsel (m) | ['ad‚vaʂəl] |
| warning sign | varselskilt (n) | ['vaʂəl‚silt] |

security	sikkerhet (m/f)	['sikər‚het]
security guard	sikkerhetsvakt (m/f)	['sikərhɛts‚vakt]
burglar alarm	tyverialarm (m)	[tyve'ri a'larm]

92. Castle. Palace

castle	borg (m)	['bɔrg]
palace	palass (n)	[pa'las]
fortress	festning (m/f)	['fɛstniŋ]
wall (round castle)	mur (m)	['mʉr]
tower	tårn (n)	['tɔːn]
keep, donjon	kjernetårn (n)	['çæːɳə'tɔːɳ]

portcullis	fallgitter (n)	['fal‚gitər]
subterranean passage	underjordisk gang (m)	['ʉnərˌjuːrdisk 'gaŋ]
moat	vollgrav (m/f)	['vɔl‚grav]
chain	kjede (m)	['çɛːde]
arrow loop	skyteskår (n)	['ʂytə‚skɔr]

magnificent (adj)	praktfull	['prakt‚fʉl]
majestic (adj)	majestetisk	[maje'stɛtisk]
impregnable (adj)	uinntakelig	[ʉən'takəli]
medieval (adj)	middelalderlig	['midel‚aldɛːˌli]

93. Flat

flat	leilighet (m/f)	['læjliˌhet]
room	rom (n)	['rʊm]
bedroom	soverom (n)	['sɔvə‚rʊm]
dining room	spisestue (m/f)	['spisəˌstʉə]
living room	dagligstue (m/f)	['dagliˌstʉə]
study (home office)	arbeidsrom (n)	['arbæjdsˌrʊm]

entry room	entré (m)	[an'trɛː]
bathroom	bad, baderom (n)	['bad], ['badəˌrʊm]
water closet	toalett, WC (n)	[tʊa'let], [vɛ'sɛ]

ceiling	tak (n)	['tak]
floor	gulv (n)	['gʉlv]
corner	hjørne (n)	['jœːɳə]

94. Flat. Cleaning

to clean (vi, vt)	å rydde	[ɔ 'rʏdə]
to put away (to stow)	å stue unna	[ɔ 'stʉə 'ʉnɑ]
dust	støv (n)	['støv]
dusty (adj)	støvet	['støvət]
to dust (vt)	å tørke støv	[ɔ 'tœrkə 'støv]
vacuum cleaner	støvsuger (m)	['støf‚sʉgər]
to vacuum (vt)	å støvsuge	[ɔ 'støf‚sʉgə]
to sweep (vi, vt)	å sope, å feie	[ɔ 'sɔpə], [ɔ 'fæjə]
sweepings	søppel (m/f/n)	['sœpəl]
order	orden (m)	['ɔrdən]
disorder, mess	uorden (m)	['ʉːˌɔrdən]
mop	mopp (m)	['mɔp]
duster	klut (m)	['klʉt]
short broom	feiekost (m)	['fæjəˌkʊst]
dustpan	feiebrett (n)	['fæjəˌbrɛt]

95. Furniture. Interior

furniture	møbler (n pl)	['møblər]
table	bord (n)	['bʊr]
chair	stol (m)	['stʊl]
bed	seng (m/f)	['sɛŋ]
sofa, settee	sofa (m)	['sʊfɑ]
armchair	lenestol (m)	['lenəˌstʊl]
bookcase	bokskap (n)	['bʊkˌskɑp]
shelf	hylle (m/f)	['hʏlə]
wardrobe	klesskap (n)	['kleˌskɑp]
coat rack (wall-mounted ~)	knaggbrett (n)	['knɑgˌbrɛt]
coat stand	stumtjener (m)	['stʉmˌtjenər]
chest of drawers	kommode (m)	[kʊ'mʊdə]
coffee table	kaffebord (n)	['kɑfəˌbʊr]
mirror	speil (n)	['spæjl]
carpet	teppe (n)	['tɛpə]
small carpet	lite teppe (n)	['litə 'tɛpə]
fireplace	peis (m), ildsted (n)	['pæjs], ['ilsted]
candle	lys (n)	['lys]
candlestick	lysestake (m)	['lysəˌstɑkə]
drapes	gardiner (m/f pl)	[gɑː'dinər]
wallpaper	tapet (n)	[tɑ'pet]
blinds (jalousie)	persienne (m)	[pæʂi'enə]
table lamp	bordlampe (m/f)	['bʊrˌlɑmpə]
wall lamp (sconce)	vegglampe (m/f)	['vɛgˌlɑmpə]

| standard lamp | gulvlampe (m/f) | ['gʉlv,lampə] |
| chandelier | lysekrone (m/f) | ['lysə,krʉnə] |

leg (of a chair, table)	bein (n)	['bæjn]
armrest	armlene (n)	['arm,lenə]
back (backrest)	rygg (m)	['rʏg]
drawer	skuff (m)	['skʉf]

96. Bedding

bedclothes	sengetøy (n)	['sɛŋə,tøj]
pillow	pute (m/f)	['pʉtə]
pillowslip	putevar, putetrekk (n)	['pʉtə,var], ['pʉtə,trɛk]
duvet	dyne (m/f)	['dynə]
sheet	laken (n)	['lakən]
bedspread	sengeteppe (n)	['sɛŋə,tɛpə]

97. Kitchen

kitchen	kjøkken (n)	['çœkən]
gas	gass (m)	['gas]
gas cooker	gasskomfyr (m)	['gas kɔm,fyr]
electric cooker	elektrisk komfyr (m)	[ɛ'lektrisk kɔm,fyr]
oven	bakeovn (m)	['bakə,ɔvn]
microwave oven	mikrobølgeovn (m)	['mikrʉ,bølgə'ɔvn]

refrigerator	kjøleskap (n)	['çœlə,skap]
freezer	fryser (m)	['frysər]
dishwasher	oppvaskmaskin (m)	['ɔpvask ma,ʂin]

mincer	kjøttkvern (m/f)	['çœt,kvɛ:ɳ]
juicer	juicepresse (m/f)	['dʒʉs,prɛsə]
toaster	brødrister (m)	['brø,ristər]
mixer	mikser (m)	['miksər]

coffee machine	kaffetrakter (m)	['kafə,traktər]
coffee pot	kaffekanne (m/f)	['kafə,kanə]
coffee grinder	kaffekvern (m/f)	['kafə,kvɛ:ɳ]

kettle	tekjele (m)	['te,çelə]
teapot	tekanne (m/f)	['te,kanə]
lid	lokk (n)	['lɔk]
tea strainer	tesil (m)	['te,sil]

spoon	skje (m)	['ʂe]
teaspoon	teskje (m)	['te,ʂe]
soup spoon	spiseskje (m)	['spisə,ʂɛ]
fork	gaffel (m)	['gafəl]
knife	kniv (m)	['kniv]

| tableware (dishes) | servise (n) | [sær'visə] |
| plate (dinner ~) | tallerken (m) | [ta'lærkən] |

saucer	**tefat** (n)	['te‚fɑt]
shot glass	**shotglass** (n)	['ʂɔt‚glɑs]
glass (tumbler)	**glass** (n)	['glɑs]
cup	**kopp** (m)	['kɔp]

sugar bowl	**sukkerskål** (m/f)	['sʉkər‚skɔl]
salt cellar	**saltbøsse** (m/f)	['salt‚bøsə]
pepper pot	**pepperbøsse** (m/f)	['pɛpər‚bøsə]
butter dish	**smørkopp** (m)	['smœr‚kɔp]

stock pot (soup pot)	**gryte** (m/f)	['grytə]
frying pan (skillet)	**steikepanne** (m/f)	['stæjkə‚panə]
ladle	**sleiv** (m/f)	['ʂlæjv]
colander	**dørslag** (n)	['dœʂlɑg]
tray (serving ~)	**brett** (n)	['brɛt]

bottle	**flaske** (m)	['flɑskə]
jar (glass)	**glasskrukke** (m/f)	['glɑs‚krʉkə]
tin (can)	**boks** (m)	['bɔks]

bottle opener	**flaskeåpner** (m)	['flɑskə‚ɔpnər]
tin opener	**konservåpner** (m)	['kʉnsəv‚ɔpnər]
corkscrew	**korketrekker** (m)	['kɔrkə‚trɛkər]
filter	**filter** (n)	['filtər]
to filter (vt)	**å filtrere**	[ɔ fil'trerə]

waste (food ~, etc.)	**søppel** (m/f/n)	['sœpəl]
waste bin (kitchen ~)	**søppelbøtte** (m/f)	['sœpəl‚bœtə]

98. Bathroom

bathroom	**bad, baderom** (n)	['bad], ['badə‚rʊm]
water	**vann** (n)	['van]
tap	**kran** (m/f)	['kran]
hot water	**varmt vann** (n)	['varmt ‚van]
cold water	**kaldt vann** (n)	['kalt van]

toothpaste	**tannpasta** (m)	['tan‚pasta]
to clean one's teeth	**å pusse tennene**	[ɔ 'pʉsə 'tɛnənə]
toothbrush	**tannbørste** (m)	['tan‚bœʂtə]

to shave (vi)	**å barbere seg**	[ɔ bar'berə sæj]
shaving foam	**barberskum** (n)	[bar'bɛ‚skʉm]
razor	**høvel** (m)	['høvəl]

to wash (one's hands, etc.)	**å vaske**	[ɔ 'vaskə]
to have a bath	**å vaske seg**	[ɔ 'vaskə sæj]
shower	**dusj** (m)	['dʉʂ]
to have a shower	**å ta en dusj**	[ɔ 'ta en 'dʉʂ]

bath	**badekar** (n)	['badə‚kar]
toilet (toilet bowl)	**toalettstol** (m)	[tʊɑ'let‚stʊl]
sink (washbasin)	**vaskeservant** (m)	['vaskə‚sɛr'vant]
soap	**såpe** (m/f)	['so:pə]

soap dish	såpeskål (m/f)	['soːpə‚skɔl]
sponge	svamp (m)	['svamp]
shampoo	sjampo (m)	['ṣam‚puʉ]
towel	håndkle (n)	['hɔn‚kle]
bathrobe	badekåpe (m/f)	['badə‚koːpə]

laundry (laundering)	vask (m)	['vɑsk]
washing machine	vaskemaskin (m)	['vɑskə mɑ‚ṣin]
to do the laundry	å vaske tøy	[ɔ 'vɑskə 'tøj]
washing powder	vaskepulver (n)	['vɑskə‚pʉlvər]

99. Household appliances

TV, telly	TV (m), TV-apparat (n)	['tɛvɛ], ['tɛvɛ apɑ'rɑt]
tape recorder	båndopptaker (m)	['bɔn‚ɔptɑkər]
video	video (m)	['videʉ]
radio	radio (m)	['rɑdiʉ]
player (CD, MP3, etc.)	spiller (m)	['spilər]

video projector	videoprojektor (m)	['videʉ prɔ'jɛktɔr]
home cinema	hjemmekino (m)	['jɛmə‚çinʉ]
DVD player	DVD-spiller (m)	[deve'de ‚spilər]
amplifier	forsterker (m)	[fo'ṣtærkər]
video game console	spillkonsoll (m)	['spil kʉn'sɔl]

video camera	videokamera (n)	['videʉ ‚kɑmerɑ]
camera (photo)	kamera (n)	['kɑmerɑ]
digital camera	digitalkamera (n)	[digi'tɑl ‚kɑmerɑ]

vacuum cleaner	støvsuger (m)	['støf‚sʉgər]
iron (e.g. steam ~)	strykejern (n)	['strykə‚jæːn̩]
ironing board	strykebrett (n)	['strykə‚brɛt]

telephone	telefon (m)	[tele'fʉn]
mobile phone	mobiltelefon (m)	[mʉ'bil tele'fʉn]
typewriter	skrivemaskin (m)	['skrivə mɑ‚ṣin]
sewing machine	symaskin (m)	['siːmɑ‚ṣin]

microphone	mikrofon (m)	[mikrʉ'fʉn]
headphones	hodetelefoner (n pl)	['hɔdetelə‚fʉnər]
remote control (TV)	fjernkontroll (m)	['fjæːn̩ kʉn'trɔl]

CD, compact disc	CD-rom (m)	['sɛdɛ‚rʉm]
cassette, tape	kassett (m)	[kɑ'sɛt]
vinyl record	plate, skive (m/f)	['plɑtə], ['ṣivə]

100. Repairs. Renovation

renovations	renovering (m/f)	[renʉ'veriŋ]
to renovate (vt)	å renovere	[ɔ renʉ'verə]
to repair, to fix (vt)	å reparere	[ɔ repɑ'rerə]
to put in order	å bringe orden	[ɔ 'briŋe 'ɔrdən]

to redo (do again)	å gjøre om	[ɔ 'jørə ɔm]
paint	maling (m/f)	['malin]
to paint (~ a wall)	å male	[ɔ 'malə]
house painter	maler (m)	['malər]
paintbrush	pensel (m)	['pɛnsəl]

| whitewash | kalkmaling (m/f) | ['kalk,malin] |
| to whitewash (vt) | å hvitmale | [ɔ 'vit,malə] |

wallpaper	tapet (n)	[ta'pet]
to wallpaper (vt)	å tapetsere	[ɔ tapet'serə]
varnish	ferniss (m)	['fæː,nis]
to varnish (vt)	å lakkere	[ɔ la'kerə]

101. Plumbing

water	vann (n)	['van]
hot water	varmt vann (n)	['varmt ,van]
cold water	kaldt vann (n)	['kalt van]
tap	kran (m/f)	['kran]

drop (of water)	dråpe (m)	['droːpə]
to drip (vi)	å dryppe	[ɔ 'drʏpə]
to leak (ab. pipe)	å lekke	[ɔ 'lekə]
leak (pipe ~)	lekk (m)	['lek]
puddle	pøl, pytt (m)	['pøl], ['pʏt]

pipe	rør (n)	['rør]
valve (e.g., ball ~)	ventil (m)	[vɛn'til]
to be clogged up	å bli tilstoppet	[ɔ 'bli til'stɔpət]

tools	verktøy (n pl)	['værk,tøj]
adjustable spanner	skiftenøkkel (m)	['şiftə,nøkəl]
to unscrew (lid, filter, etc.)	å skru ut	[ɔ 'skru ʉt]
to screw (tighten)	å skru fast	[ɔ 'skru 'fast]

to unclog (vt)	å rense	[ɔ 'rɛnsə]
plumber	rørlegger (m)	['rør,legər]
basement	kjeller (m)	['çɛlər]
sewerage (system)	avløp (n)	['av,løp]

102. Fire. Conflagration

fire (accident)	ild (m)	['il]
flame	flamme (m)	['flamə]
spark	gnist (m)	['gnist]
smoke (from fire)	røyk (m)	['røjk]
torch (flaming stick)	fakkel (m)	['fakəl]
campfire	bål (n)	['bɔl]

| petrol | bensin (m) | [bɛn'sin] |
| paraffin | parafin (m) | [para'fin] |

flammable (adj)	brennbar	['brɛnˌbar]
explosive (adj)	eksplosiv	['ɛkspluˌsiv]
NO SMOKING	RØYKING FORBUDT	['røjkiŋ for'bʉt]

safety	sikkerhet (m/f)	['sikərˌhet]
danger	fare (m)	['farə]
dangerous (adj)	farlig	['faːli̯]

to catch fire	å ta fyr	[ɔ 'ta ˌfyr]
explosion	eksplosjon (m)	[ɛksplu'ʂun]
to set fire	å sette fyr	[ɔ 'sɛtə ˌfyr]
arsonist	brannstifter (m)	['branˌstiftər]
arson	brannstiftelse (m)	['branˌstiftəlsə]

to blaze (vi)	å flamme	[ɔ 'flamə]
to burn (be on fire)	å brenne	[ɔ 'brɛnə]
to burn down	å brenne ned	[ɔ 'brɛnə ne]

to call the fire brigade	å ringe bransvesenet	[ɔ 'riŋə 'bransˌvesənə]
firefighter, fireman	brannmann (m)	['branˌman]
fire engine	brannbil (m)	['branˌbil]
fire brigade	brannkorps (n)	['branˌkɔrps]
fire engine ladder	teleskopstige (m)	['tele'skʉpˌstiːə]

fire hose	slange (m)	['ʂlaŋə]
fire extinguisher	brannslukker (n)	['branˌslʉkər]
helmet	hjelm (m)	['jɛlm]
siren	sirene (m/f)	[si'renə]

to cry (for help)	å skrike	[ɔ 'skrikə]
to call for help	å rope på hjelp	[ɔ 'rʉpə pɔ 'jɛlp]
rescuer	redningsmann (m)	['rɛdniŋsˌman]
to rescue (vt)	å redde	[ɔ 'rɛdə]

to arrive (vi)	å ankomme	[ɔ 'anˌkɔmə]
to extinguish (vt)	å slokke	[ɔ 'ʂløkə]
water	vann (n)	['van]
sand	sand (m)	['san]

ruins (destruction)	ruiner (m pl)	[rʉ'inər]
to collapse (building, etc.)	å falle sammen	[ɔ 'falə 'samən]
to fall down (vi)	å styrte ned	[ɔ 'styːʈə ne]
to cave in (ceiling, floor)	å styrte inn	[ɔ 'styːʈə in]

| piece of debris | del (m) | ['del] |
| ash | aske (m/f) | ['askə] |

| to suffocate (die) | å kveles | [ɔ 'kveləs] |
| to be killed (perish) | å omkomme | [ɔ 'ɔmˌkɔmə] |

HUMAN ACTIVITIES

Job. Business. Part 1

103. Office. Working in the office

office (company ~)	kontor (n)	[kʊn'tʊr]
office (director's ~)	kontor (n)	[kʊn'tʊr]
reception desk	resepsjon (m)	[resɛp'sʊn]
secretary	sekretær (m)	[sɛkrə'tær]
secretary (fem.)	sekretær (m)	[sɛkrə'tær]

director	direktør (m)	[dirɛk'tør]
manager	manager (m)	['mɛnidʒər]
accountant	regnskapsfører (m)	['rɛjnskaps‚førər]
employee	ansatt (n)	['an‚sat]

furniture	møbler (n pl)	['møblər]
desk	bord (n)	['bʊr]
desk chair	arbeidsstol (m)	['arbæjds‚stʊl]
drawer unit	skuffeseksjon (m)	['skʉfə‚sɛk'sʊn]
coat stand	stumtjener (m)	['stʉm‚tjenər]

computer	datamaskin (m)	['data ma‚şin]
printer	skriver (m)	['skrivər]
fax machine	faks (m)	['faks]
photocopier	kopimaskin (m)	[kʊ'pi ma‚şin]

paper	papir (n)	[pa'pir]
office supplies	kontorartikler (m pl)	[kʊn'tʊr aː'ţiklər]
mouse mat	musematte (m/f)	['mʉsə‚matə]
sheet of paper	ark (n)	['ark]
binder	mappe (m/f)	['mapə]

catalogue	katalog (m)	[kata'lɔg]
phone directory	telefonkatalog (m)	[tele'fʊn kata'lɔg]
documentation	dokumentasjon (m)	[dɔkʉmɛnta'şʊn]
brochure (e.g. 12 pages ~)	brosjyre (m)	[brɔ'şyrə]
leaflet (promotional ~)	reklameblad (n)	[rɛ'klamə‚bla]
sample	prøve (m)	['prøvə]

training meeting	trening (m/f)	['treniŋ]
meeting (of managers)	møte (n)	['møtə]
lunch time	lunsj pause (m)	['lʉnş ‚paʊsə]

to make a copy	å lage en kopi	[ɔ 'lagə en kʊ'pi]
to make multiple copies	å kopiere	[ɔ kʊ'pjerə]
to receive a fax	å motta faks	[ɔ 'mɔta ‚faks]
to send a fax	å sende faks	[ɔ 'sɛnə ‚faks]

to call (by phone)	å ringe	[ɔ 'riŋə]
to answer (vt)	å svare	[ɔ 'svarə]
to put through	å sætte over til ...	[ɔ 'sætə 'ɔvər til ...]

to arrange, to set up	å arrangere	[ɔ araŋ'ṣerə]
to demonstrate (vt)	å demonstrere	[ɔ demɔn'strerə]
to be absent	å være fraværende	[ɔ 'værə 'fra,værənə]
absence	fravær (n)	['fra,vær]

104. Business processes. Part 1

business	bedrift, handel (m)	[be'drift], ['handəl]
occupation	yrke (n)	['yrkə]
firm	firma (n)	['firma]
company	foretak (n)	['fɔrə,tak]
corporation	korporasjon (m)	[kʊrpʊra'ṣʊn]
enterprise	foretak (n)	['fɔrə,tak]
agency	agentur (n)	[agɛn'tʉr]

agreement (contract)	avtale (m)	['av,talə]
contract	kontrakt (m)	[kʊn'trakt]
deal	avtale (m)	['av,talə]
order (to place an ~)	bestilling (m)	[be'stiliŋ]
terms (of the contract)	vilkår (n)	['vil,kɔ:r]

wholesale (adv)	en gros	[ɛn 'grɔ]
wholesale (adj)	engros-	[ɛŋ'grɔ-]
wholesale (n)	engroshandel (m)	[ɛŋ'grɔ,handəl]
retail (adj)	detalj-	[de'talj-]
retail (n)	detaljhandel (m)	[de'talj,handəl]

competitor	konkurrent (m)	[kʊnkʉ'rɛnt]
competition	konkurranse (m)	[kʊnkʉ'ransə]
to compete (vi)	å konkurrere	[ɔ kʊnkʉ'rerə]

| partner (associate) | partner (m) | ['pɑ:ʈnər] |
| partnership | partnerskap (n) | ['pɑ:ʈnə,ṣkap] |

crisis	krise (m/f)	['krisə]
bankruptcy	fallitt (m)	[fa'lit]
to go bankrupt	å gå konkurs	[ɔ 'gɔ kɔn'kʉṣ]
difficulty	vanskelighet (m)	['vanskəli,het]
problem	problem (n)	[prʉ'blem]
catastrophe	katastrofe (m)	[kata'strɔfə]

economy	økonomi (m)	[økʊnʉ'mi]
economic (~ growth)	økonomisk	[økʉ'nɔmisk]
economic recession	økonomisk nedgang (m)	[økʉ'nɔmisk 'ned,gaŋ]

| goal (aim) | mål (n) | ['mol] |
| task | oppgave (m/f) | ['ɔp,gavə] |

| to trade (vi) | å handle | [ɔ 'handlə] |
| network (distribution ~) | nettverk (n) | ['nɛt,værk] |

| inventory (stock) | lager (n) | ['lagər] |
| range (assortment) | sortiment (n) | [sɔ:ʈi'mɛn] |

leader (leading company)	leder (m)	['ledər]
large (~ company)	stor	['stʊr]
monopoly	monopol (n)	[mʊnʊ'pɔl]

theory	teori (m)	[teʊ'ri]
practice	praksis (m)	['praksis]
experience (in my ~)	erfaring (m/f)	[ær'fariŋ]
trend (tendency)	tendens (m)	[tɛn'dɛns]
development	utvikling (m/f)	['ʉt͵vikliŋ]

105. Business processes. Part 2

| profit (foregone ~) | utbytte (n), fordel (m) | ['ʉt͵bʏtə], ['fɔ:dɛl] |
| profitable (~ deal) | fordelaktig | [fɔ:dɛl'akti] |

delegation (group)	delegasjon (m)	[delega'ʂʊn]
salary	lønn (m/f)	['lœn]
to correct (an error)	å rette	[ɔ 'rɛtə]
business trip	forretningsreise (m/f)	[fɔ'rɛtniŋs͵ræjsə]
commission	provisjon (m)	[prʊvi'ʂʊn]

to control (vt)	å kontrollere	[ɔ kʊntrɔ'lerə]
conference	konferanse (m)	[kʊnfə'ransə]
licence	lisens (m)	[li'sɛns]
reliable (~ partner)	pålitelig	[pɔ'liteli]

initiative (undertaking)	initiativ (n)	[initsia'tiv]
norm (standard)	norm (m)	['nɔrm]
circumstance	omstendighet (m)	[ɔm'stɛndi͵het]
duty (of an employee)	plikt (m/f)	['plikt]

organization (company)	organisasjon (m)	[ɔrganisa'ʂʊn]
organization (process)	organisering (m)	[ɔrgani'seriŋ]
organized (adj)	organisert	[ɔrgani'sɛ:t]
cancellation	avlysning (m/f)	['av͵lʏsniŋ]
to cancel (call off)	å avlyse, å annullere	[ɔ 'av͵lysə], [ɔ anʉ'lerə]
report (official ~)	rapport (m)	[ra'pɔ:t]

patent	patent (n)	[pa'tɛnt]
to patent (obtain patent)	å patentere	[ɔ paten'terə]
to plan (vt)	å planlegge	[ɔ 'plan͵legə]

bonus (money)	gratiale (n)	[gratsi'a:lə]
professional (adj)	professionel	[prʊ'fɛsiɔ͵nɛl]
procedure	prosedyre (m)	[prʊsə'dyrə]

to examine (contract, etc.)	å undersøke	[ɔ 'ʉnə͵søkə]
calculation	beregning (m/f)	[be'rɛjniŋ]
reputation	rykte (n)	['rʏktə]
risk	risiko (m)	['risikʊ]
to manage, to run	å styre, å lede	[ɔ 'styrə], [ɔ 'ledə]

95

information (report)	opplysninger (m/f pl)	['ɔpˌlʏsniŋər]
property	eiendom (m)	['æjənˌdɔm]
union	forbund (n)	['forˌbʉn]

life insurance	livsforsikring (m/f)	['lifsfoˌşikriŋ]
to insure (vt)	å forsikre	[ɔ fɔ'şikrə]
insurance	forsikring (m/f)	[fɔ'şikriŋ]

auction (~ sale)	auksjon (m)	[aʉk'şʉn]
to notify (inform)	å underrette	[ɔ 'ʉnəˌrɛtə]
management (process)	ledelse (m)	['ledəlsə]
service (~ industry)	tjeneste (m)	['tjenɛstə]

forum	forum (n)	['forum]
to function (vi)	å fungere	[ɔ fʉ'ŋerə]
stage (phase)	etappe (m)	[e'tapə]
legal (~ services)	juridisk	[jʉ'ridisk]
lawyer (legal advisor)	jurist (m)	[jʉ'rist]

106. Production. Works

plant	verk (n)	['værk]
factory	fabrikk (m)	[fa'brik]
workshop	verkstad (m)	['værkˌstɑd]
works, production site	produksjonsplass (m)	[prʉdʉk'şʉns ˌplɑs]

industry (manufacturing)	industri (m)	[indʉ'stri]
industrial (adj)	industriell	[indʉstri'ɛl]
heavy industry	tungindustri (m)	['tʉŋ ˌindʉ'stri]
light industry	lettindustri (m)	['letˌindʉ'stri]

products	produksjon (m)	[prʉdʉk'şʉn]
to produce (vt)	å produsere	[ɔ prʉdʉ'serə]
raw materials	råstoffer (n pl)	['rɔˌstɔfər]

foreman (construction ~)	formann, bas (m)	['forman], ['bɑs]
workers team (crew)	arbeidslag (n)	['ɑrbæjdsˌlɑg]
worker	arbeider (m)	['arˌbæjdər]

working day	arbeidsdag (m)	['ɑrbæjdsˌdɑ]
pause (rest break)	hvilepause (m)	['viləˌpaʉse]
meeting	møte (n)	['møtə]
to discuss (vt)	å drøfte, å diskutere	[ɔ 'drœftə], [ɔ diskʉ'terə]

plan	plan (m)	['plɑn]
to fulfil the plan	å oppfylle planen	[ɔ 'ɔpˌfʏlə 'plɑnən]
rate of output	produksjonsmål (n)	[prʉdʉk'şʉns ˌmol]
quality	kvalitet (m)	[kvɑli'tɛt]
control (checking)	kontroll (m)	[kʉn'trɔl]
quality control	kvalitetskontroll (m)	[kvɑli'tɛt kʉn'trɔl]

workplace safety	arbeidervern (n)	['ɑrbæjdərˌvæːɳ]
discipline	disiplin (m)	[disip'lin]
violation (of safety rules, etc.)	brudd (n)	['brʉd]

to violate (rules)	å bryte	[ɔ 'brytə]
strike	streik (m)	['stræjk]
striker	streiker (m)	['stræjkər]
to be on strike	å streike	[ɔ 'stræjkə]
trade union	fagforening (m/f)	['fɑgfɔˌreniŋ]

to invent (machine, etc.)	å oppfinne	[ɔ 'ɔpˌfinə]
invention	oppfinnelse (m)	['ɔpˌfinəlsə]
research	forskning (m)	['fɔːşkniŋ]
to improve (make better)	å forbedre	[ɔ fɔr'bɛdrə]
technology	teknologi (m)	[tɛknʊlʊ'gi]
technical drawing	teknisk tegning (m/f)	['tɛknisk ˌtæjniŋ]

load, cargo	last (m/f)	['lɑst]
loader (person)	lastearbeider (m)	['lɑstə'ɑrˌbæjdər]
to load (vehicle, etc.)	å laste	[ɔ 'lɑstə]
loading (process)	lasting (m/f)	['lɑstiŋ]
to unload (vi, vt)	å lesse av	[ɔ 'lesə ɑː]
unloading	avlessing (m/f)	['ɑvˌlesiŋ]

transport	transport (m)	[trɑns'pɔːt]
transport company	transportfirma (n)	[trɑns'pɔːt ˌfirmɑ]
to transport (vt)	å transportere	[ɔ trɑnspɔːˈʈerə]

wagon	godsvogn (m/f)	['gʊtsˌvɔŋn]
tank (e.g., oil ~)	tank (m)	['tɑnk]
lorry	lastebil (m)	['lɑstəˌbil]

| machine tool | verktøymaskin (m) | ['værktøj mɑˌşin] |
| mechanism | mekanisme (m) | [mekɑ'nismə] |

industrial waste	industrielt avfall (n)	[indʉstri'ɛlt 'ɑvˌfɑl]
packing (process)	pakning (m/f)	['pɑkniŋ]
to pack (vt)	å pakke	[ɔ 'pɑkə]

107. Contract. Agreement

contract	kontrakt (m)	[kʊn'trɑkt]
agreement	avtale (m)	['ɑvˌtɑlə]
addendum	tillegg, bilag (n)	['tiˌleg], ['biˌlɑg]

to sign a contract	å inngå kontrakt	[ɔ 'inˌgɔ kʊn'trɑkt]
signature	underskrift (m/f)	['ʉnəˌskrift]
to sign (vt)	å underskrive	[ɔ 'ʉnəˌskrivə]
seal (stamp)	stempel (n)	['stɛmpəl]

subject of the contract	kontraktens gjenstand (m)	[kʊn'trɑktəns 'jɛnˌstɑn]
clause	klausul (m)	[klɑʊ'sʉl]
parties (in contract)	parter (m pl)	['pɑːʈər]
legal address	juridisk adresse (m/f)	[jʉ'ridisk ɑ'drɛsə]

to violate the contract	å bryte kontrakten	[ɔ 'brytə kʊn'trɑktən]
commitment (obligation)	forpliktelse (m)	[fɔr'pliktəlsə]
responsibility	ansvar (n)	['ɑnˌsvɑr]

force majeure	force majeure (m)	[ˌfɔrs mɑ'ʒøːr]
dispute	tvist (m)	['tvist]
penalties	straffeavgifter (m pl)	['strɑfə ɑv'jiftər]

108. Import & Export

import	import (m)	[im'pɔːt]
importer	importør (m)	[impɔː'tør]
to import (vt)	å importere	[ɔ impɔː'terə]
import (as adj.)	import-	[im'pɔːt-]

export (exportation)	eksport (m)	[ɛks'pɔːt]
exporter	eksportør (m)	[ɛkspɔː'tør]
to export (vt)	å eksportere	[ɔ ɛkspɔː'terə]
export (as adj.)	eksport-	[ɛks'pɔːt-]

| goods (merchandise) | vare (m/f) | ['vɑrə] |
| consignment, lot | parti (n) | [pɑː'ʈi] |

weight	vekt (m)	['vɛkt]
volume	volum (n)	[vɔ'lʉm]
cubic metre	kubikkmeter (m)	[kʉ'bikˌmetər]

manufacturer	produsent (m)	[prʉdʉ'sɛnt]
transport company	transportfirma (n)	[trɑns'pɔːt ˌfirmɑ]
container	container (m)	[kɔn'tɛjnər]

border	grense (m/f)	['grɛnsə]
customs	toll (m)	['tɔl]
customs duty	tollavgift (m)	['tɔl ɑv'jift]
customs officer	tollbetjent (m)	['tɔlbeˌtjɛnt]
smuggling	smugling (m/f)	['smʉgliŋ]
contraband (smuggled goods)	smuglergods (n)	['smʉgləˌgʉts]

109. Finances

share, stock	aksje (m)	['akʂə]
bond (certificate)	obligasjon (m)	[ɔbligɑ'ʂun]
promissory note	veksel (m)	['vɛksəl]

| stock exchange | børs (m) | ['bœʂ] |
| stock price | aksjekurs (m) | ['akʂəˌkʉʂ] |

| to go down (become cheaper) | å gå ned | [ɔ 'gɔ ne] |
| to go up (become more expensive) | å gå opp | [ɔ 'gɔ ɔp] |

share	andel (m)	['anˌdel]
controlling interest	aksjemajoritet (m)	['akʂəˌmajori'tet]
investment	investering (m/f)	[inve'steriŋ]

to invest (vt)	å investere	[ɔ inve'sterə]
percent	prosent (m)	[prʊ'sɛnt]
interest (on investment)	rente (m/f)	['rɛntə]

profit	profitt (m), fortjeneste (m/f)	[prɔ'fit], [fɔː'tjenɛstə]
profitable (adj)	profitabel	[prɔfi'tabəl]
tax	skatt (m)	['skat]

currency (foreign ~)	valuta (m)	[va'lʉta]
national (adj)	nasjonal	[naʂʉ'nal]
exchange (currency ~)	veksling (m/f)	['vɛkʂliŋ]

| accountant | regnskapsfører (m) | ['rɛjnskaps,fører] |
| accounting | bokføring (m/f) | ['bʊk'føriŋ] |

bankruptcy	fallitt (m)	[fa'lit]
collapse, ruin	krakk (n)	['krak]
ruin	ruin (m)	[rʉ'in]
to be ruined (financially)	å ruinere seg	[ɔ rʉi'nerə sæj]
inflation	inflasjon (m)	[infla'ʂʊn]
devaluation	devaluering (m)	[devalʉ'eriŋ]

capital	kapital (m)	[kapi'tal]
income	inntekt (m/f), innkomst (m)	['in,tɛkt], ['in,kɔmst]
turnover	omsetning (m/f)	['ɔm,sɛtniŋ]
resources	ressurser (m pl)	[re'sʉsər]
monetary resources	pengemidler (m pl)	['pɛŋə,midlər]
overheads	faste utgifter (m/f pl)	['fastə 'ʉtjiftər]
to reduce (expenses)	å redusere	[ɔ redʉ'serə]

110. Marketing

marketing	markedsføring (m/f)	['markəds,føriŋ]
market	marked (n)	['markəd]
market segment	markedssegment (n)	['markəds seg'mɛnt]
product	produkt (n)	[prʊ'dʉkt]
goods (merchandise)	vare (m/f)	['varə]

brand	merkenavn (n)	['mærkə,navn]
trademark	varemerke (n)	['varə,mærkə]
logotype	firmamerke (n)	['firma,mærkə]
logo	logo (m)	['lugʊ]
demand	etterspørsel (m)	['ɛtə,spœʂəl]
supply	tilbud (n)	['til,bʉd]
need	behov (n)	[be'hʊv]
consumer	forbruker (m)	[fɔr'brʉkər]

analysis	analyse (m)	[ana'lysə]
to analyse (vt)	å analysere	[ɔ analy'serə]
positioning	posisjonering (m/f)	[pʊsiʂʊ'neriŋ]
to position (vt)	å posisjonere	[ɔ pʊsiʂʊ'nerə]
price	pris (m)	['pris]
pricing policy	prispolitikk (m)	['pris pʊli'tik]
price formation	prisdannelse (m)	['pris,danəlsə]

111. Advertising

advertising	reklame (m)	[rɛ'klɑmə]
to advertise (vt)	å reklamere	[ɔ rɛklɑ'merə]
budget	budsjett (n)	[bʉd'ʂɛt]
ad, advertisement	annonse (m)	[ɑ'nɔnsə]
TV advertising	TV-reklame (m)	['tɛvɛ rɛ'klɑmə]
radio advertising	radioreklame (m)	['rɑdiʉ rɛ'klɑmə]
outdoor advertising	utendørsreklame (m)	['ʉtən,dœʂ rɛ'klɑmə]
mass medias	massemedier (n pl)	['mɑsə,mediər]
periodical (n)	tidsskrift (n)	['tid,skrift]
image (public appearance)	image (m)	['imidʒ]
slogan	slogan (n)	['slɔgɑn]
motto (maxim)	motto (n)	['mɔtʉ]
campaign	kampanje (m)	[kɑm'pɑnjə]
advertising campaign	reklamekampanje (m)	[rɛ'klɑmə kɑm'pɑnjə]
target group	målgruppe (m/f)	['mɔːl,grʉpə]
business card	visittkort (n)	[vi'sit,kɔːt]
leaflet (promotional ~)	reklameblad (n)	[rɛ'klɑmə,blɑ]
brochure (e.g. 12 pages ~)	brosjyre (m)	[brɔ'ʂyrə]
pamphlet	folder (m)	['fɔlər]
newsletter	nyhetsbrev (n)	['nyhets,brev]
signboard (store sign, etc.)	skilt (n)	['ʂilt]
poster	plakat, poster (m)	['plɑ,kɑt], ['pɔstər]
hoarding	reklameskilt (m/f)	[rɛ'klɑmə,ʂilt]

112. Banking

bank	bank (m)	['bɑnk]
branch (of a bank)	avdeling (m)	['ɑv,deliŋ]
consultant	konsulent (m)	[kʉnsʉ'lent]
manager (director)	forstander (m)	[fɔ'ʂtɑndər]
bank account	bankkonto (m)	['bɑnk,kɔntʉ]
account number	kontonummer (n)	['kɔntʉ,nʉmər]
current account	sjekkonto (m)	['ʂɛk,kɔntʉ]
deposit account	sparekonto (m)	['spɑrə,kɔntʉ]
to open an account	å åpne en konto	[ɔ 'ɔpnə en 'kɔntʉ]
to close the account	å lukke kontoen	[ɔ 'lʉkə 'kɔntʉən]
to deposit into the account	å sette inn på kontoen	[ɔ 'sɛtə in pɔ 'kɔntʉən]
to withdraw (vt)	å ta ut fra kontoen	[ɔ 'tɑ ʉt frɑ 'kɔntʉən]
deposit	innskudd (n)	['in,skʉd]
to make a deposit	å sette inn	[ɔ 'sɛtə in]
wire transfer	overføring (m/f)	['ɔvər,føriŋ]

to wire, to transfer	å overføre	[ɔ 'ɔvər̩førə]
sum	sum (m)	['sʉm]
How much?	Hvor mye?	[vʊr 'mye]

| signature | underskrift (m/f) | ['ʉnə̩skrift] |
| to sign (vt) | å underskrive | [ɔ 'ʉnə̩skrivə] |

credit card	kredittkort (n)	[krɛ'dit̩kɔːt]
code (PIN code)	kode (m)	['kʊdə]
credit card number	kreditkortnummer (n)	[krɛ'dit̩kɔːt 'nʉmər]
cashpoint	minibank (m)	['mini̩bɑnk]

cheque	sjekk (m)	['ʂɛk]
to write a cheque	å skrive en sjekk	[ɔ 'skrivə en 'ʂɛk]
chequebook	sjekkbok (m/f)	['ʂɛk̩bʊk]

loan (bank ~)	lån (n)	['lɔn]
to apply for a loan	å søke om lån	[ɔ ˌsøkə ɔm 'lɔn]
to get a loan	å få lån	[ɔ 'fɔ 'lɔn]
to give a loan	å gi lån	[ɔ 'ji 'lɔn]
guarantee	garanti (m)	[ɡɑrɑn'ti]

113. Telephone. Phone conversation

telephone	telefon (m)	[tele'fʊn]
mobile phone	mobiltelefon (m)	[mʊ'bil tele'fʊn]
answerphone	telefonsvarer (m)	[tele'fʊn̩svɑrər]

| to call (by phone) | å ringe | [ɔ 'riŋə] |
| call, ring | telefonsamtale (m) | [tele'fʊn 'sɑm̩tɑlə] |

to dial a number	å slå et nummer	[ɔ 'ʂlɔ et 'nʉmər]
Hello!	Hallo!	[hɑ'lʊ]
to ask (vt)	å spørre	[ɔ 'spørə]
to answer (vi, vt)	å svare	[ɔ 'svɑrə]
to hear (vt)	å høre	[ɔ 'hørə]
well (adv)	godt	['ɡɔt]
not well (adv)	dårlig	['dɔːli̩]
noises (interference)	støy (m)	['støj]

receiver	telefonrør (n)	[tele'fʊn̩rør]
to pick up (~ the phone)	å ta telefonen	[ɔ 'tɑ tele'fʊnən]
to hang up (~ the phone)	å legge på røret	[ɔ 'legə pɔ 'rørə]

busy (engaged)	opptatt	['ɔp̩tɑt]
to ring (ab. phone)	å ringe	[ɔ 'riŋə]
telephone book	telefonkatalog (m)	[tele'fʊn kɑtɑ'lɔɡ]

local (adj)	lokal-	[lɔ'kɑl-]
local call	lokalsamtale (m)	[lɔ'kɑl 'sɑm̩tɑlə]
trunk (e.g. ~ call)	riks-	['riks-]
trunk call	rikssamtale (m)	['riks 'sɑm̩tɑlə]
international (adj)	internasjonal	['intɛːŋɑʂʊ̩nɑl]
international call	internasjonal samtale (m)	['intɛːŋɑʂʊ̩nɑl 'sɑm̩tɑlə]

114. Mobile telephone

mobile phone	mobiltelefon (m)	[mʉ'bil tele'fʊn]
display	skjerm (m)	['ʂærm]
button	knapp (m)	['knɑp]
SIM card	SIM-kort (n)	['sim‚kɔːt]

battery	batteri (n)	[batɛ'ri]
to be flat (battery)	å bli utladet	[ɔ 'bli 'ʉt‚lɑdət]
charger	lader (m)	['lɑdər]

menu	meny (m)	[me'ny]
settings	innstillinger (m/f pl)	['in‚stiliŋər]
tune (melody)	melodi (m)	[melɔ'di]
to select (vt)	å velge	[ɔ 'vɛlɡə]

calculator	regnemaskin (m)	['rɛjnə mɑ‚ʂin]
voice mail	telefonsvarer (m)	[tele'fʊn‚svɑrər]
alarm clock	vekkerklokka (m/f)	['vɛkər‚klɔkɑ]
contacts	kontakter (m pl)	[kʊn'tɑktər]

| SMS (text message) | SMS-beskjed (m) | [ɛsɛm'ɛs bɛ‚ʂɛ] |
| subscriber | abonnent (m) | [abɔ'nɛnt] |

115. Stationery

| ballpoint pen | kulepenn (m) | ['kʉːlə‚pɛn] |
| fountain pen | fyllepenn (m) | ['fʏlə‚pɛn] |

pencil	blyant (m)	['bly‚ant]
highlighter	merkepenn (m)	['mærkə‚pɛn]
felt-tip pen	tusjpenn (m)	['tʉʂ‚pɛn]

| notepad | notatbok (m/f) | [nʊ'tat‚bʊk] |
| diary | dagbok (m/f) | ['dɑg‚bʊk] |

ruler	linjal (m)	[li'njɑl]
calculator	regnemaskin (m)	['rɛjnə mɑ‚ʂin]
rubber	viskelær (n)	['viskə‚lær]
drawing pin	tegnestift (m)	['tæjnə‚stift]
paper clip	binders (m)	['bindɛʂ]

glue	lim (n)	['lim]
stapler	stiftemaskin (m)	['stiftə mɑ‚ʂin]
hole punch	hullemaskin (m)	['hʉlə mɑ‚ʂin]
pencil sharpener	blyantspisser (m)	['blyant‚spisər]

116. Various kinds of documents

| account (report) | rapport (m) | [rɑ'pɔːt] |
| agreement | avtale (m) | ['ɑv‚tɑlə] |

application form	søknadsskjema (n)	['søknads‚şema]
authentic (adj)	ekte	['ɛktə]
badge (identity tag)	badge (n)	['bædʒ]
business card	visittkort (n)	[vi'sit‚kɔːt]

certificate (~ of quality)	sertifikat (n)	[sæːṭifi'kɑt]
cheque (e.g. draw a ~)	sjekk (m)	['şɛk]
bill (in restaurant)	regning (m/f)	['rɛjniŋ]
constitution	grunnlov (m)	['grʉn‚lɔv]

contract (agreement)	avtale (m)	['ɑv‚tɑlə]
copy	kopi (m)	[kʉ'pi]
copy (of a contract, etc.)	eksemplar (n)	[ɛksɛm'plɑr]

customs declaration	tolldeklarasjon (m)	['tɔldɛklɑrɑ'şʉn]
document	dokument (n)	[dɔkʉ'mɛnt]
driving licence	førerkort (n)	['førər‚kɔːt]
addendum	tillegg, bilag (n)	['ti‚leg], ['bi‚lɑg]
form	skjema (n)	['şema]

ID card (e.g., warrant card)	legitimasjon (m)	[legitimɑ'şʉn]
inquiry (request)	forespørsel (m)	['forə‚spœşəl]
invitation card	invitasjonskort (n)	[invitɑ'şʉns‚kɔːt]
invoice	faktura (m)	[fɑk'tʉrɑ]

law	lov (m)	['lɔv]
letter (mail)	brev (n)	['brev]
letterhead	brevpapir (n)	['brev‚pa'pir]
list (of names, etc.)	liste (m/f)	['listə]
manuscript	manuskript (n)	[mɑnʉ'skript]
newsletter	nyhetsbrev (n)	['nyhets‚brev]
note (short letter)	lapp, seddel (m)	['lɑp], ['sɛdəl]

pass (for worker, visitor)	adgangskort (n)	['ɑdgɑŋs‚kɔːt]
passport	pass (n)	['pɑs]
permit	tillatelse (m)	['ti‚lɑtəlsə]
curriculum vitae, CV	CV (m/n)	['sɛvɛ]
debt note, IOU	skyldbrev, gjeldsbrev (m/f)	['şyl‚brev], ['jɛl‚brev]
receipt (for purchase)	kvittering (m/f)	[kvi'təriŋ]

till receipt	kassalapp (m)	['kasa‚lap]
report (mil.)	rapport (m)	[rɑ'pɔːt]

to show (ID, etc.)	å vise	[ɔ 'visə]
to sign (vt)	å underskrive	[ɔ 'ʉnə‚skrivə]
signature	underskrift (m/f)	['ʉnə‚skrift]
seal (stamp)	stempel (n)	['stɛmpəl]

text	tekst (m/f)	['tɛkst]
ticket (for entry)	billett (m)	[bi'let]

to cross out	å stryke ut	[ɔ 'strykə ʉt]
to fill in (~ a form)	å utfylle	[ɔ 'ʉt‚fʏlə]

waybill (shipping invoice)	fraktbrev (n)	['frɑkt‚brev]
will (testament)	testament (n)	[tɛstɑ'mɛnt]

117. Kinds of business

accounting services	bokføringstjenester (m pl)	['bʊkˌførɪŋs 'tjenɛstər]
advertising	reklame (m)	[rɛ'klamə]
advertising agency	reklamebyrå (n)	[rɛ'klamə byˌro]
air-conditioners	klimaanlegg (n pl)	['klima'anˌleg]
airline	flyselskap (n)	['flysəlˌskap]

alcoholic beverages	alkoholholdige drikke (m pl)	[alkʊ'hʊlˌhɔldiə 'drikə]
antiques (antique dealers)	antikviteter (m pl)	[antikvi'tetər]
art gallery (contemporary ~)	kunstgalleri (n)	['kʊnst gale'ri]
audit services	revisjonstjenester (m pl)	[revi'ʂʊnsˌtjenɛstər]

banking industry	bankvirksomhet (m/f)	['bankˌvirksɔmhet]
beauty salon	skjønnhetssalong (m)	['ʂønhɛts sa'lɔŋ]
bookshop	bokhandel (m)	['bʊkˌhandəl]
brewery	bryggeri (n)	[brʏge'ri]
business centre	forretningssenter (n)	[fo'rɛtnɪŋsˌsɛntər]
business school	handelsskole (m)	['handəlsˌskʊlə]

casino	kasino (n)	[ka'sinʊ]
chemist, pharmacy	apotek (n)	[apʊ'tek]
cinema	kino (m)	['çinʊ]
construction	byggeri (m/f)	[bʏge'ri]
consulting	konsulenttjenester (m pl)	[kʊnsu'lent ˌtjenɛstər]

dental clinic	tannklinik (m)	['tankli'nik]
design	design (m)	['desajn]
dry cleaners	renseri (n)	[rɛnse'ri]

employment agency	rekrutteringsbyrå (n)	['rekrʉˌterɪŋs byˌro]
financial services	finansielle tjenester (m pl)	[finan'sielə ˌtjenɛstər]
food products	matvarer (m/f pl)	['matˌvarər]
furniture (e.g. house ~)	møbler (n pl)	['møblər]
clothing, garment	klær (n)	['klær]
hotel	hotell (n)	[hʊ'tɛl]

ice-cream	iskrem (m)	['iskrɛm]
industry (manufacturing)	industri (m)	[indʉ'stri]
insurance	forsikring (m/f)	[fɔ'ʂikrɪŋ]
Internet	Internett	['intəˌŋɛt]
investments (finance)	investering (m/f)	[inve'sterɪŋ]
jeweller	juveler (m)	[jʉ'velər]
jewellery	smykker (n pl)	['smʏkər]

laundry (shop)	vaskeri (n)	[vaske'ri]
legal adviser	juridisk rådgiver (m pl)	[jʉ'ridisk 'rɔdˌjivər]
light industry	lettindustri (m)	['letˌindʉ'stri]

magazine	magasin, tidsskrift (n)	[maga'sin], ['tidˌskrift]
mail order selling	postordresalg (m)	['postˌordrə'salg]
medicine	medisin (m)	[medi'sin]
museum	museum (n)	[mʉ'seum]
news agency	nyhetsbyrå (n)	['nyhɛts byˌro]
newspaper	avis (m/f)	[a'vis]

nightclub	nattklubb (m)	['nat̩ˌklʉb]
oil (petroleum)	olje (m)	['ɔljə]
courier services	budtjeneste (m)	[bʉd'tjenɛstə]
pharmaceutics	legemidler (pl)	['legə'midlər]
printing (industry)	trykkeri (n)	[trʏkə'ri]
pub	bar (m)	['bar]
publishing house	forlag (n)	['fɔːlag]

radio (~ station)	radio (m)	['radiʉ]
real estate	fast eiendom (m)	[ˌfast 'æjənˌdɔm]
restaurant	restaurant (m)	[rɛstʉ'raŋ]

security company	sikkerhetsselskap (n)	['sikərhɛts 'selˌskap]
shop	forretning, butikk (m)	[fɔ'rɛtniŋ], [bʉ'tik]
sport	sport, idrett (m)	['spɔːt], ['idrɛt]
stock exchange	børs (m)	['bœʂ]
supermarket	supermarked (n)	['sʉpəˌmarket]
swimming pool (public ~)	svømmebasseng (n)	['svœməˌba'sɛŋ]

tailor shop	skredderi (n)	[skrɛde'ri]
television	televisjon (m)	['televiˌsʉn]
theatre	teater (n)	[te'atər]
trade (commerce)	handel (m)	['handəl]
transport companies	transport (m)	[trans'pɔːt]
travel	turisme (m)	[tʉ'rismə]

undertakers	begravelsesbyrå (n)	[be'gravəlsəs byˌro]
veterinary surgeon	dyrlege, veterinær (m)	['dyrˌlegə], [vetəri'nær]
warehouse	lager (n)	['lagər]
waste collection	avfallstømming (m/f)	['avfalsˌtømiŋ]

Job. Business. Part 2

118. Show. Exhibition

exhibition, show	messe (m/f)	['mɛsə]
trade show	varemesse (m/f)	['varə‚mɛsə]
participation	deltagelse (m)	['del‚tagəlsə]
to participate (vi)	å delta	[ɔ 'dɛlta]
participant (exhibitor)	deltaker (m)	['del‚takər]
director	direktør (m)	[dirɛk'tør]
organizers' office	arrangørkontor (m)	[aran'gør kun'tur]
organizer	arrangør (m)	[aran'gør]
to organize (vt)	å organisere	[ɔ ɔrgani'serə]
participation form	påmeldingsskjema (n)	['pɔmeliŋs‚sɛma]
to fill in (vt)	å utfylle	[ɔ 'ʉt‚fʏlə]
details	detaljer (m pl)	[de'taljər]
information	informasjon (m)	[infɔrma'ʂʉn]
price (cost, rate)	pris (m)	['pris]
including	inklusive	['inklʉ‚sivə]
to include (vt)	å inkludere	[ɔ inklʉ'derə]
to pay (vi, vt)	å betale	[ɔ be'talə]
registration fee	registreringsavgift (m/f)	[rɛgi'strɛriŋs av'jift]
entrance	inngang (m)	['in‚gaŋ]
pavilion, hall	paviljong (m)	[pavi'ljɔŋ]
to register (vt)	å registrere	[ɔ regi'strerə]
badge (identity tag)	badge (n)	['bædʒ]
stand	messestand (m)	['mɛsə‚stan]
to reserve, to book	å reservere	[ɔ resɛr'verə]
display case	glassmonter (m)	['glas‚mɔntər]
spotlight	lampe (m/f), spotlys (n)	['lampə], ['spɔt‚lys]
design	design (m)	['desajn]
to place (put, set)	å plassere	[ɔ pla'serə]
to be placed	å bli plasseret	[ɔ 'bli pla'serət]
distributor	distributør (m)	[distribʉ'tør]
supplier	leverandør (m)	[leveran'dør]
to supply (vt)	å levere	[ɔ le'verə]
country	land (n)	['lan]
foreign (adj)	utenlandsk	['ʉtən‚lansk]
product	produkt (n)	[prʉ'dʉkt]
association	forening (m/f)	[fɔ'reniŋ]
conference hall	konferansesal (m)	[kʉnfə'ransə‚sal]

| congress | kongress (m) | [kʊn'grɛs] |
| contest (competition) | tevling (m) | ['tɛvliŋ] |

visitor (attendee)	besøkende (m)	[be'søkenə]
to visit (attend)	å besøke	[ɔ be'søkə]
customer	kunde (m)	['kʉndə]

119. Mass Media

newspaper	avis (m/f)	[ɑ'vis]
magazine	magasin, tidsskrift (n)	[mɑgɑ'sin], ['tid‚skrift]
press (printed media)	presse (m/f)	['prɛsə]
radio	radio (m)	['rɑdiʊ]
radio station	radiostasjon (m)	['rɑdiʊ‚stɑ'ʂʊn]
television	televisjon (m)	['televi‚ʂʊn]

presenter, host	programleder (m)	[prʊ'grɑm‚ledər]
newsreader	nyhetsoppleser (m)	['nyhets'ɔp‚lesər]
commentator	kommentator (m)	[kʊmən'tɑtʊr]

journalist	journalist (m)	[ʂu:ŋɑ'list]
correspondent (reporter)	korrespondent (m)	[kʊrespɔn'dɛnt]
press photographer	pressefotograf (m)	['prɛsə fotɔ'grɑf]
reporter	reporter (m)	[re'pɔ:[ər]

| editor | redaktør (m) | [rɛdɑk'tør] |
| editor-in-chief | sjefredaktør (m) | ['ʂɛf rɛdɑk'tør] |

to subscribe (to ...)	å abonnere	[ɔ abɔ'nerə]
subscription	abonnement (n)	[abɔnə'mɑŋ]
subscriber	abonnent (m)	[abɔ'nɛnt]
to read (vi, vt)	å lese	[ɔ 'lesə]
reader	leser (m)	['lesər]

circulation (of a newspaper)	opplag (n)	['ɔp‚lɑg]
monthly (adj)	månedlig	['mo:nədli]
weekly (adj)	ukentlig	['ʉkəntli]
issue (edition)	nummer (n)	['nʉmər]
new (~ issue)	ny, fersk	['ny], ['fæʂk]

headline	overskrift (m)	['ɔvə‚skrift]
short article	notis (m)	[nʊ'tis]
column (regular article)	rubrikk (m)	[rʉ'brik]
article	artikkel (m)	[ɑ:'ʈikəl]
page	side (m/f)	['sidə]

reportage, report	reportasje (m)	[repɔ:'ʈaʂə]
event (happening)	hendelse (m)	['hɛndəlsə]
sensation (news)	sensasjon (m)	[sɛnsɑ'ʂʊn]
scandal	skandale (m)	[skan'dɑlə]
scandalous (adj)	skandaløs	[skandɑ'løs]
great (~ scandal)	stor	['stʊr]
programme (e.g. cooking ~)	program (n)	[prʊ'grɑm]
interview	intervju (n)	[intə'vjʉ:]

| live broadcast | direktesending (m/f) | [di'rɛktə,sɛniŋ] |
| channel | kanal (m) | [ka'nal] |

120. Agriculture

agriculture	landbruk (n)	['lɑn,brʉk]
peasant (masc.)	bonde (m)	['bonə]
peasant (fem.)	bondekone (m/f)	['bonə,kʉnə]
farmer	gårdbruker, bonde (m)	['gɔːr,brʉkər], ['bonə]

| tractor | traktor (m) | ['trɑktʉr] |
| combine, harvester | skurtresker (m) | ['skʉː,trɛskər] |

plough	plog (m)	['plug]
to plough (vi, vt)	å pløye	[ɔ 'pløjə]
ploughland	pløyemark (m/f)	['pløjə,mɑrk]
furrow (in field)	fure (m)	['fʉrə]

to sow (vi, vt)	å så	[ɔ 'sɔ]
seeder	såmaskin (m)	['so:mɑ,ʂin]
sowing (process)	såing (m/f)	['so:iŋ]

| scythe | ljå (m) | ['ljoː] |
| to mow, to scythe | å meie, å slå | [ɔ 'mæjə], [ɔ 'slɔ] |

| spade (tool) | spade (m) | ['spɑdə] |
| to till (vt) | å grave | [ɔ 'grɑvə] |

hoe	hakke (m/f)	['hɑkə]
to hoe, to weed	å hakke	[ɔ 'hɑkə]
weed (plant)	ugras (n)	[ʉ'grɑs]

watering can	vannkanne (f)	['vɑn,kɑnə]
to water (plants)	å vanne	[ɔ 'vɑnə]
watering (act)	vanning (m/f)	['vɑniŋ]

| pitchfork | greip (m) | ['græjp] |
| rake | rive (m/f) | ['rivə] |

fertiliser	gjødsel (m/f)	['jøtsəl]
to fertilise (vt)	å gjødsle	['ɔ 'jøtslə]
manure (fertiliser)	møkk (m/f)	['møk]

field	åker (m)	['o:ker]
meadow	eng (m/f)	['ɛŋ]
vegetable garden	kjøkkenhage (m)	['çœkən,hɑgə]
orchard (e.g. apple ~)	frukthage (m)	['frʉkt,hɑgə]

to graze (vt)	å beite	[ɔ 'bæjtə]
herdsman	gjeter, hyrde (m)	['jetər], ['hʏrdə]
pasture	beite (n), beitemark (m/f)	['bæjtə], ['bæjtə,mɑrk]

| cattle breeding | husdyrhold (n) | ['hʉsdyr,hɔl] |
| sheep farming | sauehold (n) | ['sɑʉə,hɔl] |

plantation	plantasje (m)	[plɑn'tɑʂə]
row (garden bed ~s)	rad (m/f)	['rɑd]
hothouse	drivhus (n)	['driv͵hʉs]

| drought (lack of rain) | tørke (m/f) | ['tœrkə] |
| dry (~ summer) | tørr | ['tœr] |

grain	korn (n)	['kuːn̩]
cereal crops	cerealer (n pl)	[sere'ɑlər]
to harvest, to gather	å høste	[ɔ 'høstə]

miller (person)	møller (m)	['mølər]
mill (e.g. gristmill)	mølle (m/f)	['mølə]
to grind (grain)	å male	[ɔ 'mɑlə]
flour	mel (n)	['mel]
straw	halm (m)	['hɑlm]

121. Building. Building process

building site	byggeplass (m)	['bʏgə͵plɑs]
to build (vt)	å bygge	[ɔ 'bʏgə]
building worker	bygningsarbeider (m)	['bʏgniŋʂ 'ɑr͵bæejər]

project	prosjekt (n)	[prʉ'ʂɛkt]
architect	arkitekt (m)	[ɑrki'tɛkt]
worker	arbeider (m)	['ɑr͵bæejdər]

foundations (of a building)	fundament (n)	[fʉndɑ'mɛnt]
roof	tak (n)	['tɑk]
foundation pile	pæl (m)	['pæl]
wall	mur, vegg (m)	['mʉr], ['vɛg]

| reinforcing bars | armeringsjern (n) | [ɑr'meriŋs'jæːn̩] |
| scaffolding | stillas (n) | [sti'lɑs] |

concrete	betong (m)	[be'tɔŋ]
granite	granitt (m)	[grɑ'nit]
stone	stein (m)	['stæejn]
brick	tegl (n), murstein (m)	['tæejl], ['mʉ͵stæejn]

sand	sand (m)	['sɑn]
cement	sement (m)	[se'mɛnt]
plaster (for walls)	puss (m)	['pʉs]
to plaster (vt)	å pusse	[ɔ 'pʉsə]

paint	maling (m/f)	['mɑliŋ]
to paint (~ a wall)	å male	[ɔ 'mɑlə]
barrel	tønne (m)	['tœnə]

crane	heisekran (m/f)	['hæejsə͵krɑn]
to lift, to hoist (vt)	å løfte	[ɔ 'lœftə]
to lower (vt)	å heise ned	[ɔ 'hæejsə ne]
bulldozer	bulldoser (m)	['bʉl͵dʉsər]
excavator	gravemaskin (m)	['grɑvə mɑ'ʂin]

scoop, bucket	skuffe (m/f)	['skʉfə]
to dig (excavate)	å grave	[ɔ 'grɑvə]
hard hat	hjelm (m)	['jɛlm]

122. Science. Research. Scientists

science	vitenskap (m)	['vitən‚skɑp]
scientific (adj)	vitenskapelig	['vitən‚skɑpəli]
scientist	vitenskapsmann (m)	['vitən‚skɑps mɑn]
theory	teori (m)	[teʉ'ri]

axiom	aksiom (n)	[ɑksi'ɔm]
analysis	analyse (m)	[ɑnɑ'lysə]
to analyse (vt)	å analysere	[ɔ ɑnɑly'serə]
argument (strong ~)	argument (n)	[ɑrgʉ'mɛnt]
substance (matter)	stoff (n), substans (m)	['stɔf], [sʉb'stɑns]

hypothesis	hypotese (m)	[hypʉ'tesə]
dilemma	dilemma (n)	[di'lemɑ]
dissertation	avhandling (m/f)	['ɑv‚hɑndliŋ]
dogma	dogme (n)	['dɔgmə]

doctrine	doktrine (m)	[dɔk'trinə]
research	forskning (m)	['fɔːʂkniŋ]
to research (vt)	å forske	[ɔ 'fɔːʂkə]
tests (laboratory ~)	test (m), prøve (m/f)	['tɛst], ['prøvə]
laboratory	laboratorium (n)	[lɑbʉrɑ'tʉrium]

method	metode (m)	[me'tɔdə]
molecule	molekyl (n)	[mʉle'kyl]
monitoring	overvåking (m/f)	['ɔvər‚vɔkiŋ]
discovery (act, event)	oppdagelse (m)	['ɔp‚dɑgəlsə]

postulate	postulat (n)	[pɔstʉ'lɑt]
principle	prinsipp (n)	[prin'sip]
forecast	prognose (m)	[prʉg'nʉsə]
to forecast (vt)	å prognostisere	[ɔ prʉgnʉsti'serə]

synthesis	syntese (m)	[syn'tesə]
trend (tendency)	tendens (m)	[tɛn'dɛns]
theorem	teorem (n)	[teʉ'rɛm]

| teachings | lære (m/f pl) | ['læːrə] |
| fact | faktum (n) | ['fɑktum] |

| expedition | ekspedisjon (m) | [ɛkspedi'ʂun] |
| experiment | eksperiment (n) | [ɛksperi'mɛnt] |

academician	akademiker (m)	[ɑkɑ'demikər]
bachelor (e.g. ~ of Arts)	bachelor (m)	['bɑtʂəlɔr]
doctor (PhD)	doktor (m)	['dɔktʉr]
Associate Professor	dosent (m)	[dʉ'sɛnt]
Master (e.g. ~ of Arts)	magister (m)	[mɑ'gistər]
professor	professor (m)	[prʉ'fɛsʉr]

Professions and occupations

job	arbeid (n), jobb (m)	['arbæj], ['job]
staff (work force)	ansatte (pl)	['an‚satə]
personnel	personale (n)	[pæʂu'nalə]

career	karriere (m)	[kari'ɛrə]
prospects (chances)	utsikter (m pl)	['ʉt‚siktər]
skills (mastery)	mesterskap (n)	['mɛstæ‚ʂkap]

selection (screening)	utvelgelse (m)	['ʉt‚vɛlgəlsə]
employment agency	rekrutteringsbyrå (n)	['rekrʉ‚teriŋs by‚ro]
curriculum vitae, CV	CV (m/n)	['sɛvɛ]
job interview	jobbintervju (n)	['job ‚intər'vjʉ]
vacancy	vakanse (m)	['vakansə]

salary, pay	lønn (m/f)	['lœn]
fixed salary	fastlønn (m/f)	['fast‚lœn]
pay, compensation	betaling (m/f)	[be'taliŋ]

position (job)	stilling (m/f)	['stiliŋ]
duty (of an employee)	plikt (m/f)	['plikt]
range of duties	arbeidsplikter (m/f pl)	['arbæjds‚pliktər]
busy (I'm ~)	opptatt	['ɔp‚tat]

| to fire (dismiss) | å avskjedige | [ɔ 'af‚ʂedige] |
| dismissal | avskjedigelse (m) | ['afʂe‚digəlsə] |

unemployment	arbeidsløshet (m)	['arbæjdsløs‚het]
unemployed (n)	arbeidsløs (m)	['arbæjds‚løs]
retirement	pensjon (m)	[pan'ʂun]
to retire (from job)	å gå av med pensjon	[ɔ 'gɔ a: me pan'ʂun]

director	direktør (m)	[dirɛk'tør]
manager (director)	forstander (m)	[fɔ'ʂtandər]
boss	boss (m)	['bɔs]

superior	overordnet (m)	['ɔvər‚ɔrdnet]
superiors	overordnede (pl)	['ɔvər‚ɔrdnede]
president	president (m)	[prɛsi'dɛnt]
chairman	styreformann (m)	['styrə‚fɔrman]

| deputy (substitute) | stedfortreder (m) | ['stedfɔ:‚tredər] |
| assistant | assistent (m) | [asi'stɛnt] |

secretary	sekretær (m)	[sɛkrə'tær]
personal assistant	privatsekretær (m)	[pri'vat sɛkrə'tær]
businessman	forretningsmann (m)	[fo'rɛtniŋs,man]
entrepreneur	entreprenør (m)	[ɛntreprə'nør]
founder	grunnlegger (m)	['grʉn,legər]
to found (vt)	å grunnlegge, å stifte	[ɔ 'grʉn,legə], [ɔ 'stiftə]
founding member	stifter (m)	['stiftər]
partner	partner (m)	['pɑːʈnər]
shareholder	aksjonær (m)	[akʂʉ'nær]
millionaire	millionær (m)	[milju'nær]
billionaire	milliardær (m)	[milja:'dær]
owner, proprietor	eier (m)	['æjər]
landowner	jordeier (m)	['juːr,æjər]
client	kunde (m)	['kʉndə]
regular client	fast kunde (m)	[,fast 'kʉndə]
buyer (customer)	kjøper (m)	['çœːpər]
visitor	besøkende (m)	[be'søkenə]
professional (n)	yrkesmann (m)	['yrkəs,man]
expert	ekspert (m)	[ɛks'pæːʈ]
specialist	spesialist (m)	[spesia'list]
banker	bankier (m)	[banki'e]
broker	mekler, megler (m)	['mɛklər]
cashier	kasserer (m)	[ka'serər]
accountant	regnskapsfører (m)	['rɛjnskaps,førər]
security guard	sikkerhetsvakt (m/f)	['sikərhɛts,vakt]
investor	investor (m)	[in'vɛstʉr]
debtor	skyldner (m)	['ʂylnər]
creditor	kreditor (m)	['krɛditʉr]
borrower	låntaker (m)	['lɔn,takər]
importer	importør (m)	[impɔː'ʈør]
exporter	eksportør (m)	[ɛkspɔː'ʈør]
manufacturer	produsent (m)	[prʉdʉ'sɛnt]
distributor	distributør (m)	[distribʉ'tør]
middleman	mellommann (m)	['mɛlɔ,man]
consultant	konsulent (m)	[kʉnsʉ'lent]
sales representative	representant (m)	[represɛn'tant]
agent	agent (m)	[a'gɛnt]
insurance agent	forsikringsagent (m)	[fɔ'ʂikriŋs a'gɛnt]

125. Service professions

cook	kokk (m)	['kʉk]
chef (kitchen chef)	sjefkokk (m)	['ʂɛf,kʉk]

baker	baker (m)	['bakər]
barman	bartender (m)	['bɑːˌtɛndər]
waiter	servitør (m)	['særvi'tør]
waitress	servitrise (m/f)	[særvi'trisə]

lawyer, barrister	advokat (m)	[advʊ'kat]
lawyer (legal expert)	jurist (m)	[jʉ'rist]
notary public	notar (m)	[nʊ'tar]

electrician	elektriker (m)	[ɛ'lektrikər]
plumber	rørlegger (m)	['rørˌlegər]
carpenter	tømmermann (m)	['tœmərˌman]

masseur	massør (m)	[ma'sør]
masseuse	massøse (m)	[ma'søsə]
doctor	lege (m)	['legə]

taxi driver	taxisjåfør (m)	['taksi ʂɔ'før]
driver	sjåfør (m)	[ʂɔ'før]
delivery man	bud (n)	['bʉd]

chambermaid	stuepike (m/f)	['stʉəˌpikə]
security guard	sikkerhetsvakt (m/f)	['sikərhɛtsˌvakt]
flight attendant (fem.)	flyvertinne (m/f)	[flyvɛː'ʈinə]

schoolteacher	lærer (m)	['lærər]
librarian	bibliotekar (m)	[bibliʊ'tekar]
translator	oversetter (m)	['ɔvəˌʂɛtər]
interpreter	tolk (m)	['tɔlk]
guide	guide (m)	['gajd]

hairdresser	frisør (m)	[fri'sør]
postman	postbud (n)	['pɔstˌbʉd]
salesman (store staff)	forselger (m)	[fɔ'ʂɛlər]

gardener	gartner (m)	['gaːʈnər]
domestic servant	tjener (m)	['tjenər]
maid (female servant)	tjenestepike (m/f)	['tjenɛstəˌpikə]
cleaner (cleaning lady)	vaskedame (m/f)	['vaskəˌdamə]

126. Military professions and ranks

private	menig (m)	['meni]
sergeant	sersjant (m)	[sær'ʂant]
lieutenant	løytnant (m)	['løjtˌnant]
captain	kaptein (m)	[kap'tæjn]

major	major (m)	[ma'jɔr]
colonel	oberst (m)	['ʊbɛʂt]
general	general (m)	[gene'ral]
marshal	marskalk (m)	['marʂal]
admiral	admiral (m)	[admi'ral]
military (n)	militær (m)	[mili'tær]
soldier	soldat (m)	[sʊl'dat]

113

| officer | offiser (m) | [ɔfi'sɛr] |
| commander | befalshaver (m) | [be'fals,havər] |

border guard	grensevakt (m/f)	['grɛnsə,vakt]
radio operator	radiooperatør (m)	['radiʊ ʊpəra'tør]
scout (searcher)	oppklaringssoldat (m)	['ɔp,klariŋ sʊl'dat]
pioneer (sapper)	pioner (m)	[piʊ'ner]
marksman	skytter (m)	['ṣytər]
navigator	styrmann (m)	['styr,man]

127. Officials. Priests

| king | konge (m) | ['kʊŋə] |
| queen | dronning (m/f) | ['drɔniŋ] |

| prince | prins (m) | ['prins] |
| princess | prinsesse (m/f) | [prin'sɛsə] |

| czar | tsar (m) | ['tsar] |
| czarina | tsarina (m) | [tsa'rina] |

president	president (m)	[prɛsi'dɛnt]
Secretary (minister)	minister (m)	[mi'nistər]
prime minister	statsminister (m)	['stats mi'nistər]
senator	senator (m)	[se'natʊr]

diplomat	diplomat (m)	[diplʊ'mat]
consul	konsul (m)	['kʊn,sʉl]
ambassador	ambassadør (m)	[ambasa'dør]
counselor (diplomatic officer)	rådgiver (m)	['rɔdˌjivər]

official, functionary (civil servant)	embetsmann (m)	['ɛmbets,man]
prefect	prefekt (m)	[prɛ'fɛkt]
mayor	borgermester (m)	[bɔrgər'mɛstər]

| judge | dommer (m) | ['dɔmər] |
| prosecutor | anklager (m) | ['an,klagər] |

missionary	misjonær (m)	[miṣʊ'nær]
monk	munk (m)	['mʉnk]
abbot	abbed (m)	['abed]
rabbi	rabbiner (m)	[ra'binər]

vizier	vesir (m)	[vɛ'sir]
shah	sjah (m)	['ṣa]
sheikh	sjeik (m)	['ṣæjk]

128. Agricultural professions

| beekeeper | birøkter (m) | ['biˌrøktər] |
| shepherd | gjeter, hyrde (m) | ['jetər], ['hʏrdə] |

agronomist	agronom (m)	[agrʉ'nʉm]
cattle breeder	husdyrholder (m)	['hʉsdyrˌhɔldər]
veterinary surgeon	dyrlege, veterinær (m)	['dyrˌlegə], [vetəri'nær]

farmer	gårdbruker, bonde (m)	['gɔːrˌbrʉkər], ['bɔnə]
winemaker	vinmaker (m)	['vinˌmakər]
zoologist	zoolog (m)	[sʉ:'lɔg]
cowboy	cowboy (m)	['kawˌbɔj]

129. Art professions

| actor | skuespiller (m) | ['skʉəˌspilər] |
| actress | skuespillerinne (m/f) | ['skʉəˌspilə'rinə] |

| singer (masc.) | sanger (m) | ['saŋər] |
| singer (fem.) | sangerinne (m/f) | [saŋə'rinə] |

| dancer (masc.) | danser (m) | ['dansər] |
| dancer (fem.) | danserinne (m/f) | [danse'rinə] |

| performer (masc.) | skuespiller (m) | ['skʉəˌspilər] |
| performer (fem.) | skuespillerinne (m/f) | ['skʉəˌspilə'rinə] |

musician	musiker (m)	['mʉsikər]
pianist	pianist (m)	[pia'nist]
guitar player	gitarspiller (m)	[gi'tarˌspilər]

conductor (orchestra ~)	dirigent (m)	[diri'gɛnt]
composer	komponist (m)	[kʉmpʉ'nist]
impresario	impresario (m)	[impre'sariʉ]

film director	regissør (m)	[rɛʂi'sør]
producer	produsent (m)	[prʉdʉ'sɛnt]
scriptwriter	manusforfatter (m)	['manʉs fɔr'fatər]
critic	kritiker (m)	['kritikər]

writer	forfatter (m)	[fɔr'fatər]
poet	poet, dikter (m)	['pɔɛt], ['diktər]
sculptor	skulptør (m)	[skʉlp'tør]
artist (painter)	kunstner (m)	['kʉnstnər]

juggler	sjonglør (m)	[ʂɔŋ'lør]
clown	klovn (m)	['klɔvn]
acrobat	akrobat (m)	[akrʉ'bat]
magician	tryllekunstner (m)	['trʏləˌkʉnstnər]

130. Various professions

doctor	lege (m)	['legə]
nurse	sykepleierske (m/f)	['sykəˌplæjeʂkə]
psychiatrist	psykiater (m)	[syki'atər]
dentist	tannlege (m)	['tanˌlegə]

surgeon	kirurg (m)	[çi'rʉrg]
astronaut	astronaut (m)	[astrʉ'naʊt]
astronomer	astronom (m)	[astrʉ'nʊm]

driver (of a taxi, etc.)	fører (m)	['fører]
train driver	lokfører (m)	['lʊk‚fører]
mechanic	mekaniker (m)	[me'kaniker]

miner	gruvearbeider (m)	['grʉve'ar‚bæjder]
worker	arbeider (m)	['ar‚bæjder]
locksmith	låsesmed (m)	['lo:se‚sme]
joiner (carpenter)	snekker (m)	['snɛker]
turner (lathe operator)	dreier (m)	['dræjer]
building worker	bygningsarbeider (m)	['bygniŋs 'ar‚bæjer]
welder	sveiser (m)	['svæjser]

professor (title)	professor (m)	[prʉ'fɛsʉr]
architect	arkitekt (m)	[arki'tɛkt]
historian	historiker (m)	[hi'stʉriker]
scientist	vitenskapsmann (m)	['viten‚skaps man]
physicist	fysiker (m)	['fysiker]
chemist (scientist)	kjemiker (m)	['çemiker]

archaeologist	arkeolog (m)	[‚arkeʊ'lɔg]
geologist	geolog (m)	[geʊ'lɔg]
researcher (scientist)	forsker (m)	['fɔşker]

| babysitter | babysitter (m) | ['bɛby‚siter] |
| teacher, educator | lærer, pedagog (m) | [lærer], [peda'gɔg] |

editor	redaktør (m)	[rɛdak'tør]
editor-in-chief	sjefredaktør (m)	['şɛf rɛdak'tør]
correspondent	korrespondent (m)	[kʉrespɔn'dɛnt]
typist (fem.)	maskinskriverske (m)	[ma'şin ‚skrivɛşke]

designer	designer (m)	[de'sajner]
computer expert	dataekspert (m)	['data ɛks'pɛ:t]
programmer	programmerer (m)	[prʉgra'merer]
engineer (designer)	ingeniør (m)	[inşe'njør]

sailor	sjømann (m)	['şø‚man]
seaman	matros (m)	[ma'trʊs]
rescuer	redningsmann (m)	['rɛdniŋs‚man]

firefighter	brannmann (m)	['bran‚man]
police officer	politi (m)	[pʉli'ti]
watchman	nattvakt (m)	['nat‚vakt]
detective	detektiv (m)	[detɛk'tiv]

customs officer	tollbetjent (m)	['tɔlbe‚tjɛnt]
bodyguard	livvakt (m/f)	['liv‚vakt]
prison officer	fangevokter (m)	['faŋe‚vɔkter]
inspector	inspektør (m)	[inspɛk'tør]

| sportsman | idrettsmann (m) | ['idrɛts‚man] |
| trainer, coach | trener (m) | ['trener] |

butcher	slakter (m)	['ʂlaktər]
cobbler (shoe repairer)	skomaker (m)	['skʉˌmakər]
merchant	handelsmann (m)	['handəlsˌman]
loader (person)	lastearbeider (m)	['lastəˈarˌbæjdər]

| fashion designer | moteskaper (m) | ['mʉtəˌskapər] |
| model (fem.) | modell (m) | [mʉ'dɛl] |

131. Occupations. Social status

| schoolboy | skolegutt (m) | ['skʉləˌgʉt] |
| student (college ~) | student (m) | [stʉ'dɛnt] |

philosopher	filosof (m)	[filu'sʊf]
economist	økonom (m)	[økʉ'nʉm]
inventor	oppfinner (m)	['ɔpˌfinər]

unemployed (n)	arbeidsløs (m)	['arbæjdsˌløs]
retiree, pensioner	pensjonist (m)	[panʂu'nist]
spy, secret agent	spion (m)	[spi'un]

prisoner	fange (m)	['faŋə]
striker	streiker (m)	['stræjkər]
bureaucrat	byråkrat (m)	[byrɔ'krat]
traveller (globetrotter)	reisende (m)	['ræjsenə]

gay, homosexual (n)	homofil (m)	['hʉmʉˌfil]
hacker	hacker (m)	['hakər]
hippie	hippie (m)	['hipi]

bandit	banditt (m)	[ban'dit]
hit man, killer	leiemorder (m)	['læjəˌmʉrdər]
drug addict	narkoman (m)	[narkʉ'man]
drug dealer	narkolanger (m)	['narkɔˌlaŋər]
prostitute (fem.)	prostituert (m)	[prʊstitʉ'e:t]
pimp	hallik (m)	['halik]

sorcerer	trollmann (m)	['trɔlˌman]
sorceress (evil ~)	trollkjerring (m/f)	['trɔlˌçæriŋ]
pirate	pirat, sjørøver (m)	['pi'rat], ['ʂøˌrøvər]
slave	slave (m)	['slavə]
samurai	samurai (m)	[samʉ'raj]
savage (primitive)	villmann (m)	['vilˌman]

Sports

sportsman	idrettsmann (m)	['idrɛts,man]
kind of sport	idrettsgren (m/f)	['idrɛts,gren]
basketball	basketball (m)	['basketbal]
basketball player	basketballspiller (m)	['basketbal,spilər]
baseball	baseball (m)	['bɛjsbɔl]
baseball player	baseballspiller (m)	['bɛjsbɔl,spilər]
football	fotball (m)	['fʊtbal]
football player	fotballspiller (m)	['fʊtbal,spilər]
goalkeeper	målmann (m)	['moːl,man]
ice hockey	ishockey (m)	['is,hɔki]
ice hockey player	ishockeyspiller (m)	['is,hɔki 'spilər]
volleyball	volleyball (m)	['vɔlibal]
volleyball player	volleyballspiller (m)	['vɔlibal,spilər]
boxing	boksing (m)	['bɔksiŋ]
boxer	bokser (m)	['bɔksər]
wrestling	bryting (m/f)	['brytiŋ]
wrestler	bryter (m)	['brytər]
karate	karate (m)	[ka'ratə]
karate fighter	karateutøver (m)	[ka'ratə 'ʉ,tøvər]
judo	judo (m)	['jʉdɔ]
judo athlete	judobryter (m)	['jʉdɔ,brytər]
tennis	tennis (m)	['tɛnis]
tennis player	tennisspiller (m)	['tɛnis,spilər]
swimming	svømming (m/f)	['svœmiŋ]
swimmer	svømmer (m)	['svœmər]
fencing	fekting (m)	['fɛktiŋ]
fencer	fekter (m)	['fɛktər]
chess	sjakk (m)	['ʂak]
chess player	sjakkspiller (m)	['ʂak,spilər]
alpinism	alpinisme (m)	[alpi'nismə]
alpinist	alpinist (m)	[alpi'nist]
running	løp (n)	['løp]

runner	løper (m)	['løpər]
athletics	friidrett (m)	['fri: 'i‚drɛt]
athlete	atlet (m)	[at'let]

horse riding	ridesport (m)	['ridə‚spɔ:t]
horse rider	rytter (m)	['rʏtər]

figure skating	kunstløp (n)	['kʉnst‚løp]
figure skater (masc.)	kunstløper (m)	['kʉnst‚løpər]
figure skater (fem.)	kunstløperske (m/f)	['kʉnst‚løpəʂkə]

powerlifting	vektløfting (m/f)	['vɛkt‚lœftiŋ]
powerlifter	vektløfter (m)	['vɛkt‚lœftər]

car racing	billøp (m), bilrace (n)	['bil‚løp], ['bil‚ras]
racer (driver)	racerfører (m)	['resə‚førər]

cycling	sykkelsport (m)	['sʏkəl‚spɔ:t]
cyclist	syklist (m)	[sʏk'list]

long jump	lengdehopp (n pl)	['leŋdə‚hɔp]
pole vaulting	stavhopp (n)	['stɑv‚hɔp]
jumper	hopper (m)	['hɔpər]

133. Kinds of sports. Miscellaneous

American football	amerikansk fotball (m)	[ameri'kansk 'fʊtbal]
badminton	badminton (m)	['bɛdmintɔn]
biathlon	skiskyting (m/f)	['ʂi‚sytiŋ]
billiards	biljard (m)	[bil'ja:d̥]

bobsleigh	bobsleigh (m)	['bobslej]
bodybuilding	kroppsbygging (m/f)	['krɔps‚bʏgiŋ]
water polo	vannpolo (m)	['van‚pʊlʉ]
handball	håndball (m)	['hɔn‚bal]
golf	golf (m)	['gɔlf]

rowing	roing (m/f)	['rʉiŋ]
scuba diving	dykking (m/f)	['dʏkiŋ]
cross-country skiing	langrenn (n), skirenn (n)	['laŋ‚rɛn], ['ʂi‚rɛn]
table tennis (ping-pong)	bordtennis (m)	['bʊr‚tɛnis]

sailing	seiling (m/f)	['sæjliŋ]
rally	rally (n)	['rɛli]
rugby	rugby (m)	['rygbi]
snowboarding	snøbrett (n)	['snø‚brɛt]
archery	bueskyting (m/f)	['bʉ:ə‚sytiŋ]

134. Gym

barbell	vektstang (m/f)	['vɛkt‚staŋ]
dumbbells	manualer (m pl)	['manʉ‚alər]

training machine	treningsapparat (n)	['treniŋs apɑ'rɑt]
exercise bicycle	trimsykkel (m)	['trim‚sʏkəl]
treadmill	løpebånd (n)	['løpə‚bɔːn]

horizontal bar	svingstang (m/f)	['sviŋstɑŋ]
parallel bars	barre (m)	['bɑrə]
vault (vaulting horse)	hest (m)	['hɛst]
mat (exercise ~)	matte (m/f)	['mɑtə]

skipping rope	hoppetau (n)	['hɔpə‚tɑʊ]
aerobics	aerobic (m)	[ɑɛ'rɔbik]
yoga	yoga (m)	['joɡɑ]

135. Ice hockey

ice hockey	ishockey (m)	['is‚hɔki]
ice hockey player	ishockeyspiller (m)	['is‚hɔki 'spilər]
to play ice hockey	å spille ishockey	[ɔ 'spilə 'is‚hɔki]
ice	is (m)	['is]

puck	puck (m)	['puk]
ice hockey stick	kølle (m/f)	['kølə]
ice skates	skøyter (m/f pl)	['ʂøjtər]

| board (ice hockey rink ~) | vant (n) | ['vɑnt] |
| shot | skudd (n) | ['skʉd] |

goaltender	målvakt (m/f)	['moːl‚vɑkt]
goal (score)	mål (n)	['mol]
to score a goal	å score mål	[ɔ 'skɔrə ‚mol]

period	periode (m)	[pæri'ʉdə]
second period	andre periode (m)	['ɑndrə pæri'ʉdə]
substitutes bench	reservebenk (m)	[re'sɛrvə‚bɛnk]

136. Football

football	fotball (m)	['fʊtbɑl]
football player	fotballspiller (m)	['fʊtbɑl‚spilər]
to play football	å spille fotball	[ɔ 'spilə 'fʊtbɑl]

major league	øverste liga (m)	['øvəʂtə ‚liɡɑ]
football club	fotballklubb (m)	['fʊtbɑl‚klʉb]
coach	trener (m)	['trenər]
owner, proprietor	eier (m)	['æjər]

team	lag (n)	['lɑɡ]
team captain	kaptein (m) på laget	[kɑp'tæjn pɔ 'lɑɡe]
player	spiller (m)	['spilər]
substitute	reservespiller (m)	[re'sɛrvə‚spilər]
forward	spiss, angriper (m)	['spis], ['ɑn‚ɡripər]
centre forward	sentral spiss (m)	[sɛn'trɑl ‚spis]

scorer	målscorer (m)	['moːl‚skɔrər]
defender, back	forsvarer, back (m)	['fɔ‚svarər], ['bɛk]
midfielder, halfback	midtbanespiller (m)	['mit‚banə 'spilər]

match	kamp (m)	['kamp]
to meet (vi, vt)	å møtes	[ɔ 'møtəs]
final	finale (m)	[fi'nalə]
semi-final	semifinale (m)	[‚semifi'nalə]
championship	mesterskap (n)	['mɛstæ‚skap]

period, half	omgang (m)	['ɔmgaŋ]
first period	første omgang (m)	['fœ̞ʂtə ‚ɔmgaŋ]
half-time	halvtid (m)	['hal‚tid]

goal	mål (n)	['mol]
goalkeeper	målmann (m), målvakt (m/f)	['moːl‚man], ['moːl‚vakt]
goalpost	stolpe (m)	['stɔlpə]
crossbar	tverrligger (m)	['tvæː‚ligər]
net	nett (n)	['nɛt]
to concede a goal	å slippe inn et mål	[ɔ 'ʂlipə in et 'mol]

ball	ball (m)	['bal]
pass	pasning (m/f)	['pasniŋ]
kick	spark (m/n)	['spark]
to kick (~ the ball)	å sparke	[ɔ 'sparkə]
free kick (direct ~)	frispark (m/n)	['fri‚spark]
corner kick	hjørnespark (m/n)	['jœː‚ŋə‚spark]

attack	angrep (n)	['an‚grɛp]
counterattack	kontring (m/f)	['kɔntriŋ]
combination	kombinasjon (m)	[kʊmbina'ʂʊn]

referee	dommer (m)	['dɔmər]
to blow the whistle	å blåse i fløyte	[ɔ 'blɔːsə i 'fløjtə]
whistle (sound)	plystring (m/f)	['plʏstriŋ]
foul, misconduct	brudd (n), forseelse (m)	['brʊd], [fɔ'ʂeəlsə]
to commit a foul	å begå en forseelse	[ɔ be'gɔ en fɔ'ʂeəlsə]
to send off	å utvise	[ɔ 'ʉt‚visə]

yellow card	gult kort (n)	['gʉlt ‚kɔːt]
red card	rødt kort (n)	['røt kɔːt]
disqualification	diskvalifisering (m)	['diskvalifi‚seriŋ]
to disqualify (vt)	å diskvalifisere	[ɔ 'diskvalifi‚serə]

penalty kick	straffespark (m/n)	['strafə‚spark]
wall	mur (m)	['mʉr]
to score (vi, vt)	å score	[ɔ 'skɔrə]
goal (score)	mål (n)	['mol]
to score a goal	å score mål	[ɔ 'skɔrə ‚mol]

substitution	erstatning (m)	['æ‚statniŋ]
to replace (a player)	å bytte ut	[ɔ 'bʏtə ʉt]
rules	regler (m pl)	['rɛglər]
tactics	taktikk (m)	[tak'tik]
stadium	stadion (m/n)	['stadiɔn]
terrace	tribune (m)	[tri'bʉnə]

| fan, supporter | fan (m) | ['fæn] |
| to shout (vi) | å skrike | [ɔ 'skrikə] |

| scoreboard | måltavle (m/f) | ['moːlˌtavlə] |
| score | resultat (n) | [resʉl'tɑt] |

| defeat | nederlag (n) | ['nedəˌlɑg] |
| to lose (not win) | å tape | [ɔ 'tɑpə] |

| draw | uavgjort (m) | [ʉːav'jɔːt] |
| to draw (vi) | å spille uavgjort | [ɔ 'spilə ʉːav'jɔːt] |

victory	seier (m)	['sæjər]
to win (vi, vt)	å vinne	[ɔ 'vinə]
champion	mester (m)	['mɛstər]
best (adj)	best	['bɛst]
to congratulate (vt)	å gratulere	[ɔ gratʉ'lerə]

commentator	kommentator (m)	[kʊmən'tatʊr]
to commentate (vt)	å kommentere	[ɔ kʊmən'terə]
broadcast	sending (m/f)	['sɛniŋ]

137. Alpine skiing

skis	ski (m/f pl)	['ʂi]
to ski (vi)	å gå på ski	[ɔ 'gɔ pɔ 'ʂi]
mountain-ski resort	skisted (n)	['ʂistəd]
ski lift	skiheis (m)	['ʂiˌhæjs]

ski poles	skistaver (m pl)	['ʂiˌstavər]
slope	skråning (m)	['skrɔniŋ]
slalom	slalåm (m)	['ʂlɑlɔm]

138. Tennis. Golf

golf	golf (m)	['gɔlf]
golf club	golfklubb (m)	['gɔlfˌklʉb]
golfer	golfspiller (m)	['gɔlfˌspilər]

hole	hull (n)	['hʉl]
club	kølle (m/f)	['kølə]
golf trolley	golftralle (m/f)	['gɔlfˌtrɑlə]

| tennis | tennis (m) | ['tɛnis] |
| tennis court | tennisbane (m) | ['tɛnisˌbɑnə] |

| serve | serve (m) | ['sɛrv] |
| to serve (vt) | å serve | [ɔ 'sɛrvə] |

racket	racket (m)	['rɛket]
net	nett (n)	['nɛt]
ball	ball (m)	['bɑl]

139. Chess

chess	sjakk (m)	['ʂak]
chessmen	sjakkbrikker (m/f pl)	['ʂak͵brikər]
chess player	sjakkspiller (m)	['ʂak͵spilər]
chessboard	sjakkbrett (n)	['ʂak͵brɛt]
chessman	sjakbrikke (m/f)	['ʂak͵brikə]

| White (white pieces) | hvite brikker (m/f pl) | ['vitə ͵brikər] |
| Black (black pieces) | svarte brikker (m/f pl) | ['sva:tə ͵brikər] |

pawn	bonde (m)	['bɔnə]
bishop	løper (m)	['løpər]
knight	springer (m)	['spriŋər]
rook	tårn (n)	['tɔ:ɳ]
queen	dronning (m/f)	['drɔniŋ]
king	konge (m)	['kʊŋə]

move	trekk (n)	['trɛk]
to move (vi, vt)	å flytte	[ɔ 'flʏtə]
to sacrifice (vt)	å ofre	[ɔ 'ɔfrə]
castling	rokade (m)	[rʊ'kadə]
check	sjakk (m)	['ʂak]
checkmate	matt (m)	['mat]

chess tournament	sjakkturnering (m/f)	['ʂak tʉr͵neriŋ]
Grand Master	stormester (m)	['stʊr͵mɛstər]
combination	kombinasjon (m)	[kʊmbina'ʂʊn]
game (in chess)	parti (n)	[pa:'ʈi]
draughts	damspill (n)	['dam͵spil]

140. Boxing

boxing	boksing (m)	['bɔksiŋ]
fight (bout)	kamp (m)	['kamp]
boxing match	boksekamp (m)	['bɔksə͵kamp]
round (in boxing)	runde (m)	['rʉndə]

| ring | ring (m) | ['riŋ] |
| gong | gong (m) | ['gɔŋ] |

| punch | støt, slag (n) | ['støt], ['ʂlag] |
| knockdown | knockdown (m) | [nɔk'daʊn] |

| knockout | knockout (m) | [nɔk'aʊt] |
| to knock out | å slå ut | [ɔ 'ʂlɔ ʉt] |

| boxing glove | boksehanske (m) | ['bɔksə͵hanskə] |
| referee | dommer (m) | ['dɔmər] |

lightweight	lettvekt (m/f)	['let͵vɛkt]
middleweight	mellomvekt (m/f)	['mɛlɔm͵vɛkt]
heavyweight	tungvekt (m/f)	['tʉŋ͵vɛkt]

141. Sports. Miscellaneous

Olympic Games	de olympiske leker	[de u'lʏmpiskə 'lekər]
winner	seierherre (m)	['sæjər‚hɛrə]
to be winning	å vinne, å seire	[ɔ 'vinə], [ɔ 'sæjrə]
to win (vi)	å vinne	[ɔ 'vinə]
leader	leder (m)	['ledər]
to lead (vi)	å lede	[ɔ 'ledə]
first place	førsteplass (m)	['fœʂtə‚plɑs]
second place	annenplass (m)	['ɑnən‚plɑs]
third place	tredjeplass (m)	['trɛdjə‚plɑs]
medal	medalje (m)	[me'dɑljə]
trophy	trofé (m/n)	[trɔ'fe]
prize cup (trophy)	pokal (m)	[pɔ'kɑl]
prize (in game)	pris (m)	['pris]
main prize	hovedpris (m)	['hʊvəd‚pris]
record	rekord (m)	[re'kɔrd]
to set a record	å sette rekord	[ɔ 'sɛtə re'kɔrd]
final	finale (m)	[fi'nɑlə]
final (adj)	finale-	[fi'nɑlə-]
champion	mester (m)	['mɛstər]
championship	mesterskap (n)	['mɛstæ‚skɑp]
stadium	stadion (m/n)	['stɑdiɔn]
terrace	tribune (m)	[tri'bʉnə]
fan, supporter	fan (m)	['fæn]
opponent, rival	motstander (m)	['mʊt‚stɑnər]
start (start line)	start (m)	['stɑːt]
finish line	mål (n), målstrek (m)	['mɔːl], ['mɔːl‚strek]
defeat	nederlag (n)	['nedə‚lɑg]
to lose (not win)	å tape	[ɔ 'tɑpə]
referee	dommer (m)	['dɔmər]
jury (judges)	jury (m)	['jʉry]
score	resultat (n)	[resʉl'tɑt]
draw	uavgjort (m)	[ʉːav'jɔːt]
to draw (vi)	å spille uavgjort	[ɔ 'spilə ʉːav'jɔːt]
point	poeng (n)	[pɔ'ɛŋ]
result (final score)	resultat (n)	[resʉl'tɑt]
period	periode (m)	[pæri'ʊdə]
half-time	halvtid (m)	['hɑl‚tid]
doping	doping (m)	['dʊpiŋ]
to penalise (vt)	å straffe	[ɔ 'strɑfə]
to disqualify (vt)	å diskvalifisere	[ɔ 'diskvɑlifi‚serə]
apparatus	redskap (m/n)	['rɛd‚skɑp]

javelin	spyd (n)	['spyd]
shot (metal ball)	kule (m/f)	['kʉ:lə]
ball (snooker, etc.)	kule (m/f), ball (m)	['kʉ:lə], ['bɑl]
aim (target)	mål (n)	['mol]
target	målskive (m/f)	['mo:lˌsivə]
to shoot (vi)	å skyte	[ɔ 'ʂytə]
accurate (~ shot)	fulltreffer	['fʉlˌtrɛfər]
trainer, coach	trener (m)	['trenər]
to train (sb)	å trene	[ɔ 'trenə]
to train (vi)	å trene	[ɔ 'trenə]
training	trening (m/f)	['treniŋ]
gym	idrettssal (m)	['idrɛtsˌsɑl]
exercise (physical)	øvelse (m)	['øvəlsə]
warm-up (athlete ~)	oppvarming (m/f)	['ɔpˌvarmiŋ]

Education

| school | skole (m/f) | ['skʊlə] |
| headmaster | rektor (m) | ['rektʊr] |

student (m)	elev (m)	[e'lev]
student (f)	elev (m)	[e'lev]
schoolboy	skolegutt (m)	['skʊlə‚gʊt]
schoolgirl	skolepike (m)	['skʊlə‚pikə]

to teach (sb)	å undervise	[ɔ 'ʉnər‚visə]
to learn (language, etc.)	å lære	[ɔ 'lærə]
to learn by heart	å lære utenat	[ɔ 'lærə 'ʉtənat]

to learn (~ to count, etc.)	å lære	[ɔ 'lærə]
to be at school	å gå på skolen	[ɔ 'gɔ pɔ 'skʊlən]
to go to school	å gå på skolen	[ɔ 'gɔ pɔ 'skʊlən]

| alphabet | alfabet (n) | [alfa'bet] |
| subject (at school) | fag (n) | ['fag] |

classroom	klasserom (m/f)	['klɑsə‚rʊm]
lesson	time (m)	['timə]
playtime, break	frikvarter (n)	['frikvɑː‚ter]
school bell	skoleklokke (m/f)	['skʊlə‚klɔkə]
school desk	skolepult (m)	['skʊlə‚pʉlt]
blackboard	tavle (m/f)	['tɑvlə]

mark	karakter (m)	[kɑrɑk'ter]
good mark	god karakter (m)	['gʊ kɑrɑk'ter]
bad mark	dårlig karakter (m)	['doːli̥ kɑrɑk'ter]
to give a mark	å gi en karakter	[ɔ 'ji en kɑrɑk'ter]

mistake, error	feil (m)	['fæjl]
to make mistakes	å gjøre feil	[ɔ 'jørə ‚fæjl]
to correct (an error)	å rette	[ɔ 'rɛtə]
crib	fuskelapp (m)	['fʉskə‚lɑp]

| homework | lekser (m/f pl) | ['leksər] |
| exercise (in education) | øvelse (m) | ['øvəlsə] |

to be present	å være til stede	[ɔ 'værə til 'stedə]
to be absent	å være fraværende	[ɔ 'værə 'frɑ‚værənə]
to miss school	å skulke skolen	[ɔ 'skʉlkə 'skʊlən]

to punish (vt)	å straffe	[ɔ 'strɑfə]
punishment	straff, avstraffelse (m)	['strɑf], ['ɑf‚strɑfəlsə]
conduct (behaviour)	oppførsel (m)	['ɔp‚fœʂəl]

school report	karakterbok (m/f)	[karak'ter‚buk]
pencil	blyant (m)	['bly‚ant]
rubber	viskelær (n)	['viskə‚lær]
chalk	kritt (n)	['krit]
pencil case	pennal (n)	[pɛ'nal]

schoolbag	skoleveske (m/f)	['skulə‚vɛskə]
pen	penn (m)	['pɛn]
exercise book	skrivebok (m/f)	['skrivə‚buk]
textbook	lærebok (m/f)	['lærə‚buk]
compasses	passer (m)	['pasər]

| to make technical drawings | å tegne | [ɔ 'tæjnə] |
| technical drawing | teknisk tegning (m/f) | ['tɛknisk ‚tæjniŋ] |

poem	dikt (n)	['dikt]
by heart (adv)	utenat	['ʉtən‚at]
to learn by heart	å lære utenat	[ɔ 'lærə 'ʉtənat]

school holidays	skoleferie (m)	['skulə‚fɛriə]
to be on holiday	å være på ferie	[ɔ 'værə pɔ 'fɛriə]
to spend holidays	å tilbringe ferien	[ɔ 'til‚briŋə 'fɛriən]

test (at school)	prøve (m/f)	['prøvə]
essay (composition)	essay (n)	[ɛ'sɛj]
dictation	diktat (m)	[dik'tat]
exam (examination)	eksamen (m)	[ɛk'samən]
to do an exam	å ta eksamen	[ɔ 'ta ɛk'samən]
experiment (e.g., chemistry ~)	forsøk (n)	['fɔ'søk]

143. College. University

academy	akademi (n)	[akade'mi]
university	universitet (n)	[ʉnivæṣi'tet]
faculty (e.g., ~ of Medicine)	fakultet (n)	[fakʉl'tet]

student (masc.)	student (m)	[stʉ'dɛnt]
student (fem.)	kvinnelig student (m)	['kvinəli stʉ'dɛnt]
lecturer (teacher)	lærer, foreleser (m)	['lærər], ['fʉrə‚lesər]

| lecture hall, room | auditorium (n) | [‚aʉdi'tʉrium] |
| graduate | alumn (m) | [a'lʉmn] |

| diploma | diplom (n) | [di'plʉm] |
| dissertation | avhandling (m/f) | ['av‚handliŋ] |

| study (report) | studie (m) | ['stʉdiə] |
| laboratory | laboratorium (n) | [labʉra'tɔrium] |

lecture	forelesning (m)	['fɔrə‚lesniŋ]
coursemate	studiekamerat (m)	['stʉdiə kame‚rat]
scholarship, bursary	stipendium (n)	[sti'pɛndium]
academic degree	akademisk grad (m)	[aka'demisk ‚grad]

144. Sciences. Disciplines

mathematics	matematikk (m)	[matəmɑ'tik]
algebra	algebra (m)	['ɑlgə‚brɑ]
geometry	geometri (m)	[geʊme'tri]
astronomy	astronomi (m)	[ɑstrʊnʊ'mi]
biology	biologi (m)	[biʊlʊ'gi]
geography	geografi (m)	[geʊgrɑ'fi]
geology	geologi (m)	[geʊlʊ'gi]
history	historie (m/f)	[hi'stʊriə]
medicine	medisin (m)	[medi'sin]
pedagogy	pedagogikk (m)	[pedɑgʊ'gik]
law	rett (m)	['rɛt]
physics	fysikk (m)	[fy'sik]
chemistry	kjemi (m)	[çe'mi]
philosophy	filosofi (m)	[filʊsʊ'fi]
psychology	psykologi (m)	[sikʊlʊ'gi]

145. Writing system. Orthography

grammar	grammatikk (m)	[grɑmɑ'tik]
vocabulary	ordforråd (n)	['uːrfʊ‚rɔd]
phonetics	fonetikk (m)	[fʊne'tik]
noun	substantiv (n)	['sʉbstɑn‚tiv]
adjective	adjektiv (n)	['ɑdjɛk‚tiv]
verb	verb (n)	['værb]
adverb	adverb (n)	[ɑd'væːb]
pronoun	pronomen (n)	[prʊ'nʊmən]
interjection	interjeksjon (m)	[interjɛk'ʂʊn]
preposition	preposisjon (m)	[prɛpʊsi'ʂʊn]
root	rot (m/f)	['rʊt]
ending	endelse (m)	['ɛnəlsə]
prefix	prefiks (n)	[prɛ'fiks]
syllable	stavelse (m)	['stɑvəlsə]
suffix	suffiks (n)	[sʉ'fiks]
stress mark	betoning (m), trykk (n)	['be'tɔniŋ], ['trʏk]
apostrophe	apostrof (m)	[ɑpʊ'strɔf]
full stop	punktum (n)	['pʉnktum]
comma	komma (n)	['kɔmɑ]
semicolon	semikolon (n)	[‚semikʊ'lɔn]
colon	kolon (n)	['kʊlɔn]
ellipsis	tre prikker (m pl)	['tre 'prikər]
question mark	spørsmålstegn (n)	['spœʂmɔls‚tæjn]
exclamation mark	utropstegn (n)	['ʉtrʊps‚tæjn]

inverted commas	anførselstegn (n pl)	[ɑnˈfœṣɛlsˌtejn]
in inverted commas	i anførselstegn	[i ɑnˈfœṣɛlsˌtejn]
parenthesis	parentes (m)	[pɑrɛnˈtes]
in parenthesis	i parentes	[i pɑrɛnˈtes]

hyphen	bindestrek (m)	[ˈbinəˌstrek]
dash	tankestrek (m)	[ˈtɑnkəˌstrek]
space (between words)	mellomrom (n)	[ˈmɛlɔmˌrʊm]

| letter | bokstav (m) | [ˈbʊkstɑv] |
| capital letter | stor bokstav (m) | [ˈstʊr ˈbʊkstɑv] |

| vowel (n) | vokal (m) | [vʊˈkɑl] |
| consonant (n) | konsonant (m) | [kʊnsʊˈnɑnt] |

sentence	setning (m)	[ˈsɛtniŋ]
subject	subjekt (n)	[sʉbˈjɛkt]
predicate	predikat (n)	[prɛdiˈkɑt]

line	linje (m)	[ˈlinjə]
on a new line	på ny linje	[pɔ ny ˈlinjə]
paragraph	avsnitt (n)	[ˈɑfˌsnit]

word	ord (n)	[ˈuːr]
group of words	ordgruppe (m/f)	[ˈuːrˌgrʉpə]
expression	uttrykk (n)	[ˈʉtˌtrʏk]
synonym	synonym (n)	[synʊˈnym]
antonym	antonym (n)	[ɑntʊˈnym]

rule	regel (m)	[ˈrɛgəl]
exception	unntak (n)	[ˈʉnˌtɑk]
correct (adj)	riktig	[ˈrikti]

conjugation	bøyning (m/f)	[ˈbøjniŋ]
declension	bøyning (m/f)	[ˈbøjniŋ]
nominal case	kasus (m)	[ˈkɑsʉs]
question	spørsmål (n)	[ˈspœṣˌmol]
to underline (vt)	å understreke	[ɔ ˈʉnəˌstrekə]
dotted line	prikket linje (m)	[ˈprikət ˈlinjə]

146. Foreign languages

language	språk (n)	[ˈsprɔk]
foreign (adj)	fremmed-	[ˈfremə-]
foreign language	fremmedspråk (n)	[ˈfremedˌsprɔk]
to study (vt)	å studere	[ɔ stʉˈderə]
to learn (language, etc.)	å lære	[ɔ ˈlærə]

to read (vi, vt)	å lese	[ɔ ˈlesə]
to speak (vi, vt)	å tale	[ɔ ˈtɑlə]
to understand (vt)	å forstå	[ɔ fɔˈṣtɔ]
to write (vt)	å skrive	[ɔ ˈskrivə]
fast (adv)	fort	[ˈfʊːt]
slowly (adv)	langsomt	[ˈlɑŋsɔmt]

fluently (adv)	**flytende**	['flytnə]
rules	**regler** (m pl)	['rɛglər]
grammar	**grammatikk** (m)	[gramɑ'tik]
vocabulary	**ordforråd** (n)	['uːrfʊˌrɔd]
phonetics	**fonetikk** (m)	[fʊne'tik]
textbook	**lærebok** (m/f)	['læreˌbʊk]
dictionary	**ordbok** (m/f)	['uːrˌbʊk]
teach-yourself book	**lærebok** (m/f) **for selvstudium**	['læreˌbʊk fɔ 'selˌstʉdium]
phrasebook	**parlør** (m)	[pɑː'ʟør]
cassette, tape	**kassett** (m)	[kɑ'sɛt]
videotape	**videokassett** (m)	['videʊ kɑ'sɛt]
CD, compact disc	**CD-rom** (m)	['sɛdɛˌrʊm]
DVD	**DVD** (m)	[deve'de]
alphabet	**alfabet** (n)	[ɑlfɑ'bet]
to spell (vt)	**å stave**	[ɔ 'stɑvə]
pronunciation	**uttale** (m)	['ʉtˌtɑlə]
accent	**aksent** (m)	[ɑk'sɑŋ]
with an accent	**med aksent**	[me ɑk'sɑŋ]
without an accent	**uten aksent**	['ʉtən ɑk'sɑŋ]
word	**ord** (n)	['uːr]
meaning	**betydning** (m)	[be'tʏdniŋ]
course (e.g. a French ~)	**kurs** (n)	['kʉʂ]
to sign up	**å anmelde seg**	[ɔ 'anˌmɛlə sæj]
teacher	**lærer** (m)	['lærər]
translation (process)	**oversettelse** (m)	['ɔvəˌsɛtəlsə]
translation (text, etc.)	**oversettelse** (m)	['ɔvəˌsɛtəlsə]
translator	**oversetter** (m)	['ɔvəˌsɛtər]
interpreter	**tolk** (m)	['tɔlk]
polyglot	**polyglott** (m)	[pʊlʏ'glɔt]
memory	**minne** (n), **hukommelse** (m)	['minə], [hʉ'kɔməlsə]

147. Fairy tale characters

Father Christmas	**Julenissen**	['jʉləˌnisən]
Cinderella	**Askepott**	['askəˌpɔt]
mermaid	**havfrue** (m/f)	['hɑvˌfrʉə]
Neptune	**Neptun**	[nɛp'tʉn]
magician, wizard	**trollmann** (m)	['trɔlˌman]
fairy	**fe** (m)	['fe]
magic (adj)	**trylle-**	['trʏlə-]
magic wand	**tryllestav** (m)	['trʏləˌstɑv]
fairy tale	**eventyr** (n)	['ɛvənˌtyr]
miracle	**mirakel** (n)	[mi'rɑkəl]

| dwarf | gnom, dverg (m) | ['gnʊm], ['dvɛrg] |
| to turn into ... | å forvandle seg til ... | [ɔ fɔr'vandlə sæj til ...] |

ghost	spøkelse (n)	['spøkəlsə]
phantom	fantom (m)	[fan'tɔm]
monster	monster (n)	['mɔnstər]
dragon	drage (m)	['dragə]
giant	gigant (m)	[gi'gant]

148. Zodiac Signs

Aries	Væren (m)	['værən]
Taurus	Tyren (m)	['tyrən]
Gemini	Tvillingene (m pl)	['tviliŋənə]
Cancer	Krepsen (m)	['krɛpsən]
Leo	Løven (m)	['løvən]
Virgo	Jomfruen (m)	['ʉmfrʉən]

Libra	Vekten (m)	['vɛktən]
Scorpio	Skorpionen	[skɔrpi'ʉnən]
Sagittarius	Skytten (m)	['ʂytən]
Capricorn	Steinbukken (m)	['stæjn,bʉkən]
Aquarius	Vannmannen (m)	['van,manən]
Pisces	Fiskene (pl)	['fiskenə]

character	karakter (m)	[karak'ter]
character traits	karaktertrekk (n pl)	[karak'ter,trɛk]
behaviour	oppførsel (m)	['ɔp,fœʂəl]
to tell fortunes	å spå	[ɔ 'spɔ]
fortune-teller	spåkone (m/f)	['spo:,kɔnə]
horoscope	horoskop (n)	[hʉrʉ'skɔp]

Arts

theatre	**teater** (n)	[te'ɑtər]
opera	**opera** (m)	['ʊpera]
operetta	**operette** (m)	[ʊpe'rɛtə]
ballet	**ballett** (m)	[bɑ'let]
theatre poster	**plakat** (m)	[plɑ'kɑt]
theatre company	**teatertrupp** (m)	[te'ɑtər͵trʉp]
tour	**turné** (m)	[tʉr'ne:]
to be on tour	**å være på turné**	[ɔ 'væːrə pɔ tʉr'ne:]
to rehearse (vi, vt)	**å repetere**	[ɔ repe'terə]
rehearsal	**repetisjon** (m)	[repeti'ʂʊn]
repertoire	**repertoar** (n)	[repæː͟tʊ'ɑr]
performance	**forestilling** (m/f)	['fɔrə͵stiliŋ]
theatrical show	**teaterstykke** (n)	[te'ɑtər͵stʏkə]
play	**skuespill** (n)	['skʉə͵spil]
ticket	**billett** (m)	[bi'let]
booking office	**billettluke** (m/f)	[bi'let͵lʉkə]
lobby, foyer	**lobby, foajé** (m)	['lɔbi], [fʊɑ'je]
coat check (cloakroom)	**garderobe** (m)	[gɑ:d̥ə'rʉbə]
cloakroom ticket	**garderobemerke** (n)	[gɑ:d̥ə'rʉbə 'mærkə]
binoculars	**kikkert** (m)	['çikɛ:t]
usher	**plassanviser** (m)	['plɑs ɑn͵viser]
stalls (orchestra seats)	**parkett** (m)	[pɑr'kɛt]
balcony	**balkong** (m)	[bɑl'kɔŋ]
dress circle	**første losjerad** (m)	['fœʂtə ͵lʉʂɛrɑd]
box	**losje** (m)	['lʉʂə]
row	**rad** (m/f)	['rɑd]
seat	**plass** (m)	['plɑs]
audience	**publikum** (n)	['pʉblikum]
spectator	**tilskuer** (m)	['til͵skʉər]
to clap (vi, vt)	**å klappe**	[ɔ 'klɑpə]
applause	**applaus** (m)	[ɑ'plaʊs]
ovation	**bifall** (n)	['bi͵fɑl]
stage	**scene** (m)	['se:nə]
curtain	**teppe** (n)	['tɛpə]
scenery	**dekorasjon** (m)	[dekʊrɑ'ʂʊn]
backstage	**kulisser** (m pl)	[kʉ'lisər]
scene (e.g. the last ~)	**scene** (m)	['se:nə]
act	**akt** (m)	['ɑkt]
interval	**mellomakt** (m)	['mɛlɔm͵ɑkt]

150. Cinema

actor	skuespiller (m)	['skʉəˌspilər]
actress	skuespillerinne (m/f)	['skʉəˌspilə'rinə]
cinema (industry)	filmindustri (m)	['film indʉ'stri]
film	film (m)	['film]
episode	del (m)	['del]
detective film	kriminalfilm (m)	[krimi'nalˌfilm]
action film	actionfilm (m)	['ɛkʂənˌfilm]
adventure film	eventyrfilm (m)	['ɛvəntyrˌfilm]
science fiction film	Sci-Fi film (m)	['sɑjˌfɑj film]
horror film	skrekkfilm (m)	['skrɛkˌfilm]
comedy film	komedie (m)	['kʉ'mediə]
melodrama	melodrama (n)	[melɔ'drɑmɑ]
drama	drama (n)	['drɑmɑ]
fictional film	spillefilm (m)	['spiləˌfilm]
documentary	dokumentarfilm (m)	[dɔkʉmɛn'tɑr ˌfilm]
cartoon	tegnefilm (m)	['tæjnəˌfilm]
silent films	stumfilm (m)	['stʉmˌfilm]
role (part)	rolle (m/f)	['rɔlə]
leading role	hovedrolle (m)	['hʉvədˌrɔle]
to play (vi, vt)	å spille	[ɔ 'spilə]
film star	filmstjerne (m)	['filmˌstjæːŋə]
well-known (adj)	kjent	['çɛnt]
famous (adj)	berømt	[be'rømt]
popular (adj)	populær	[pʉpʉ'lær]
script (screenplay)	manus (n)	['mɑnʉs]
scriptwriter	manusforfatter (m)	['mɑnʉs fɔr'fɑtər]
film director	regissør (m)	[rɛʂi'sør]
producer	produsent (m)	[prʉdʉ'sɛnt]
assistant	assistent (m)	[ɑsi'stɛnt]
cameraman	kameramann (m)	['kɑmerɑˌmɑn]
stuntman	stuntmann (m)	['stɑntˌmɑn]
double (body double)	stand-in (m)	[ˌstɑnd'in]
to shoot a film	å spille inn en film	[ɔ 'spilə in en 'film]
audition, screen test	prøve (m/f)	['prøvə]
shooting	opptak (n)	['ɔpˌtɑk]
film crew	filmteam (n)	['filmˌtim]
film set	opptaksplass (m)	['ɔptɑksˌplɑs]
camera	filmkamera (n)	['filmˌkɑmerɑ]
cinema	kino (m)	['çinʉ]
screen (e.g. big ~)	filmduk (m)	['filmˌdʉk]
to show a film	å vise en film	[ɔ 'visə en 'film]
soundtrack	lydspor (n)	['lydˌspʉr]
special effects	spesialeffekter (m pl)	['spesi'ɑl e'fɛktər]

133

subtitles	undertekster (m/f)	['ʉnəˌtɛkstər]
credits	rulletekst (m)	['rʉləˌtɛkst]
translation	oversettelse (m)	['ɔvəˌsɛtəlsə]

151. Painting

art	kunst (m)	['kʉnst]
fine arts	de skjønne kunster	[de 'ʂønə 'kʉnstər]
art gallery	kunstgalleri (n)	['kʉnst galeˈri]
art exhibition	maleriutstilling (m/f)	[ˌmaleˈri ʉtˌstiliŋ]

painting (art)	malerkunst (m)	['malərˌkʉnst]
graphic art	grafikk (m)	[graˈfik]
abstract art	abstrakt kunst (m)	[abˈstrakt 'kʉnst]
impressionism	impresjonisme (m)	[imprɛʂʉˈnismə]

picture (painting)	maleri (m/f)	[ˌmaleˈri]
drawing	tegning (m/f)	['tæjniŋ]
poster	plakat, poster (m)	['plaˌkat], ['pɔstər]

illustration (picture)	illustrasjon (m)	[ilʉstraˈʂʉn]
miniature	miniatyr (m)	[miniaˈtyr]
copy (of painting, etc.)	kopi (m)	[kʉˈpi]
reproduction	reproduksjon (m)	[reprʉdʉkˈʂʉn]

mosaic	mosaikk (m)	[mʉsaˈik]
stained glass window	glassmaleri (n)	['glasˌmaleˈri]
fresco	freske (m)	['frɛskə]
engraving	gravyr (m)	[graˈvyr]

bust (sculpture)	byste (m)	['bystə]
sculpture	skulptur (m)	[skʉlpˈtʉr]
statue	statue (m)	['statʉə]
plaster of Paris	gips (m)	['jips]
plaster (as adj)	gips-	['jips-]

portrait	portrett (n)	[pɔːˈʈrɛt]
self-portrait	selvportrett (n)	['sɛlˌpɔːˈʈrɛt]
landscape painting	landskapsmaleri (n)	['lanskapsˌmaleˈri]
still life	stilleben (n)	['stilˌlebən]
caricature	karikatur (m)	[karikaˈtʉr]
sketch	skisse (m/f)	['ʂisə]

paint	maling (m/f)	['maliŋ]
watercolor paint	akvarell (m)	[akvaˈrɛl]
oil (paint)	olje (m)	['ɔljə]
pencil	blyant (m)	['blyˌant]
Indian ink	tusj (m/n)	['tʉʂ]
charcoal	kull (n)	['kʉl]

to draw (vi, vt)	å tegne	[ɔ 'tæjnə]
to paint (vi, vt)	å male	[ɔ 'malə]
to pose (vi)	å posere	[ɔ pɔˈserə]
artist's model (masc.)	modell (m)	[mʉˈdɛl]

artist's model (fem.)	modell (m)	[mʊ'dɛl]
artist (painter)	kunstner (m)	['kʉnstnər]
work of art	kunstverk (n)	['kʉnst‚værk]
masterpiece	mesterverk (n)	['mɛstɛr‚værk]
studio (artist's workroom)	atelier (n)	[ate'lje]

canvas (cloth)	kanvas (m/n), lerret (n)	['kɑnvɑs], ['leret]
easel	staffeli (n)	[stɑfe'li]
palette	palett (m)	[pɑ'let]

frame (picture ~, etc.)	ramme (m/f)	['rɑmə]
restoration	restaurering (m)	[rɛstaʊ'reriŋ]
to restore (vt)	å restaurere	[ɔ rɛstaʊ'rerə]

152. Literature & Poetry

literature	litteratur (m)	[litərɑ'tʉr]
author (writer)	forfatter (m)	[fɔr'fɑtər]
pseudonym	pseudonym (n)	[sewdʊ'nym]

book	bok (m/f)	['bʊk]
volume	bind (n)	['bin]
table of contents	innholdsfortegnelse (m)	['inhɔls fɔː'ʈæjnəlsə]
page	side (m/f)	['sidə]
main character	hovedperson (m)	['hʊvəd pæ'şʊn]
autograph	autograf (m)	[aʊtʊ'grɑf]

short story	novelle (m/f)	[nʊ'vɛlə]
story (novella)	kortroman (m)	['kʊːʈ rʊ‚mɑn]
novel	roman (m)	[rʊ'mɑn]
work (writing)	verk (n)	['værk]
fable	fabel (m)	['fɑbəl]
detective novel	kriminalroman (m)	[krimi'nɑl rʊ‚mɑn]

poem (verse)	dikt (n)	['dikt]
poetry	poesi (m)	[pɔɛ'si]
poem (epic, ballad)	epos (n)	['ɛpɔs]
poet	poet, dikter (m)	['pɔɛt], ['diktər]

fiction	skjønnlitteratur (m)	['şøn litərɑ'tʉr]
science fiction	science fiction (m)	['sɑjəns ‚fikşn]
adventures	eventyr (n pl)	['ɛvən‚tyr]
educational literature	undervisningslitteratur (m)	['ʉnər‚visniŋs litərɑ'tʉr]
children's literature	barnelitteratur (m)	['bɑːn̩ə litərɑ'tʉr]

153. Circus

circus	sirkus (m/n)	['sirkʉs]
travelling circus	ambulerende sirkus (n)	['ɑmbʉ‚lerɛnə 'sirkʉs]
programme	program (n)	[prʊ'grɑm]
performance	forestilling (m/f)	['fɔrə‚stiliŋ]
act (circus ~)	nummer (n)	['nʉmmər]

circus ring	manesje, arena (m)	[ma'neʂə], [a'rena]
pantomime (act)	pantomime (m)	[pantʉ'mimə]
clown	klovn (m)	['klɔvn]

acrobat	akrobat (m)	[akrʉ'bat]
acrobatics	akrobatikk (m)	[akrʉba'tik]
gymnast	gymnast (m)	[gʏm'nast]
acrobatic gymnastics	gymnastikk (m)	[gʏmna'stik]
somersault	salto (m)	['saltʉ]

strongman	atlet (m)	[at'let]
tamer (e.g., lion ~)	dyretemmer (m)	['dyrə‚tɛmər]
rider (circus horse ~)	rytter (m)	['rʏtər]
assistant	assistent (m)	[asi'stɛnt]

stunt	trikk, triks (n)	['trik], ['triks]
magic trick	trylletriks (n)	['trʏlə‚triks]
conjurer, magician	tryllekunstner (m)	['trʏlə‚kʉnstnər]

juggler	sjonglør (m)	[ʂɔŋ'lør]
to juggle (vi, vt)	å sjonglere	[ɔ 'ʂɔŋ‚lerə]
animal trainer	dressør (m)	[drɛ'sør]
animal training	dressur (m)	[drɛ'sʉr]
to train (animals)	å dressere	[ɔ drɛ'serə]

154. Music. Pop music

music	musikk (m)	[mʉ'sik]
musician	musiker (m)	['mʉsikər]
musical instrument	musikkinstrument (n)	[mʉ'sik instrʉ'mɛnt]
to play ...	å spille ...	[ɔ 'spilə ...]

guitar	gitar (m)	['gi‚tar]
violin	fiolin (m)	[fiʉ'lin]
cello	cello (m)	['sɛlʉ]
double bass	kontrabass (m)	['kʉntra‚bas]
harp	harpe (m)	['harpə]

piano	piano (n)	[pi'anʉ]
grand piano	flygel (n)	['flygəl]
organ	orgel (n)	['ɔrgəl]

wind instruments	blåseinstrumenter (n pl)	['blo:sə instrʉ'mɛntər]
oboe	obo (m)	[ʉ'bʉ]
saxophone	saksofon (m)	[saksʉ'fʉn]
clarinet	klarinett (m)	[klari'nɛt]
flute	fløyte (m)	['fløjtə]
trumpet	trompet (m)	[trʉm'pet]

| accordion | trekkspill (n) | ['trɛk‚spil] |
| drum | tromme (m) | ['trʉmə] |

| duo | duett (m) | [dʉ'ɛt] |
| trio | trio (m) | ['triʉ] |

quartet	kvartett (m)	[kvɑːˈtɛt]
choir	kor (n)	[ˈkʊr]
orchestra	orkester (n)	[ɔrˈkɛstər]

pop music	popmusikk (m)	[ˈpɔp mʉˈsik]
rock music	rockmusikk (m)	[ˈrɔk mʉˈsik]
rock group	rockeband (n)	[ˈrɔkəˌbɛnd]
jazz	jazz (m)	[ˈjas]

| idol | idol (n) | [iˈdʊl] |
| admirer, fan | beundrer (m) | [beˈʉndrər] |

concert	konsert (m)	[kʊnˈsæːt]
symphony	symfoni (m)	[sʏmfʉˈni]
composition	komposisjon (m)	[kʊmpʊziˈʂʊn]
to compose (write)	å komponere	[ɔ kʊmpʉˈnerə]

singing (n)	synging (m/f)	[ˈsʏŋiŋ]
song	sang (m)	[ˈsɑŋ]
tune (melody)	melodi (m)	[melɔˈdi]
rhythm	rytme (m)	[ˈrʏtmə]
blues	blues (m)	[ˈblʉs]

sheet music	noter (m pl)	[ˈnʊtər]
baton	taktstokk (m)	[ˈtɑktˌstɔk]
bow	bue, boge (m)	[ˈbʉːə], [ˈbɔgə]
string	streng (m)	[ˈstrɛŋ]
case (e.g. guitar ~)	futteral (n), kasse (m/f)	[ˈfʉteˈrɑl], [ˈkɑsə]

Rest. Entertainment. Travel

155. Trip. Travel

tourism, travel	turisme (m)	[tʉ'rismə]
tourist	turist (m)	[tʉ'rist]
trip, voyage	reise (m/f)	['ræjsə]
adventure	eventyr (n)	['ɛvənˌtyr]
trip, journey	tripp (m)	['trip]
holiday	ferie (m)	['fɛriə]
to be on holiday	å være på ferie	[ɔ 'værə pɔ 'fɛriə]
rest	hvile (m/f)	['vilə]
train	tog (n)	['tɔg]
by train	med tog	[me 'tɔg]
aeroplane	fly (n)	['fly]
by aeroplane	med fly	[me 'fly]
by car	med bil	[me 'bil]
by ship	med skip	[me 'ʂip]
luggage	bagasje (m)	[bɑ'gɑʂə]
suitcase	koffert (m)	['kʊfɛːt]
luggage trolley	bagasjetralle (m/f)	[bɑ'gɑʂəˌtrɑlə]
passport	pass (n)	['pɑs]
visa	visum (n)	['visʉm]
ticket	billett (m)	[bi'let]
air ticket	flybillett (m)	['fly bi'let]
guidebook	reisehåndbok (m/f)	['ræjsəˌhɔnbʊk]
map (tourist ~)	kart (n)	['kɑːt]
area (rural ~)	område (n)	['ɔmˌroːdə]
place, site	sted (n)	['sted]
exotic (adj)	eksotisk	[ɛk'sʉtisk]
amazing (adj)	forunderlig	[fo'rʉndeːli̞]
group	gruppe (m)	['grʉpə]
excursion, sightseeing tour	utflukt (m/f)	['ʉtˌflʉkt]
guide (person)	guide (m)	['gɑjd]

156. Hotel

hotel	hotell (n)	[hʊ'tɛl]
motel	motell (n)	[mʊ'tɛl]
three-star (~ hotel)	trestjernet	['treˌstjæːŋə]
five-star	femstjernet	['fɛmˌstjæːŋə]

to stay (in a hotel, etc.)	å bo	[ɔ 'buː]
room	rom (n)	['rʊm]
single room	enkeltrom (n)	['ɛnkelt,rʊm]
double room	dobbeltrom (n)	['dɔbəlt,rʊm]
to book a room	å reservere rom	[ɔ resɛr'verə 'rʊm]

| half board | halvpensjon (m) | ['hal pan,ʂʊn] |
| full board | fullpensjon (m) | ['fʉl pan,ʂʊn] |

with bath	med badekar	[me 'badə,kar]
with shower	med dusj	[me 'dʉʂ]
satellite television	satellitt-TV (m)	[satɛ'lit 'tɛvɛ]
air-conditioner	klimaanlegg (n)	['klimɑ'an,leg]
towel	håndkle (n)	['hɔn,kle]
key	nøkkel (m)	['nøkəl]

administrator	administrator (m)	[admini'straːtʊr]
chambermaid	stuepike (m/f)	['stʉə,pikə]
porter	pikkolo (m)	['pikɔlɔ]
doorman	portier (m)	[pɔː'tje]

restaurant	restaurant (m)	[rɛstʉ'raŋ]
pub, bar	bar (m)	['bar]
breakfast	frokost (m)	['frʊkɔst]
dinner	middag (m)	['mi,da]
buffet	buffet (m)	[bʉ'fɛ]

| lobby | hall, lobby (m) | ['hal], ['lɔbi] |
| lift | heis (m) | ['hæjs] |

| DO NOT DISTURB | VENNLIGST IKKE FORSTYRR! | ['vɛnligt ikə fɔ'ʂtyr] |
| NO SMOKING | RØYKING FORBUDT | ['røjkiŋ fɔr'bʉt] |

157. Books. Reading

book	bok (m/f)	['bʊk]
author	forfatter (m)	[fɔr'fɑtər]
writer	forfatter (m)	[fɔr'fɑtər]
to write (~ a book)	å skrive	[ɔ 'skrivə]

reader	leser (m)	['lesər]
to read (vi, vt)	å lese	[ɔ 'lesə]
reading (activity)	lesning (m/f)	['lesniŋ]

| silently (to oneself) | for seg selv | [fɔr sæj 'sɛl] |
| aloud (adv) | høyt | ['højt] |

to publish (vt)	å publisere	[ɔ pʉbli'serə]
publishing (process)	publisering (m/f)	[pʉbli'seriŋ]
publisher	forlegger (m)	['fɔː,legər]
publishing house	forlag (n)	['fɔːlag]
to come out (be released)	å komme ut	[ɔ 'kɔmə ʉt]
release (of a book)	utgivelse (m)	['ʉtjivəlsə]

print run	opplag (n)	['ɔpˌlɑg]
bookshop	bokhandel (m)	['bʊkˌhandəl]
library	bibliotek (n)	[bibliʊ'tek]

story (novella)	kortroman (m)	['kʊːʈ rʊˌmɑn]
short story	novelle (m/f)	[nʊ'vɛlə]
novel	roman (m)	[rʊ'mɑn]
detective novel	kriminalroman (m)	[krimi'nɑl rʊˌmɑn]

memoirs	memoarer (pl)	[memʊ'ɑrər]
legend	legende (m)	['le'gɛndə]
myth	myte (m)	['myːtə]

poetry, poems	dikt (n pl)	['dikt]
autobiography	selvbiografi (m)	['sɛlˌbiʊgrɑ'fi]
selected works	utvalgte verker (n pl)	['ʉtˌvalgtə 'værkər]
science fiction	science fiction (m)	['sajəns ˌfikʂn]

title	tittel (m)	['titəl]
introduction	innledning (m)	['inˌledniŋ]
title page	tittelblad (n)	['titəlˌblɑ]

chapter	kapitel (n)	[ka'pitəl]
extract	utdrag (n)	['ʉtˌdrɑg]
episode	episode (m)	[ɛpi'sʊdə]

plot (storyline)	handling (m/f)	['handliŋ]
contents	innhold (n)	['inˌhɔl]
table of contents	innholdsfortegnelse (m)	['inhɔls fɔː'ʈæjnəlsə]
main character	hovedperson (m)	['hʊvəd pæ'ʂʊn]

volume	bind (n)	['bin]
cover	omslag (n)	['ɔmˌslɑg]
binding	bokbind (n)	['bʊkˌbin]
bookmark	bokmerke (n)	['bʊkˌmærkə]

page	side (m/f)	['sidə]
to page through	å bla	[ɔ 'blɑ]
margins	marger (m pl)	['mɑrgər]
annotation (marginal note, etc.)	annotering (n)	[anʊ'tɛriŋ]
footnote	anmerkning (m)	['anˌmærkniŋ]

text	tekst (m/f)	['tɛkst]
type, fount	skrift, font (m)	['skrift], ['font]
misprint, typo	trykkfeil (m)	['trʏkˌfæjl]

translation	oversettelse (m)	['ɔveˌsɛtəlsə]
to translate (vt)	å oversette	[ɔ 'ɔveˌsɛtə]
original (n)	original (m)	[ɔrigi'nɑl]

famous (adj)	berømt	[be'rømt]
unknown (not famous)	ukjent	['ʉˌçɛnt]
interesting (adj)	interessant	[intere'san]
bestseller	bestselger (m)	['bɛstˌsɛlər]
dictionary	ordbok (m/f)	['uːrˌbʊk]

| textbook | lærebok (m/f) | ['læɾəˌbʊk] |
| encyclopedia | encyklopedi (m) | [ɛnsʏklɔpe'di] |

158. Hunting. Fishing

hunting	jakt (m/f)	['jakt]
to hunt (vi, vt)	å jage	[ɔ 'jagə]
hunter	jeger (m)	['jɛ:gər]

to shoot (vi)	å skyte	[ɔ 'ʂytə]
rifle	gevær (n)	[ge'vær]
bullet (shell)	patron (m)	[pɑ'trʊn]
shot (lead balls)	hagl (n)	['hɑgl]

steel trap	saks (m/f)	['sɑks]
snare (for birds, etc.)	felle (m/f)	['fɛlə]
to fall into the steel trap	å fanges i felle	[ɔ 'fɑŋəs i 'fɛlə]
to lay a steel trap	å sette opp felle	[ɔ 'sɛtə ɔp 'fɛlə]

poacher	tyvskytter (m)	['tyfˌʂytər]
game (in hunting)	vilt (n)	['vilt]
hound dog	jakthund (m)	['jaktˌhʉn]

| safari | safari (m) | [sɑ'fɑri] |
| mounted animal | utstoppet dyr (n) | ['ʉtˌstɔpet ˌdyr] |

fisherman	fisker (m)	['fiskər]
fishing (angling)	fiske (n)	['fiskə]
to fish (vi)	å fiske	[ɔ 'fiskə]

fishing rod	fiskestang (m/f)	['fiskəˌstɑŋ]
fishing line	fiskesnøre (n)	['fiskəˌsnøre]
hook	krok (m)	['krʊk]

| float | dupp (m) | ['dʉp] |
| bait | agn (m) | ['ɑŋn] |

| to cast a line | å kaste ut | [ɔ 'kɑstə ʉt] |
| to bite (ab. fish) | å bite | [ɔ 'bitə] |

| catch (of fish) | fangst (m) | ['fɑŋst] |
| ice-hole | hull (n) i isen | ['hʉl i ˌisən] |

fishing net	nett (n)	['nɛt]
boat	båt (m)	['bɔt]
to net (to fish with a net)	å fiske med nett	[ɔ 'fiskə me 'nɛt]
to cast[throw] the net	å kaste nettet	[ɔ 'kɑstə 'nɛtə]

| to haul the net in | å hale opp nettet | [ɔ 'hɑlə ɔp 'nɛtə] |
| to fall into the net | å bli fanget i nett | [ɔ 'bli 'fɑŋet i 'nɛt] |

whaler (person)	hvalfanger (m)	['vɑlˌfɑŋər]
whaleboat	hvalbåt (m)	['vɑlˌbɔt]
harpoon	harpun (m)	[hɑr'pʉn]

159. Games. Billiards

billiards	biljard (m)	[bil'ja:ɖ]
billiard room, hall	biljardsalong (m)	[bil'ja:ɖsɑ‚lɔŋ]
ball (snooker, etc.)	biljardkule (m/f)	[bil'ja:ɖ‚kʉ:lə]

to pocket a ball	å støte en kule	[ɔ 'støtə en 'kʉ:lə]
cue	kø (m)	['kø]
pocket	hull (n)	['hʉl]

160. Games. Playing cards

diamonds	ruter (m pl)	['rʉtər]
spades	spar (m pl)	['spɑr]
hearts	hjerter (m)	['jæ:ʈər]
clubs	kløver (m)	['kløvər]

ace	ess (n)	['ɛs]
king	konge (m)	['kʊŋə]
queen	dame (m/f)	['dɑmə]
jack, knave	knekt (m)	['knɛkt]

playing card	kort (n)	['kɔ:t]
cards	kort (n pl)	['kɔ:t]
trump	trumf (m)	['trʉmf]
pack of cards	kortstokk (m)	['kɔ:t‚stɔk]

point	poeng (n)	[pɔ'ɛŋ]
to deal (vi, vt)	å gi, å dele ut	[ɔ 'ji], [ɔ 'delə ʉt]
to shuffle (cards)	å blande	[ɔ 'blɑnə]
lead, turn (n)	trekk (n)	['trɛk]
cardsharp	falskspiller (m)	['fɑlsk‚spilər]

161. Casino. Roulette

casino	kasino (n)	[kɑ'sinʊ]
roulette (game)	rulett (m)	[rʉ'let]
bet	innsats (m)	['in‚sɑts]
to place bets	å satse	[ɔ 'sɑtsə]

red	rød (m)	['rø]
black	svart (m)	['svɑ:t]
to bet on red	å satse på rød	[ɔ 'sɑtsə pɔ 'rø]
to bet on black	å satse på svart	[ɔ 'sɑtsə pɔ 'svɑ:t]

croupier (dealer)	croupier, dealer (m)	[kru'pje], ['dilər]
to spin the wheel	å snurre hjulet	[ɔ 'snʉrə 'jʉlə]
rules (~ of the game)	spilleregler (m pl)	['spilə‚rɛglər]
chip	sjetong (m)	[ʂɛ'tɔŋ]
to win (vi, vt)	å vinne	[ɔ 'vinə]
win (winnings)	gevinst (m)	[ge'vinst]

| to lose (~ 100 dollars) | å tape | [ɔ 'tapə] |
| loss (losses) | tap (n) | ['tap] |

player	spiller (m)	['spilər]
blackjack (card game)	blackjack (m)	['blek‚sɛk]
craps (dice game)	terningspill (n)	['tæːŋiŋ‚spil]
dice (a pair of ~)	terninger (m/f pl)	['tæːŋiŋər]
fruit machine	spilleautomat (m)	['spilə aʊtʊ'mat]

162. Rest. Games. Miscellaneous

to stroll (vi, vt)	å spasere	[ɔ spa'serə]
stroll (leisurely walk)	spasertur (m)	[spa'sɛː‚tʉr]
car ride	kjøretur (m)	['çœːrə‚tʉr]
adventure	eventyr (n)	['ɛvən‚tyr]
picnic	piknik (m)	['piknik]

game (chess, etc.)	spill (n)	['spil]
player	spiller (m)	['spilər]
game (one ~ of chess)	parti (n)	[pɑː'ti]

collector (e.g. philatelist)	samler (m)	['sɑmlər]
to collect (stamps, etc.)	å samle	[ɔ 'sɑmlə]
collection	samling (m/f)	['sɑmliŋ]

crossword puzzle	kryssord (n)	['krʏs‚ʊːr]
racecourse (hippodrome)	travbane (m)	['trɑv‚bɑnə]
disco (discotheque)	diskotek (n)	[diskʊ'tek]

| sauna | sauna (m) | ['saʊna] |
| lottery | lotteri (n) | [lɔte'ri] |

camping trip	campingtur (m)	['kɑmpiŋ‚tʉr]
camp	leir (m)	['læjr]
tent (for camping)	telt (n)	['tɛlt]
compass	kompass (m/n)	[kʊm'pɑs]
camper	camper (m)	['kɑmpər]

to watch (film, etc.)	å se på	[ɔ 'se pɔ]
viewer	TV-seer (m)	['tɛvɛ ‚seːər]
TV show (TV program)	TV-show (n)	['tɛvɛ ‚ɕɔːw]

163. Photography

| camera (photo) | kamera (n) | ['kɑmera] |
| photo, picture | foto, fotografi (n) | ['fɔtɔ], ['fɔtɔgra'fi] |

photographer	fotograf (m)	[fɔtɔ'grɑf]
photo studio	fotostudio (n)	['fɔtɔ‚stʉdiɔ]
photo album	fotoalbum (n)	['fɔtɔ‚albʉm]
camera lens	objektiv (n)	[ɔbjɛk'tiv]
telephoto lens	teleobjektiv (n)	['teleɔbjek'tiv]

| filter | filter (n) | ['filtər] |
| lens | linse (m/f) | ['linsə] |

optics (high-quality ~)	optikk (m)	[ɔp'tik]
diaphragm (aperture)	blender (m)	['blenər]
exposure time (shutter speed)	eksponeringstid (m/f)	[ɛkspu'neriŋs,tid]
viewfinder	søker (m)	['søkər]

digital camera	digitalkamera (n)	[digi'tal ,kamera]
tripod	stativ (m)	[sta'tiv]
flash	blits (m)	['blits]

to photograph (vt)	å fotografere	[ɔ fotɔgra'ferə]
to take pictures	å ta bilder	[ɔ 'ta 'bildər]
to have one's picture taken	å bli fotografert	[ɔ 'bli fotɔgra'fɛːt]

focus	fokus (n)	['fokʉs]
to focus	å stille skarphet	[ɔ 'stilə 'skarp,het]
sharp, in focus (adj)	skarp	['skarp]
sharpness	skarphet (m)	['skarp,het]

| contrast | kontrast (m) | [kʉn'trast] |
| contrast (as adj) | kontrast- | [kʉn'trast-] |

picture (photo)	bilde (n)	['bildə]
negative (n)	negativ (m/n)	['nega,tiv]
film (a roll of ~)	film (m)	['film]
frame (still)	bilde (n)	['bildə]
to print (photos)	å skrive ut	[ɔ skrivə ʉt]

164. Beach. Swimming

beach	badestrand (m/f)	['badə,stran]
sand	sand (m)	['san]
deserted (beach)	øde	['ødə]

suntan	solbrenthet (m)	['sʉlbrɛnt,het]
to get a tan	å sole seg	[ɔ 'sʉlə sæj]
tanned (adj)	solbrent	['sʉl,brɛnt]
sunscreen	solkrem (m)	['sʉl,krɛm]

bikini	bikini (m)	[bi'kini]
swimsuit, bikini	badedrakt (m/f)	['badə,drakt]
swim trunks	badebukser (m/f)	['badə,bʉksər]

swimming pool	svømmebasseng (n)	['svœmə,ba'sɛŋ]
to swim (vi)	å svømme	[ɔ 'svœmə]
shower	dusj (m)	['dʉʂ]
to change (one's clothes)	å kle seg om	[ɔ 'kle sæj ,om]
towel	håndkle (n)	['hɔn,kle]

| boat | båt (m) | ['bɔt] |
| motorboat | motorbåt (m) | ['motʉr,bot] |

water ski	vannski (m pl)	['vɑnˌʂi]
pedalo	pedalbåt (m)	['pe'dɑlˌbɔt]
surfing	surfing (m/f)	['sørfiŋ]
surfer	surfer (m)	['sørfər]

scuba set	scuba (n)	['skʉbɑ]
flippers (swim fins)	svømmeføtter (m pl)	['svœməˌfœtər]
mask (diving ~)	maske (m/f)	['mɑskə]
diver	dykker (m)	['dʏkər]
to dive (vi)	å dykke	[ɔ 'dʏkə]
underwater (adv)	under vannet	['ʉnər 'vɑnə]

beach umbrella	parasoll (m)	[pɑrɑ'sɔl]
beach chair (sun lounger)	liggestol (m)	['ligəˌstʉl]
sunglasses	solbriller (m pl)	['sʉlˌbrilər]
air mattress	luftmadrass (m)	['lʉftmɑˌdrɑs]

| to play (amuse oneself) | å leke | [ɔ 'lekə] |
| to go for a swim | å bade | [ɔ 'bɑdə] |

beach ball	ball (m)	['bɑl]
to inflate (vt)	å blåse opp	[ɔ 'blɔːsə ɔp]
inflatable, air (adj)	luft-, oppblåsbar	['lʉft-], [ɔp'blɔːsbɑr]

wave	bølge (m)	['bølgə]
buoy (line of ~s)	bøye (m)	['bøjə]
to drown (ab. person)	å drukne	[ɔ 'drʉknə]

to save, to rescue	å redde	[ɔ 'rɛdə]
life jacket	redningsvest (m)	['rɛdniŋsˌvɛst]
to observe, to watch	å observere	[ɔ ɔbsɛr'verə]
lifeguard	badevakt (m/f)	['bɑdəˌvɑkt]

TECHNICAL EQUIPMENT. TRANSPORT

Technical equipment

165. Computer

computer	datamaskin (m)	['dɑtɑ mɑˌʂin]
notebook, laptop	bærbar, laptop (m)	['bærˌbɑr], ['lɑptɔp]
to turn on	å slå på	[ɔ 'ʂlɔ pɔ]
to turn off	å slå av	[ɔ 'ʂlɔ ɑː]
keyboard	tastatur (n)	[tɑstɑ'tʉr]
key	tast (m)	['tɑst]
mouse	mus (m/f)	['mʉs]
mouse mat	musematte (m/f)	['mʉseˌmɑtə]
button	knapp (m)	['knɑp]
cursor	markør (m)	[mɑr'kør]
monitor	monitor (m)	['mɔnitɔr]
screen	skjerm (m)	['ʂærm]
hard disk	harddisk (m)	['hɑrˌdisk]
hard disk capacity	harddiskkapasitet (m)	['hɑrˌdisk kɑpɑsi'tet]
memory	minne (n)	['minə]
random access memory	hovedminne (n)	['hɔvedˌminə]
file	fil (m)	['fil]
folder	mappe (m/f)	['mɑpə]
to open (vt)	å åpne	[ɔ 'ɔpnə]
to close (vt)	å lukke	[ɔ 'lʉkə]
to save (vt)	å lagre	[ɔ 'lɑgrə]
to delete (vt)	å slette, å fjerne	[ɔ 'ʂletə], [ɔ 'fjæːɳə]
to copy (vt)	å kopiere	[ɔ kʉ'pjerə]
to sort (vt)	å sortere	[ɔ sɔːˈʈerə]
to transfer (copy)	å overføre	[ɔ 'ɔverˌførə]
programme	program (n)	[prʉ'grɑm]
software	programvare (m/f)	[prʉ'grɑmˌvɑrə]
programmer	programmerer (m)	[prʉgrɑ'merər]
to program (vt)	å programmere	[ɔ prʉgrɑ'merə]
hacker	hacker (m)	['hɑkər]
password	passord (n)	['pɑsˌuːr]
virus	virus (m)	['virʉs]
to find, to detect	å oppdage	[ɔ 'ɔpˌdɑgə]
byte	byte (m)	['bɑjt]

146

megabyte	megabyte (m)	['mega,bajt]
data	data (m pl)	['data]
database	database (m)	['data,base]

cable (USB, etc.)	kabel (m)	['kabəl]
to disconnect (vt)	å koble fra	[ɔ 'kɔblə fra]
to connect (sth to sth)	å koble	[ɔ 'kɔblə]

166. Internet. E-mail

Internet	Internett	['intə,nɛt]
browser	nettleser (m)	['nɛt,lesər]
search engine	søkemotor (m)	['søkə,motʊr]
provider	leverandør (m)	[levəran'dør]

webmaster	webmaster (m)	['vɛb,mastər]
website	webside, hjemmeside (m/f)	['vɛb,sidə], ['jɛmə,sidə]
web page	nettside (m)	['nɛt,sidə]

| address (e-mail ~) | adresse (m) | [a'drɛsə] |
| address book | adressebok (f) | [a'drɛsə,bʊk] |

postbox	postkasse (m/f)	['pɔst,kasə]
post	post (m)	['pɔst]
full (adj)	full	['fʊl]

message	melding (m/f)	['mɛliŋ]
incoming messages	innkommende meldinger	['in,kɔmənə 'mɛliŋər]
outgoing messages	utgående meldinger	['ʊt,gɔənə 'mɛliŋər]
sender	avsender (m)	['af,sɛnər]
to send (vt)	å sende	[ɔ 'sɛnə]
sending (of mail)	avsending (m)	['af,sɛniŋ]
receiver	mottaker (m)	['mɔt,takər]
to receive (vt)	å motta	[ɔ 'mɔta]

| correspondence | korrespondanse (m) | [kʊrespɔn'dansə] |
| to correspond (vi) | å brevveksle | [ɔ 'brɛv,vɛkslə] |

file	fil (m)	['fil]
to download (vt)	å laste ned	[ɔ 'lastə 'ne]
to create (vt)	å opprette	[ɔ 'ɔp,rɛtə]
to delete (vt)	å slette, å fjerne	[ɔ 'ʂletə], [ɔ 'fjæːɳə]
deleted (adj)	slettet	['ʂletət]

connection (ADSL, etc.)	forbindelse (m)	[fɔr'binəlsə]
speed	hastighet (m/f)	['hasti,het]
modem	modem (n)	['mʊ'dɛm]
access	tilgang (m)	['til,gaŋ]
port (e.g. input ~)	port (m)	['pɔːt]

connection (make a ~)	tilkobling (m/f)	['til,kɔbliŋ]
to connect to ... (vi)	å koble	[ɔ 'kɔblə]
to select (vt)	å velge	[ɔ 'vɛlgə]
to search (for ...)	å søke etter ...	[ɔ 'søkə ,ɛtər ...]

167. Electricity

electricity	elektrisitet (m)	[ɛlektrisi'tet]
electric, electrical (adj)	elektrisk	[ɛ'lektrisk]
electric power station	kraftverk (n)	['kraft,værk]
energy	energi (m)	[ɛnær'gi]
electric power	elkraft (m/f)	['ɛl,kraft]

light bulb	lyspære (m/f)	['lys,pærə]
torch	lommelykt (m/f)	['lʊmə,lʏkt]
street light	gatelykt (m/f)	['gatə,lʏkt]

light	lys (n)	['lys]
to turn on	å slå på	[ɔ 'ʂlɔ pɔ]
to turn off	å slå av	[ɔ 'ʂlɔ aː]
to turn off the light	å slokke lyset	[ɔ 'ʂløkə 'lysə]

to burn out (vi)	å brenne ut	[ɔ 'brɛnə ʉt]
short circuit	kortslutning (m)	['kʊː,tslʉtniŋ]
broken wire	kabelbrudd (n)	['kabəl,brʉd]
contact (electrical ~)	kontakt (m)	[kʊn'takt]

light switch	strømbryter (m)	['strøm,brytər]
socket outlet	stikkontakt (m)	['stik kʊn,takt]
plug	støpsel (n)	['støpsəl]
extension lead	skjøteledning (m)	['ʂøtə,ledniŋ]

fuse	sikring (m)	['sikriŋ]
cable, wire	ledning (m)	['ledniŋ]
wiring	ledningsnett (n)	['ledniŋs,nɛt]

ampere	ampere (m)	[am'pɛr]
amperage	strømstyrke (m)	['strøm,styrkə]
volt	volt (m)	['vɔlt]
voltage	spenning (m/f)	['spɛniŋ]

| electrical device | elektrisk apparat (n) | [ɛ'lektrisk apa'rat] |
| indicator | indikator (m) | [indi'katʊr] |

electrician	elektriker (m)	[ɛ'lektrikər]
to solder (vt)	å lodde	[ɔ 'lɔdə]
soldering iron	loddebolt (m)	['lɔdə,bɔlt]
electric current	strøm (m)	['strøm]

168. Tools

tool, instrument	verktøy (n)	['værk,tøj]
tools	verktøy (n pl)	['værk,tøj]
equipment (factory ~)	utstyr (n)	['ʉt,styr]

hammer	hammer (m)	['hamər]
screwdriver	skrutrekker (m)	['skrʉ,trɛkər]
axe	øks (m/f)	['øks]

saw	sag (m/f)	['sag]
to saw (vt)	å sage	[ɔ 'sagə]
plane (tool)	høvel (m)	['høvəl]
to plane (vt)	å høvle	[ɔ 'høvlə]
soldering iron	loddebolt (m)	['lɔdə,bɔlt]
to solder (vt)	å lodde	[ɔ 'lɔdə]

file (tool)	fil (m/f)	['fil]
carpenter pincers	knipetang (m/f)	['knipə,taŋ]
combination pliers	flattang (m/f)	['flat,taŋ]
chisel	hoggjern, huggjern (n)	['hʊg,jæ:ɳ]

drill bit	bor (m/n)	['bʊr]
electric drill	boremaskin (m)	['bɔre ma,ʂin]
to drill (vi, vt)	å bore	[ɔ 'bɔrə]

| knife | kniv (m) | ['kniv] |
| blade | blad (n) | ['bla] |

sharp (blade, etc.)	skarp	['skarp]
dull, blunt (adj)	sløv	['sløv]
to get blunt (dull)	å bli sløv	[ɔ 'bli 'sløv]
to sharpen (vt)	å skjerpe, å slipe	[ɔ 'ʂɛrpə], [ɔ 'ʂlipə]

bolt	bolt (m)	['bɔlt]
nut	mutter (m)	['mʉtər]
thread (of a screw)	gjenge (n)	['jɛŋə]
wood screw	skrue (m)	['skrʉə]

| nail | spiker (m) | ['spikər] |
| nailhead | spikerhode (n) | ['spikər,hʊdə] |

ruler (for measuring)	linjal (m)	[li'njal]
tape measure	målebånd (n)	['mo:lə,bɔn]
spirit level	vater, vaterpass (n)	['vatər], ['vatər,pas]
magnifying glass	lupe (m/f)	['lʉpə]

measuring instrument	måleinstrument (n)	['mo:lə instrʉ'mɛnt]
to measure (vt)	å måle	[ɔ 'mo:lə]
scale (temperature ~, etc.)	skala (m)	['skala]
readings	avlesninger (m/f pl)	['av,lesniŋər]

| compressor | kompressor (m) | [kʊm'presʊr] |
| microscope | mikroskop (n) | [mikrʊ'skʊp] |

pump (e.g. water ~)	pumpe (m/f)	['pʉmpə]
robot	robot (m)	['rɔbot]
laser	laser (m)	['lasər]

spanner	skrunøkkel (m)	['skrʉ,nøkəl]
adhesive tape	pakketeip (m)	['pakə,tɛjp]
glue	lim (n)	['lim]

sandpaper	sandpapir (n)	['sanpa,pir]
spring	fjær (m/f)	['fjær]
magnet	magnet (m)	[maŋ'net]

gloves	hansker (m pl)	['hɑnskər]
rope	reip, rep (n)	['ræjp], ['rɛp]
cord	snor (m/f)	['snʊr]
wire (e.g. telephone ~)	ledning (m)	['ledniŋ]
cable	kabel (m)	['kɑbəl]

sledgehammer	slegge (m/f)	['ʂlegə]
prybar	spett, jernspett (n)	['spɛt], ['jæ:rˌspɛt]
ladder	stige (m)	['sti:ə]
stepladder	trappstige (m/f)	['trɑpˌsti:ə]

to screw (tighten)	å skru fast	[ɔ 'skrʉ 'fɑst]
to unscrew (lid, filter, etc.)	å skru løs	[ɔ 'skrʉ ˌløs]
to tighten (e.g. with a clamp)	å klemme	[ɔ 'klemə]
to glue, to stick	å klistre, å lime	[ɔ 'klistrə], [ɔ 'limə]
to cut (vt)	å skjære	[ɔ 'ʂæ:rə]

malfunction (fault)	funksjonsfeil (m)	['fʉnkʂɔnsˌfæjl]
repair (mending)	reparasjon (m)	[repɑrɑ'ʂʊn]
to repair, to fix (vt)	å reparere	[ɔ repɑ'rerə]
to adjust (machine, etc.)	å justere	[ɔ jʉ'sterə]

to check (to examine)	å sjekke	[ɔ 'ʂɛkə]
checking	kontroll (m)	[kʊn'trɔl]
readings	avlesninger (m/f pl)	['ɑvˌlesniŋər]

reliable, solid (machine)	pålitelig	[pɔ'liteli]
complex (adj)	komplisert	[kʊmpli'sɛ:t]

to rust (get rusted)	å ruste	[ɔ 'rʉstə]
rusty (adj)	rusten, rustet	['rʉstən], ['rʉstət]
rust	rust (m/f)	['rʉst]

Transport

aeroplane	fly (n)	['fly]
air ticket	flybillett (m)	['fly bi'let]
airline	flyselskap (n)	['flysel‚skap]
airport	flyplass (m)	['fly‚plas]
supersonic (adj)	overlyds-	['ɔvə‚lyds-]

captain	kaptein (m)	[kap'tæjn]
crew	besetning (m/f)	[be'sɛtniŋ]
pilot	pilot (m)	[pi'lɔt]
stewardess	flyvertinne (m/f)	[flyvɛ:'ʈinə]
navigator	styrmann (m)	['styr‚man]

wings	vinger (m pl)	['viŋər]
tail	hale (m)	['halə]
cockpit	cockpit, førerkabin (m)	['kɔkpit], ['førərka‚bin]
engine	motor (m)	['mɔtʉr]
undercarriage (landing gear)	landingshjul (n)	['laniŋsjʉl]
turbine	turbin (m)	[tʉr'bin]

propeller	propell (m)	[prʉ'pɛl]
black box	svart boks (m)	['sva:ʈ bɔks]
yoke (control column)	ratt (n)	['rat]
fuel	brensel (n)	['brɛnsəl]

safety card	sikkerhetsbrosjyre (m)	['sikərhɛts‚brɔ'syrə]
oxygen mask	oksygenmaske (m/f)	['ɔksygən‚maskə]
uniform	uniform (m)	[ʉni'fɔrm]

| lifejacket | redningsvest (m) | ['rɛdniŋs‚vɛst] |
| parachute | fallskjerm (m) | ['fal‚særm] |

takeoff	start (m)	['sta:ʈ]
to take off (vi)	å løfte	[ɔ 'lœftə]
runway	startbane (m)	['sta:ʈ‚banə]

| visibility | siktbarhet (m) | ['siktbar‚het] |
| flight (act of flying) | flyging (m/f) | ['flygiŋ] |

| altitude | høyde (m) | ['højdə] |
| air pocket | lufthull (n) | ['lʉft‚hʉl] |

seat	plass (m)	['plas]
headphones	hodetelefoner (n pl)	['hɔdətelə‚fʉnər]
folding tray (tray table)	klappbord (n)	['klap‚bʉr]
airplane window	vindu (n)	['vindʉ]
aisle	midtgang (m)	['mit‚gaŋ]

170. Train

train	tog (n)	['tɔg]
commuter train	lokaltog (n)	[lo'kal‚tɔg]
express train	ekspresstog (n)	[ɛks'prɛs‚tɔg]
diesel locomotive	diesellokomotiv (n)	['disəl lʊkɔmɔ'tiv]
steam locomotive	damplokomotiv (n)	['damp lʊkɔmɔ'tiv]

coach, carriage	vogn (m)	['vɔŋn]
buffet car	restaurantvogn (m/f)	[rɛstʊ'raŋ‚vɔŋn]

rails	skinner (m/f pl)	['ʂinər]
railway	jernbane (m)	['jæː‚n‚banə]
sleeper (track support)	sville (m/f)	['svilə]

platform (railway ~)	perrong, plattform (m/f)	[pɛ'rɔŋ], ['platfɔrm]
platform (~ 1, 2, etc.)	spor (n)	['spʊr]
semaphore	semafor (m)	[sema'fʊr]
station	stasjon (m)	[sta'ʂʊn]

train driver	lokfører (m)	['lʊk‚førər]
porter (of luggage)	bærer (m)	['bærər]
carriage attendant	betjent (m)	['be'tjɛnt]
passenger	passasjer (m)	[pɑsɑ'ʂɛr]
ticket inspector	billett inspektør (m)	[bi'let inspɛk'tør]

corridor (in train)	korridor (m)	[kʊri'dɔr]
emergency brake	nødbrems (m)	['nød‚brɛms]

compartment	kupé (m)	[kʉ'pe]
berth	køye (m/f)	['køjə]
upper berth	overkøye (m/f)	['ɔvər‚køjə]
lower berth	underkøye (m/f)	['ʉnər‚køjə]
bed linen, bedding	sengetøy (n)	['sɛŋə‚tøj]

ticket	billett (m)	[bi'let]
timetable	rutetabell (m)	['rʉtə‚ta'bɛl]
information display	informasjonstavle (m/f)	[informa'ʂʉns ‚tavlə]

to leave, to depart	å avgå	[ɔ 'avgɔ]
departure (of a train)	avgang (m)	['av‚gɑŋ]

to arrive (ab. train)	å ankomme	[ɔ 'an‚kɔmə]
arrival	ankomst (m)	['an‚kɔmst]

to arrive by train	å ankomme med toget	[ɔ 'an‚kɔmə me 'tɔgə]
to get on the train	å gå på toget	[ɔ 'gɔ pɔ 'tɔgə]
to get off the train	å gå av toget	[ɔ 'gɔ ɑː 'tɔgə]

train crash	togulykke (m/n)	['tɔg ʉ'lʏkə]
to derail (vi)	å spore av	[ɔ 'spʉrə ɑː]
steam locomotive	damplokomotiv (n)	['damp lʊkɔmɔ'tiv]
stoker, fireman	fyrbøter (m)	['fyr‚bøtər]
firebox	fyrrom (n)	['fyr‚rʊm]
coal	kull (n)	['kʉl]

171. Ship

ship	**skip** (n)	['ʂip]
vessel	**fartøy** (n)	['fɑːˌtøj]
steamship	**dampskip** (n)	['dɑmpˌʂip]
riverboat	**elvebåt** (m)	['ɛlvəˌbot]
cruise ship	**cruiseskip** (n)	['krʉsˌʂip]
cruiser	**krysser** (m)	['krʏsər]
yacht	**jakt** (m/f)	['jakt]
tugboat	**bukserbåt** (m)	[bʉk'serˌbot]
barge	**lastepram** (m)	['lɑstəˌprɑm]
ferry	**ferje, ferge** (m/f)	['færjə], ['færgə]
sailing ship	**seilbåt** (n)	['sæjlˌbot]
brigantine	**brigantin** (m)	[brigɑn'tin]
ice breaker	**isbryter** (m)	['isˌbrytər]
submarine	**ubåt** (m)	['ʉːˌbot]
boat (flat-bottomed ~)	**båt** (m)	['bot]
dinghy (lifeboat)	**jolle** (m/f)	['jolə]
lifeboat	**livbåt** (m)	['livˌbot]
motorboat	**motorbåt** (m)	['motʉrˌbot]
captain	**kaptein** (m)	[kɑp'tæjn]
seaman	**matros** (m)	[mɑ'trʉs]
sailor	**sjømann** (m)	['ʂøˌmɑn]
crew	**besetning** (m/f)	[be'sɛtniŋ]
boatswain	**båtsmann** (m)	['bosˌmɑn]
ship's boy	**skipsgutt, jungmann** (m)	['ʂipsˌgʉt], ['jʉŋˌmɑn]
cook	**kokk** (m)	['kʉk]
ship's doctor	**skipslege** (m)	['ʂipsˌlegə]
deck	**dekk** (n)	['dɛk]
mast	**mast** (m/f)	['mɑst]
sail	**seil** (n)	['sæjl]
hold	**lasterom** (n)	['lɑstəˌrʉm]
bow (prow)	**baug** (m)	['bæu]
stern	**akterende** (m)	['ɑktəˌrɛnə]
oar	**åre** (m)	['oːrə]
screw propeller	**propell** (m)	[prʉ'pɛl]
cabin	**hytte** (m)	['hʏte]
wardroom	**offisersmesse** (m/f)	[ɔfi'sɛrsˌmɛsə]
engine room	**maskinrom** (n)	[mɑ'ʂinˌrʉm]
bridge	**kommandobro** (m/f)	[kɔ'mɑndʉˌbrʉ]
radio room	**radiorom** (m)	['rɑdiʉˌrʉm]
wave (radio)	**bølge** (m)	['bølgə]
logbook	**loggbok** (m/f)	['lɔgˌbʉk]
spyglass	**langkikkert** (m)	['lɑŋˌkikeːt]
bell	**klokke** (m/f)	['klɔkə]

flag	flagg (n)	['flɑg]
hawser (mooring ~)	trosse (m/f)	['trʊsə]
knot (bowline, etc.)	knute (m)	['knʉtə]

| deckrails | rekkverk (n) | ['rɛkˌværk] |
| gangway | landgang (m) | ['lanˌgɑŋ] |

anchor	anker (n)	['ɑnkər]
to weigh anchor	å lette anker	[ɔ 'letə 'ɑnkər]
to drop anchor	å kaste anker	[ɔ 'kɑstə 'ɑnkər]
anchor chain	ankerkjetting (m)	['ɑnkərˌçɛtiŋ]

port (harbour)	havn (m/f)	['hɑvn]
quay, wharf	kai (m/f)	['kɑj]
to berth (moor)	å fortøye	[ɔ fɔːˈʈøjə]
to cast off	å kaste loss	[ɔ 'kɑstə lɔs]

trip, voyage	reise (m/f)	['ræjsə]
cruise (sea trip)	cruise (n)	['krʉs]
course (route)	kurs (m)	['kʉʂ]
route (itinerary)	rute (m/f)	['rʉtə]

fairway (safe water channel)	seilrende (m)	['sæjlˌrɛnə]
shallows	grunne (m/f)	['grʉnə]
to run aground	å gå på grunn	[ɔ 'gɔ pɔ 'grʉn]

storm	storm (m)	['stɔrm]
signal	signal (n)	[siŋ'nɑl]
to sink (vi)	å synke	[ɔ 'sʏnkə]
Man overboard!	Mann over bord!	['man ˌɔvər 'bʊr]
SOS (distress signal)	SOS (n)	[ɛsʊˈɛs]
ring buoy	livbøye (m/f)	['livˌbøjə]

172. Airport

airport	flyplass (m)	['flyˌplɑs]
aeroplane	fly (n)	['fly]
airline	flyselskap (n)	['flysəlˌskɑp]
air traffic controller	flygeleder (m)	['flygəˌledər]

departure	avgang (m)	['ɑvˌgɑŋ]
arrival	ankomst (m)	['anˌkɔmst]
to arrive (by plane)	å ankomme	[ɔ 'anˌkɔmə]

| departure time | avgangstid (m/f) | ['ɑvgɑŋsˌtid] |
| arrival time | ankomsttid (m/f) | [an'kɔmsˌtid] |

| to be delayed | å bli forsinket | [ɔ 'bli fɔˈʂinkət] |
| flight delay | avgangsforsinkelse (m) | ['ɑvgɑŋs fɔˈʂinkəlsə] |

information board	informasjonstavle (m/f)	[infɔrmɑˈʂuns ˌtɑvlə]
information	informasjon (m)	[infɔrmɑˈʂun]
to announce (vt)	å meddele	[ɔ 'mɛdˌdelə]
flight (e.g. next ~)	fly (n)	['fly]

| customs | toll (m) | ['tɔl] |
| customs officer | tollbetjent (m) | ['tɔlbeˌtjɛnt] |

customs declaration	tolldeklarasjon (m)	['tɔldɛklɑrɑ'ʂʊn]
to fill in (vt)	å utfylle	[ɔ 'ʉtˌfʏlə]
to fill in the declaration	å utfylle en tolldeklarasjon	[ɔ 'ʉtˌfʏlə en 'tɔldɛklɑrɑˌʂʊn]
passport control	passkontroll (m)	['pɑskʊnˌtrɔl]

luggage	bagasje (m)	[bɑ'gɑʂə]
hand luggage	håndbagasje (m)	['hɔnˌbɑ'gɑʂə]
luggage trolley	bagasjetralle (m/f)	[bɑ'gɑʂəˌtrɑlə]

landing	landing (m)	['lɑniŋ]
landing strip	landingsbane (m)	['lɑniŋsˌbɑnə]
to land (vi)	å lande	[ɔ 'lɑnə]
airstair (passenger stair)	trapp (m/f)	['trɑp]

check-in	innsjekking (m/f)	['inˌʂɛkiŋ]
check-in counter	innsjekkingsskranke (m)	['inˌʂɛkiŋs ˌskrɑnkə]
to check-in (vi)	å sjekke inn	[ɔ 'ʂɛkə in]
boarding card	boardingkort (n)	['bɔːdiŋˌkɔːt]
departure gate	gate (m/f)	['gejt]

transit	transitt (m)	[trɑn'sit]
to wait (vt)	å vente	[ɔ 'vɛntə]
departure lounge	ventehall (m)	['vɛntəˌhɑl]
to see off	å ta avskjed	[ɔ 'tɑ 'ɑfˌʂɛd]
to say goodbye	å si farvel	[ɔ 'si fɑr'vɛl]

173. Bicycle. Motorcycle

bicycle	sykkel (m)	['sʏkəl]
scooter	skooter (m)	['skutər]
motorbike	motorsykkel (m)	['mɔtʊrˌsʏkəl]

to go by bicycle	å sykle	[ɔ 'sʏklə]
handlebars	styre (n)	['styrə]
pedal	pedal (m)	[pe'dɑl]
brakes	bremser (m pl)	['brɛmsər]
bicycle seat (saddle)	sete (n)	['setə]

pump	pumpe (m/f)	['pʉmpə]
pannier rack	bagasjebrett (n)	[bɑ'gɑʂəˌbrɛt]
front lamp	lykt (m/f)	['lʏkt]
helmet	hjelm (m)	['jɛlm]

wheel	hjul (n)	['jʉl]
mudguard	skjerm (m)	['ʂærm]
rim	felg (m)	['fɛlg]
spoke	eik (m/f)	['æjk]

Cars

car	bil (m)	['bil]
sports car	sportsbil (m)	['spɔːʦˌbil]
limousine	limousin (m)	[limʉ'sin]
off-road vehicle	terrengbil (m)	[tɛ'rɛŋˌbil]
drophead coupé (convertible)	kabriolet (m)	[kabriʉ'le]
minibus	minibuss (m)	['miniˌbʉs]
ambulance	ambulanse (m)	[ambʉ'lɑnsə]
snowplough	snøplog (m)	['snøˌplɔg]
lorry	lastebil (m)	['lɑstəˌbil]
road tanker	tankbil (m)	['tɑŋkˌbil]
van (small truck)	skapbil (m)	['skɑpˌbil]
tractor unit	trekkvogn (m/f)	['trɛkˌvɔŋn]
trailer	tilhenger (m)	['tilˌhɛŋər]
comfortable (adj)	komfortabel	[kʉmfɔ:'tɑbəl]
used (adj)	brukt	['brʉkt]

bonnet	panser (n)	['pɑnsər]
wing	skjerm (m)	['ʂærm]
roof	tak (n)	['tɑk]
windscreen	frontrute (m/f)	['frɔntˌrʉtə]
rear-view mirror	bakspeil (n)	['bɑkˌspæjl]
windscreen washer	vindusspyler (m)	['vindʉsˌspylər]
windscreen wipers	viskerblader (n pl)	['viskəblɑər]
side window	siderute (m/f)	['sidəˌrʉtə]
electric window	vindusheis (m)	['vindʉsˌhæjs]
aerial	antenne (m)	[ɑn'tɛnə]
sunroof	takluke (m/f), soltak (n)	['tɑkˌlʉkə], ['sʉlˌtɑk]
bumper	støtfanger (m)	['støtˌfɑŋər]
boot	bagasjerom (n)	[bɑ'gɑʂəˌrʉm]
roof luggage rack	takgrind (m/f)	['tɑkˌgrin]
door	dør (m/f)	['dœr]
door handle	dørhåndtak (n)	['dœrˌhɔntɑk]
door lock	dørlås (m/n)	['dœrˌlɔs]
number plate	nummerskilt (n)	['nʉmərˌʂilt]
silencer	lyddemper (m)	['lydˌdɛmpər]

| petrol tank | bensintank (m) | [bɛn'sin‚taŋk] |
| exhaust pipe | eksosrør (n) | ['ɛksʊs‚rør] |

accelerator	gass (m)	['gɑs]
pedal	pedal (m)	[pe'dɑl]
accelerator pedal	gasspedal (m)	['gɑs pe'dɑl]

brake	brems (m)	['brɛms]
brake pedal	bremsepedal (m)	['brɛmsə pe'dɑl]
to brake (use the brake)	å bremse	[ɔ 'brɛmsə]
handbrake	håndbrekk (n)	['hɔn‚brɛk]

clutch	koppling (m)	['kɔpliŋ]
clutch pedal	kopplingspedal (m)	['kɔpliŋs pe'dɑl]
clutch disc	koplingsskive (m/f)	['kɔpliŋs‚ʂivə]
shock absorber	støtdemper (m)	['støt‚dɛmpər]

wheel	hjul (n)	['jʉl]
spare tyre	reservehjul (n)	[re'sɛrvə jʉl]
tyre	dekk (n)	['dɛk]
wheel cover (hubcap)	hjulkapsel (m)	['jʉl‚kapsəl]

driving wheels	drivhjul (n pl)	['driv jʉl]
front-wheel drive (as adj)	forhjulsdrevet	['fɔrjʉls‚drevət]
rear-wheel drive (as adj)	bakhjulsdrevet	['bɑkjʉls‚drevət]
all-wheel drive (as adj)	firehjulsdrevet	['firəjʉls‚drevət]

gearbox	girkasse (m/f)	['gir‚kɑsə]
automatic (adj)	automatisk	[aʊtʊ'mɑtisk]
mechanical (adj)	mekanisk	[me'kɑnisk]
gear lever	girspak (m)	['gi‚spɑk]

| headlamp | lyskaster (m) | ['lys‚kɑstər] |
| headlights | lyskastere (m pl) | ['lys‚kɑstərə] |

dipped headlights	nærlys (n)	['nær‚lys]
full headlights	fjernlys (n)	['fjæːn‚lys]
brake light	stopplys, bremselys (n)	['stɔp‚lys], ['brɛmsə‚lys]

sidelights	parkeringslys (n)	[par'keriŋs‚lys]
hazard lights	varselblinklys (n)	['vɑʂəl‚blink lys]
fog lights	tåkelys (n)	['to:kə‚lys]
turn indicator	blinklys (n)	['blink‚lys]
reversing light	baklys (n)	['bɑk‚lys]

176. Cars. Passenger compartment

car interior	interiør (n), innredning (m/f)	[inter'jør], ['in‚rɛdniŋ]
leather (as adj)	lær-	['lær-]
velour (as adj)	velur	[ve'lʉr]
upholstery	trekk (n)	['trɛk]

| instrument (gage) | instrument (n) | [instrʉ'mɛnt] |
| dashboard | dashbord (n) | ['daʂbɔ:d] |

| speedometer | speedometer (n) | [spidʊ'metər] |
| needle (pointer) | viser (m) | ['visər] |

mileometer	kilometerteller (m)	[çilu'metər‚tɛlər]
indicator (sensor)	indikator (m)	[indi'katʊr]
level	nivå (n)	[ni'vo]
warning light	varsellampe (m/f)	['vaʂəl‚lampə]

steering wheel	ratt (n)	['rat]
horn	horn (n)	['hʊːɳ]
button	knapp (m)	['knap]
switch	bryter (m)	['brytər]

seat	sete (n)	['setə]
backrest	seterygg (m)	['setə‚rʏg]
headrest	nakkestøtte (m/f)	['nakə‚stœtə]
seat belt	sikkerhetsbelte (m)	['sikərhɛts‚bɛltə]
to fasten the belt	å spenne fast sikkerhetsbeltet	[ɔ 'spɛnə fast 'sikərhets‚bɛltə]
adjustment (of seats)	justering (m/f)	[jʉ'steriŋ]

| airbag | kollisjonspute (m/f) | ['kʉliʂʊns‚pʉtə] |
| air-conditioner | klimaanlegg (n) | ['klima'an‚leg] |

radio	radio (m)	['radiʊ]
CD player	CD-spiller (m)	['sɛdɛ ‚spilər]
to turn on	å slå på	[ɔ 'ʂlɔ pɔ]
aerial	antenne (m)	[an'tɛnə]
glove box	hanskerom (n)	['hanskə‚rʊm]
ashtray	askebeger (n)	['askə‚begər]

177. Cars. Engine

engine, motor	motor (m)	['mɔtʊr]
diesel (as adj)	diesel-	['disəl-]
petrol (as adj)	bensin-	[bɛn'sin-]

engine volume	motorvolum (n)	['mɔtʊr vɔ'lʉm]
power	styrke (m)	['styrkə]
horsepower	hestekraft (m/f)	['hɛstə‚kraft]
piston	stempel (n)	['stɛmpəl]
cylinder	sylinder (m)	[sy'lindər]
valve	ventil (m)	[vɛn'til]

injector	injektor (m)	[i'njɛktʊr]
generator (alternator)	generator (m)	[gene'ratʊr]
carburettor	forgasser (m)	[fɔr'gasər]
motor oil	motorolje (m)	['mɔtʊr‚ɔljə]

radiator	radiator (m)	[radi'atʊr]
coolant	kjølevæske (m/f)	['çøːlə‚væskə]
cooling fan	vifte (m/f)	['viftə]
battery (accumulator)	batteri (n)	[batɛ'ri]
starter	starter (m)	['staːʈər]

| ignition | tenning (m/f) | ['tɛniŋ] |
| sparking plug | tennplugg (m) | ['tɛn͵plʉg] |

terminal (battery ~)	klemme (m/f)	['klemə]
positive terminal	plussklemme (m/f)	['plʉs͵klemə]
negative terminal	minusklemme (m/f)	['minʉs͵klemə]
fuse	sikring (m)	['sikriŋ]

air filter	luftfilter (n)	['lʉft͵filtər]
oil filter	oljefilter (n)	['ɔljə͵filtər]
fuel filter	brenselsfilter (n)	['brɛnsəls͵filtər]

178. Cars. Crash. Repair

car crash	bilulykke (m/f)	['bil ʉ'lykə]
traffic accident	trafikkulykke (m/f)	[trɑ'fik ʉ'lykə]
to crash (into the wall, etc.)	å kjøre inn i ...	[ɔ 'çœːrə in i ...]
to get smashed up	å havarere	[ɔ hɑvɑ'rerə]
damage	skade (m)	['skɑdə]
intact (unscathed)	uskadd	['ʉ͵skɑd]

breakdown	havari (n)	[hɑvɑ'ri]
to break down (vi)	å bryte sammen	[ɔ 'brytə 'sɑmən]
towrope	slepetau (n)	['ʂlepə͵taʉ]

puncture	punktering (m)	[pʉn'teriŋ]
to have a puncture	å være punktert	[ɔ 'værə pʉnk'tɛːţ]
to pump up	å pumpe opp	[ɔ 'pʉmpə ɔp]
pressure	trykk (n)	['trvk]
to check (to examine)	å sjekke	[ɔ 'ʂɛkə]

repair	reparasjon (m)	[repɑrɑ'ʂʉn]
garage (auto service shop)	bilverksted (n)	['bil 'værk͵sted]
spare part	reservedel (m)	[re'sɛrvə͵del]
part	del (m)	['del]

bolt (with nut)	bolt (m)	['bɔlt]
screw (fastener)	skrue (m)	['skrʉə]
nut	mutter (m)	['mʉtər]
washer	skive (m/f)	['ʂivə]
bearing (e.g. ball ~)	lager (n)	['lɑgər]

tube	rør (m)	['rør]
gasket (head ~)	pakning (m/f)	['pɑkniŋ]
cable, wire	ledning (m)	['ledniŋ]

jack	jekk (m), donkraft (m/f)	['jɛk], ['dɔn͵krɑft]
spanner	skrunøkkel (m)	['skrʉ͵nøkəl]
hammer	hammer (m)	['hɑmər]
pump	pumpe (m/f)	['pʉmpə]
screwdriver	skrutrekker (m)	['skrʉ͵trɛkər]

| fire extinguisher | brannslukker (n) | ['brɑn͵ʂlʉkər] |
| warning triangle | varseltrekant (m) | ['vɑʂəl 'trɛ͵kɑnt] |

to stall (vi)	å skjære	[ɔ 'ʂæːrə]
stall (n)	stans (m), stopp (m/n)	['stɑns], ['stɔp]
to be broken	å være ødelagt	[ɔ 'væːrə 'ødəˌlɑkt]
to overheat (vi)	å bli overopphetet	[ɔ 'bli 'ɔvərɔpˌhetət]
to be clogged up	å bli tilstoppet	[ɔ 'bli til'stɔpət]
to freeze up (pipes, etc.)	å fryse	[ɔ 'fryʂə]
to burst (vi, ab. tube)	å sprekke, å briste	[ɔ 'sprɛkə], [ɔ 'bristə]
pressure	trykk (n)	['trʏk]
level	nivå (n)	[ni'vo]
slack (~ belt)	slakk	['ʂlɑk]
dent	bulk (m)	['bʉlk]
knocking noise (engine)	bankelyd (m), dunk (m/n)	['bɑnkəˌlyd], ['dʉnk]
crack	sprekk (m)	['sprɛk]
scratch	ripe (m/f)	['ripə]

179. Cars. Road

road	vei (m)	['væj]
motorway	hovedvei (m)	['hʉvədˌvæj]
highway	motorvei (m)	['mɔtʉrˌvæj]
direction (way)	retning (m/f)	['rɛtniŋ]
distance	avstand (m)	['ɑfˌstɑn]
bridge	bro (m/f)	['brʉ]
car park	parkeringsplass (m)	[pɑr'keriŋsˌplɑs]
square	torg (n)	['tɔr]
road junction	trafikkmaskin (m)	[trɑ'fik mɑˌʂin]
tunnel	tunnel (m)	['tʉnəl]
petrol station	bensinstasjon (m)	[bɛn'sinˌstɑ'ʂʉn]
car park	parkeringsplass (m)	[pɑr'keriŋsˌplɑs]
petrol pump	bensinpumpe (m/f)	[bɛn'sinˌpʉmpə]
auto repair shop	bilverksted (n)	['bil 'værkˌsted]
to fill up	å tanke opp	[ɔ 'tɑnkə ɔp]
fuel	brensel (n)	['brɛnsəl]
jerrycan	bensinkanne (m/f)	[bɛn'sinˌkɑnə]
asphalt, tarmac	asfalt (m)	['ɑsˌfɑlt]
road markings	vegoppmerking (m/f)	['veg 'ɔpˌmærkiŋ]
kerb	fortauskant (m)	['foːʈɑʉsˌkɑnt]
crash barrier	autovern, veirekkverk (n)	['ɑʉtɔˌvæːɳ], ['væjˌrekværk]
ditch	veigrøft (m/f)	['væjˌgrœft]
roadside (shoulder)	veikant (m)	['væjˌkɑnt]
lamppost	lyktestolpe (m)	['lʏktəˌstɔlpə]
to drive (a car)	å kjøre	[ɔ 'çœːrə]
to turn (e.g., ~ left)	å svinge	[ɔ 'sviŋə]
to make a U-turn	å ta en U-sving	[ɔ 'tɑ en 'ʉːˌsviŋ]
reverse (~ gear)	revers (m)	[re'væʂ]
to honk (vi)	å tute	[ɔ 'tʉtə]
honk (sound)	tut (n)	['tʉt]

to get stuck (in the mud, etc.)	å kjøre seg fast	[ɔ 'çœ:rə sæj 'fɑst]
to spin the wheels	å spinne	[ɔ 'spinə]
to cut, to turn off (vt)	å stanse	[ɔ 'stɑnsə]

speed	hastighet (m/f)	['hɑsti,het]
to exceed the speed limit	å overskride fartsgrensen	[ɔ 'ʌvə,skridə 'fɑ:ʦ,grɛnsən]
to give a ticket	å gi bot	[ɔ 'ji 'bʉt]
traffic lights	trafikklys (n)	[trɑ'fik,lys]
driving licence	førerkort (n)	['fører,kɔ:t]

level crossing	planovergang (m)	['plɑn 'ʌver,gɑŋ]
crossroads	veikryss (n)	['væjkrʏs]
zebra crossing	fotgjengerovergang (m)	['fʉtjɛŋər 'ʌver,gɑŋ]
bend, curve	kurve (m)	['kʉrvə]
pedestrian precinct	gågate (m/f)	['go:,gɑtə]

180. Signs

Highway Code	trafikkregler (m pl)	[trɑ'fik,rɛglər]
road sign (traffic sign)	trafikkskilt (n)	[trɑ'fik,ʂilt]
overtaking	forbikjøring (m/f)	['forbi,çœriŋ]
curve	Sving	['sviŋ]
U-turn	u-sving, u-vending	['ʉ:,sviŋ], ['ʉ:,vɛniŋ]
roundabout	rundkjøring	['rʉn,çœriŋ]

No entry	Innkjøring forbudt	['in'çœriŋ for'bʉt]
All vehicles prohibited	Trafikkforbud	[trɑ'fik for,bʉt]
No overtaking	Forbikjøring forbudt	['forbi,çœriŋ for'bʉt]
No parking	Parkering forbudt	[pɑr'keriŋ for'bʉt]
No stopping	Stans forbudt	['stɑns for'bʉt]

dangerous curve	Farlig sving	['fɑ:ļi ,sviŋ]
steep descent	Bratt bakke	['brɑt ,bɑkə]
one-way traffic	Enveiskjøring	['ɛnvæjs,søriŋ]
zebra crossing	fotgjengerovergang (m)	['fʉtjɛŋər 'ʌver,gɑŋ]
slippery road	Glatt kjørebane	['glɑt 'çœ:rə,bɑnə]
GIVE WAY	Vikeplikt	['vikə,plikt]

PEOPLE. LIFE EVENTS

181. Holidays. Event

celebration, holiday	**fest** (m)	['fɛst]
national day	**nasjonaldag** (m)	[naʂʉ'nal‚da]
public holiday	**festdag** (m)	['fɛst‚da]
to commemorate (vt)	**å feire**	[ɔ 'fæjrə]
event (happening)	**begivenhet** (m/f)	[be'jiven‚het]
event (organized activity)	**evenement** (n)	[ɛvenə'maŋ]
banquet (party)	**bankett** (m)	[ban'kɛt]
reception (formal party)	**resepsjon** (m)	[resɛp'ʂʉn]
feast	**fest** (n)	['fɛst]
anniversary	**årsdag** (m)	['oːʂ‚da]
jubilee	**jubileum** (n)	[jʉbi'leʉm]
to celebrate (vt)	**å feire**	[ɔ 'fæjrə]
New Year	**nytt år** (n)	['nʏt ‚oːr]
Happy New Year!	**Godt nytt år!**	['gɔt nʏt ‚oːr]
Father Christmas	**Julenissen**	['jʉlə‚nisən]
Christmas	**Jul** (m/f)	['jʉl]
Merry Christmas!	**Gledelig jul!**	['gledəli 'jʉl]
Christmas tree	**juletre** (n)	['jʉlə‚trɛ]
fireworks (fireworks show)	**fyrverkeri** (n)	[‚fyrværkə'ri]
wedding	**bryllup** (n)	['brʏlʉp]
groom	**brudgom** (m)	['brʉd‚gɔm]
bride	**brud** (m/f)	['brʉd]
to invite (vt)	**å innby, å invitere**	[ɔ 'inby], [ɔ invi'terə]
invitation card	**innbydelse** (m)	[in'bydəlse]
guest	**gjest** (m)	['jɛst]
to visit (~ your parents, etc.)	**å besøke**	[ɔ be'søkə]
to meet the guests	**å hilse på gjestene**	[ɔ 'hilsə pɔ 'jɛstenə]
gift, present	**gave** (m/f)	['gavə]
to give (sth as present)	**å gi**	[ɔ 'ji]
to receive gifts	**å få gaver**	[ɔ 'fɔ 'gavər]
bouquet (of flowers)	**bukett** (m)	[bʉ'kɛt]
congratulations	**lykkønskning** (m/f)	['lʏk‚ønskniŋ]
to congratulate (vt)	**å gratulere**	[ɔ gratʉ'lerə]
greetings card	**gratulasjonskort** (n)	[gratʉla'ʂʉns‚koːt]
to send a postcard	**å sende postkort**	[ɔ 'sɛnə 'post‚koːt]
to get a postcard	**å få postkort**	[ɔ 'fɔ 'post‚koːt]

toast	skål (m/f)	['skɔl]
to offer (a drink, etc.)	å tilby	[ɔ 'tilby]
champagne	champagne (m)	[ʂamˈpanjə]

to enjoy oneself	å more seg	[ɔ 'mʊrə sæj]
merriment (gaiety)	munterhet (m)	['mʉntərˌhet]
joy (emotion)	glede (m/f)	['gledə]

| dance | dans (m) | ['dɑns] |
| to dance (vi, vt) | å danse | [ɔ 'dɑnsə] |

| waltz | vals (m) | ['vɑls] |
| tango | tango (m) | ['taŋgʊ] |

182. Funerals. Burial

cemetery	gravplass, kirkegård (m)	['gravˌplɑs], ['çirkəˌgɔːr]
grave, tomb	grav (m)	['grav]
cross	kors (n)	['kɔːʂ]
gravestone	gravstein (m)	['grafˌstæjn]
fence	gjerde (n)	['jærə]
chapel	kapell (n)	[kaˈpɛl]

death	død (m)	['dø]
to die (vi)	å dø	[ɔ 'dø]
the deceased	den avdøde	[den 'avˌdødə]
mourning	sorg (m/f)	['sɔr]

to bury (vt)	å begrave	[ɔ beˈgravə]
undertakers	begravelsesbyrå (n)	[beˈgravəlsəs byˌro]
funeral	begravelse (m)	[beˈgravəlsə]

wreath	krans (m)	['krɑns]
coffin	likkiste (m/f)	['likˌçistə]
hearse	likbil (m)	['likˌbil]
shroud	likklede (n)	['likˌkledə]

funeral procession	gravfølge (n)	['gravˌfølgə]
funerary urn	askeurne (m/f)	['askəˌʉːnə]
crematorium	krematorium (n)	[krɛmaˈtʊrium]

obituary	nekrolog (m)	[nekrʊˈlɔg]
to cry (weep)	å gråte	[ɔ 'groːtə]
to sob (vi)	å hulke	[ɔ 'hʉlkə]

183. War. Soldiers

platoon	tropp (m)	['trɔp]
company	kompani (n)	[kʊmpaˈni]
regiment	regiment (n)	[rɛgiˈmɛnt]
army	hær (m)	['hær]
division	divisjon (m)	[diviˈʂʊn]

section, squad	tropp (m)	['trɔp]
host (army)	hær (m)	['hær]

soldier	soldat (m)	[sʊl'dɑt]
officer	offiser (m)	[ɔfi'sɛr]

private	menig (m)	['meni]
sergeant	sersjant (m)	[sær'ʂɑnt]
lieutenant	løytnant (m)	['løjt,nɑnt]
captain	kaptein (m)	[kɑp'tæjn]
major	major (m)	[mɑ'jɔr]
colonel	oberst (m)	['ʊbɛʂt]
general	general (m)	[gene'rɑl]

sailor	sjømann (m)	['ʂø,mɑn]
captain	kaptein (m)	[kɑp'tæjn]
boatswain	båtsmann (m)	['bɔs,mɑn]

artilleryman	artillerist (m)	[,ɑ:ʈile'rist]
paratrooper	fallskjermjeger (m)	['fɑl,ʂærm 'jɛ:gər]
pilot	flyger, flyver (m)	['flygər], ['flyvər]
navigator	styrmann (m)	['styr,mɑn]
mechanic	mekaniker (m)	[me'kɑnikər]

pioneer (sapper)	pioner (m)	[piʊ'ner]
parachutist	fallskjermhopper (m)	['fɑl,ʂærm 'hɔpər]
reconnaissance scout	oppklaringssoldat (m)	['ɔp,klɑriŋ sʊl'dɑt]
sniper	skarpskytte (m)	['skɑrp,ʂytə]
patrol (group)	patrulje (m)	[pɑ'trʊljə]
to patrol (vt)	å patruljere	[ɔ patrʊ'ljerə]
sentry, guard	vakt (m)	['vɑkt]

warrior	kriger (m)	['krigər]
patriot	patriot (m)	[patri'ɔt]
hero	helt (m)	['hɛlt]
heroine	heltinne (m)	['hɛlt,inə]

traitor	forræder (m)	[fɔ'rædər]
to betray (vt)	å forråde	[ɔ fɔ'rɔ:də]
deserter	desertør (m)	[desæ:'ʈør]
to desert (vi)	å desertere	[ɔ desæ:'ʈerə]

mercenary	leiesoldat (m)	['læjəsʊl,dɑt]
recruit	rekrutt (m)	[re'krʊt]
volunteer	frivillig (m)	['fri,vili]

dead (n)	drept (m)	['drɛpt]
wounded (n)	såret (m)	['so:rə]
prisoner of war	fange (m)	['faŋə]

184. War. Military actions. Part 1

war	krig (m)	['krig]
to be at war	å være i krig	[ɔ 'værə i ,krig]

civil war	borgerkrig (m)	['borgər,krig]
treacherously (adv)	lumsk, forræderisk	['lumsk], [fo'ræderisk]
declaration of war	krigserklæring (m)	['krigs ær,klæriŋ]
to declare (~ war)	å erklære	[ɔ ær'klærə]
aggression	aggresjon (m)	[agre'ʂun]
to attack (invade)	å angripe	[ɔ 'an,gripə]
to invade (vt)	å invadere	[ɔ inva'derə]
invader	angriper (m)	['an,gripər]
conqueror	erobrer (m)	[ɛ'rubrər]
defence	forsvar (n)	['fu,ʂvar]
to defend (a country, etc.)	å forsvare	[ɔ fo'ʂvarə]
to defend (against ...)	å forsvare seg	[ɔ fo'ʂvarə sæj]
enemy	fiende (m)	['fiɛndə]
foe, adversary	motstander (m)	['mut,stanər]
enemy (as adj)	fiendtlig	['fjɛntli]
strategy	strategi (m)	[strate'gi]
tactics	taktikk (m)	[tak'tik]
order	ordre (m)	['ordrə]
command (order)	ordre, kommando (m/f)	['ordrə], ['ku'mandu]
to order (vt)	å beordre	[ɔ be'ordrə]
mission	oppdrag (m)	['opdrag]
secret (adj)	hemmelig	['hɛməli]
battle	batalje (m)	[ba'taljə]
battle	slag (n)	['ʂlag]
combat	kamp (m)	['kamp]
attack	angrep (n)	['an,grɛp]
charge (assault)	storm (m)	['storm]
to storm (vt)	å storme	[ɔ 'stormə]
siege (to be under ~)	beleiring (m/f)	[be'læjriŋ]
offensive (n)	offensiv (m), angrep (n)	['ofen,sif], ['an,grɛp]
to go on the offensive	å angripe	[ɔ 'an,gripə]
retreat	retrett (m)	[rɛ'trɛt]
to retreat (vi)	å retirere	[ɔ reti'rerə]
encirclement	omringing (m/f)	['om,riŋiŋ]
to encircle (vt)	å omringe	[ɔ 'om,riŋə]
bombing (by aircraft)	bombing (m/f)	['bumbiŋ]
to drop a bomb	å slippe bombe	[ɔ 'ʂlipə 'bumbə]
to bomb (vt)	å bombardere	[ɔ bumba:'derə]
explosion	eksplosjon (m)	[ɛksplu'ʂun]
shot	skudd (n)	['skud]
to fire (~ a shot)	å skyte av	[ɔ 'ʂytə a:]
firing (burst of ~)	skytning (m/f)	['ʂytniŋ]
to aim (to point a weapon)	å sikte på ...	[ɔ 'siktə pɔ ...]
to point (a gun)	å rette	[ɔ 'rɛtə]

to hit (the target)	å treffe	[ɔ 'trɛfə]
to sink (~ a ship)	å senke	[ɔ 'sɛnkə]
hole (in a ship)	hull (n)	['hʉl]
to founder, to sink (vi)	å synke	[ɔ 'sʏnkə]

front (war ~)	front (m)	['frɔnt]
evacuation	evakuering (m/f)	[ɛvɑkʉ'eriŋ]
to evacuate (vt)	å evakuere	[ɔ ɛvɑkʉ'erə]

trench	skyttergrav (m)	['ʂʏtə‚grɑv]
barbed wire	piggtråd (m)	['pig‚trɔd]
barrier (anti tank ~)	hinder (n), sperring (m/f)	['hindər], ['spɛriŋ]
watchtower	vakttårn (n)	['vɑkt‚tɔ:ŋ]

military hospital	militærsykehus (n)	[mili'tær‚sykə'hʉs]
to wound (vt)	å såre	[ɔ 'so:rə]
wound	sår (n)	['sɔr]
wounded (n)	såret (n)	['so:rə]
to be wounded	å bli såret	[ɔ 'bli 'so:rət]
serious (wound)	alvorlig	[al'vɔ:ḻi]

185. War. Military actions. Part 2

captivity	fangeskap (n)	['faŋə‚skɑp]
to take captive	å ta til fange	[ɔ 'ta til 'faŋə]
to be held captive	å være i fangeskap	[ɔ 'værə i 'faŋə‚skɑp]
to be taken captive	å bli tatt til fange	[ɔ 'bli tat til 'faŋə]

concentration camp	konsentrasjonsleir (m)	[kʉnsɛntrɑ'ʂʉns‚læjr]
prisoner of war	fange (m)	['faŋə]
to escape (vi)	å flykte	[ɔ 'flʏktə]

to betray (vt)	å forråde	[ɔ fɔ'rɔ:də]
betrayer	forræder (m)	[fɔ'rædər]
betrayal	forræderi (n)	[forædə'ri]

| to execute (by firing squad) | å henrette ved skyting | [ɔ 'hɛn‚rɛtə ve 'ʂytiŋ] |
| execution (by firing squad) | skyting (m/f) | ['ʂytiŋ] |

equipment (military gear)	mundering (m/f)	[mʉn'dɛriŋ]
shoulder board	skulderklaff (m)	['skʉldər‚klɑf]
gas mask	gassmaske (m/f)	['gas‚maskə]

field radio	feltradio (m)	['fɛlt‚rɑdiʉ]
cipher, code	chiffer (n)	['ʂifər]
secrecy	hemmeligholdelse (m)	['hɛmə‚liˌhɔləlsə]
password	passord (n)	['pas‚u:r]

land mine	mine (m/f)	['minə]
to mine (road, etc.)	å minelegge	[ɔ 'minə‚legə]
minefield	minefelt (n)	['minə‚fɛlt]

| air-raid warning | flyalarm (m) | ['fly a'lɑrm] |
| alarm (alert signal) | alarm (m) | [a'lɑrm] |

signal	signal (n)	[sɪŋ'nɑl]
signal flare	signalrakett (m)	[sɪŋ'nɑl rɑ'kɛt]
headquarters	stab (m)	['stɑb]
reconnaissance	oppklaring (m/f)	['ɔp‚klɑrɪŋ]
situation	situasjon (m)	[sɪtʉɑ'ʂʉn]
report	rapport (m)	[rɑ'pɔːt]
ambush	bakhold (n)	['bɑk‚hɔl]
reinforcement (army)	forsterkning (m/f)	[fɔ'ʂtærknɪŋ]
target	mål (n)	['mɔl]
training area	skytefelt (n)	['ʂytə‚fɛlt]
military exercise	manøverer (m pl)	[mɑ'nøvər]
panic	panikk (m)	[pɑ'nik]
devastation	ødeleggelse (m)	['ødə‚legəlsə]
destruction, ruins	ruiner (m pl)	[rʉ'inər]
to destroy (vt)	å ødelegge	[ɔ 'ødə‚legə]
to survive (vi, vt)	å overleve	[ɔ 'ɔvə‚levə]
to disarm (vt)	å avvæpne	[ɔ 'ɑv‚væpnə]
to handle (~ a gun)	å handtere	[ɔ hɑn'terə]
Attention!	Rett! | Gi-akt!	['rɛt], ['jiː'ɑkt]
At ease!	Hvil!	['vil]
feat, act of courage	bedrift (m)	[be'drift]
oath (vow)	ed (m)	['ɛd]
to swear (an oath)	å sverge	[ɔ 'sværgə]
decoration (medal, etc.)	belønning (m/f)	[be'lœnɪŋ]
to award (give a medal to)	å belønne	[ɔ be'lœnə]
medal	medalje (m)	[me'dɑljə]
order (e.g. ~ of Merit)	orden (m)	['ɔrdən]
victory	seier (m)	['sæjər]
defeat	nederlag (n)	['nedə‚lɑg]
armistice	våpenhvile (m)	['vɔpən‚vilə]
standard (battle flag)	fane (m)	['fɑnə]
glory (honour, fame)	berømmelse (m)	[be'rœməlsə]
parade	parade (m)	[pɑ'rɑdə]
to march (on parade)	å marsjere	[ɔ mɑ'ʂerə]

186. Weapons

weapons	våpen (n)	['vɔpən]
firearms	skytevåpen (n)	['ʂytə‚vɔpən]
cold weapons (knives, etc.)	blankvåpen (n)	['blɑnk‚vɔpən]
chemical weapons	kjemisk våpen (n)	['çemisk ‚vɔpən]
nuclear (adj)	kjerne-	['çæːɳə-]
nuclear weapons	kjernevåpen (n)	['çæːɳə‚vɔpən]
bomb	bombe (m)	['bʊmbə]

atomic bomb	atombombe (m)	[ɑ'tʉmˌbʉmbə]
pistol (gun)	pistol (m)	[pi'stʉl]
rifle	gevær (n)	[ge'vær]
submachine gun	maskinpistol (m)	[mɑ'ʂin piˌstʉl]
machine gun	maskingevær (n)	[mɑ'ʂin geˌvær]

muzzle	munning (m)	['mʉniŋ]
barrel	løp (n)	['løp]
calibre	kaliber (m/n)	[kɑ'libər]

trigger	avtrekker (m)	['ɑvˌtrɛkər]
sight (aiming device)	sikte (n)	['siktə]
magazine	magasin (n)	[mɑgɑ'sin]
butt (shoulder stock)	kolbe (m)	['kɔlbə]

hand grenade	håndgranat (m)	['hɔnˌgrɑ'nɑt]
explosive	sprengstoff (n)	['sprɛŋˌstɔf]

bullet	kule (m/f)	['kʉ:lə]
cartridge	patron (m)	[pɑ'trʉn]
charge	ladning (m)	['lɑdniŋ]
ammunition	ammunisjon (m)	[amʉni'ʂʉn]

bomber (aircraft)	bombefly (n)	['bʉmbəˌfly]
fighter	jagerfly (n)	['jagərˌfly]
helicopter	helikopter (n)	[heli'kɔptər]

anti-aircraft gun	luftvernkanon (m)	['lʉftvɛːɳ kɑ'nʉn]
tank	stridsvogn (m/f)	['stridsˌvɔŋn]
tank gun	kanon (m)	[kɑ'nʉn]

artillery	artilleri (n)	[ˌɑ:ʈile'ri]
gun (cannon, howitzer)	kanon (m)	[kɑ'nʉn]
to lay (a gun)	å rette	[ɔ 'rɛtə]

shell (projectile)	projektil (m)	[prʉek'til]
mortar bomb	granat (m/f)	[grɑ'nɑt]
mortar	granatkaster (m)	[grɑ'nɑtˌkɑstər]
splinter (shell fragment)	splint (m)	['splint]

submarine	ubåt (m)	['ʉːˌbɔt]
torpedo	torpedo (m)	[tʉr'pedʉ]
missile	rakett (m)	[rɑ'kɛt]

to load (gun)	å lade	[ɔ 'lɑdə]
to shoot (vi)	å skyte	[ɔ 'ʂytə]
to point at (the cannon)	å sikte på ...	[ɔ 'siktə pɔ ...]
bayonet	bajonett (m)	[bajo'nɛt]

rapier	kårde (m)	['ko:rdə]
sabre (e.g. cavalry ~)	sabel (m)	['sabəl]
spear (weapon)	spyd (n)	['spyd]
bow	bue (m)	['bʉːə]
arrow	pil (m/f)	['pil]
musket	muskett (m)	[mʉ'skɛt]
crossbow	armbrøst (m)	['ɑrmˌbrøst]

187. Ancient people

primitive (prehistoric)	ur-	['ʉr-]
prehistoric (adj)	forhistorisk	['fɔrhiˌstʉrisk]
ancient (~ civilization)	oldtidens, antikkens	['ɔlˌtidəns], [an'tikəns]
Stone Age	Steinalderen	['stæjnˌalderən]
Bronze Age	bronsealder (m)	['brɔnsəˌalder]
Ice Age	istid (m/f)	['isˌtid]
tribe	stamme (m)	['stamə]
cannibal	kannibal (m)	[kani'bal]
hunter	jeger (m)	['jɛːgər]
to hunt (vi, vt)	å jage	[ɔ 'jagə]
mammoth	mammut (m)	['mamʉt]
cave	grotte (m/f)	['grɔtə]
fire	ild (m)	['il]
campfire	bål (n)	['bɔl]
cave painting	helleristning (m/f)	['hɛləˌristniŋ]
tool (e.g. stone axe)	redskap (m/n)	['rɛdˌskap]
spear	spyd (n)	['spyd]
stone axe	steinøks (m/f)	['stæjnˌøks]
to be at war	å være i krig	[ɔ 'værə i ˌkrig]
to domesticate (vt)	å temme	[ɔ 'tɛmə]
idol	idol (n)	[i'dʉl]
to worship (vt)	å dyrke	[ɔ 'dyrkə]
superstition	overtro (m)	['ɔvəˌtrʉ]
rite	ritual (n)	[ritʉ'al]
evolution	evolusjon (m)	[ɛvɔlʉ'ʂʉn]
development	utvikling (m/f)	['ʉtˌvikliŋ]
disappearance (extinction)	forsvinning (m/f)	[fɔ'ʂvinin]
to adapt oneself	å tilpasse seg	[ɔ 'tilˌpasə sæj]
archaeology	arkeologi (m)	[ˌarkeʉlʉ'gi]
archaeologist	arkeolog (m)	[ˌarkeʉ'lɔg]
archaeological (adj)	arkeologisk	[ˌarkeʉ'lɔgisk]
excavation site	utgravingssted (n)	['ʉtˌgraviŋs ˌsted]
excavations	utgravinger (m/f pl)	['ʉtˌgraviŋər]
find (object)	funn (n)	['fʉn]
fragment	fragment (n)	[frag'mɛnt]

188. Middle Ages

people (ethnic group)	folk (n)	['fɔlk]
peoples	folk (n pl)	['fɔlk]
tribe	stamme (m)	['stamə]
tribes	stammer (m pl)	['stamər]
barbarians	barbarer (m pl)	[bar'barər]

Gauls	gallere (m pl)	['galere]
Goths	gotere (m pl)	['gɔterə]
Slavs	slavere (m pl)	['slavɛrə]
Vikings	vikinger (m pl)	['vikiŋər]

Romans	romere (m pl)	['rʊmerə]
Roman (adj)	romersk	['rʊmæʂk]

Byzantines	bysantiner (m pl)	[bysan'tinər]
Byzantium	Bysants	[by'sants]
Byzantine (adj)	bysantinsk	[bysan'tinsk]

emperor	keiser (m)	['kæjsər]
leader, chief (tribal ~)	høvding (m)	['høvdiŋ]
powerful (~ king)	mektig	['mɛkti]
king	konge (m)	['kuŋə]
ruler (sovereign)	hersker (m)	['hæʂkər]

knight	ridder (m)	['ridər]
feudal lord	føydalherre (m)	['føjdal͜hɛrə]
feudal (adj)	føydal	['føjdal]
vassal	vasall (m)	[va'sal]

duke	hertug (m)	['hæːʈʉg]
earl	greve (m)	['grevə]
baron	baron (m)	[ba'rʊn]
bishop	biskop (m)	['biskɔp]

armour	rustning (m/f)	['rʉstniŋ]
shield	skjold (n)	['ʂɔl]
sword	sverd (n)	['sværd]
visor	visir (n)	[vi'sir]
chainmail	ringbrynje (m/f)	['riŋ͜brynjə]

Crusade	korstog (n)	['kɔːʂ͜tɔg]
crusader	korsfarer (m)	['kɔːʂ͜farər]

territory	territorium (n)	[tɛri'tʊrium]
to attack (invade)	å angripe	[ɔ 'an͜gripə]
to conquer (vt)	å erobre	[ɔ ɛ'rʊbrə]
to occupy (invade)	å okkupere	[ɔ ɔkʉ'perə]

siege (to be under ~)	beleiring (m/f)	[be'læjriŋ]
besieged (adj)	beleiret	[be'læjrət]
to besiege (vt)	å beleire	[ɔ be'læjre]

inquisition	inkvisisjon (m)	[inkvisi'ʂʊn]
inquisitor	inkvisitor (m)	[inkvi'sitʊr]
torture	tortur (m)	[tɔːˈʈʉr]
cruel (adj)	brutal	[brʉ'tal]
heretic	kjetter (m)	['çɛtər]
heresy	kjetteri (n)	[çɛtə'ri]

seafaring	sjøfart (m)	['ʂøˌfaːʈ]
pirate	pirat, sjørøver (m)	['pi'rat], ['ʂøˌrøvər]
piracy	sjørøveri (n)	['ʂø røvɛ'ri]

boarding (attack)	entring (m/f)	['ɛntriŋ]
loot, booty	bytte (n)	['bʏtə]
treasure	skatter (m pl)	['skatər]

discovery	oppdagelse (m)	['ɔp,dagəlsə]
to discover (new land, etc.)	å oppdage	[ɔ 'ɔp,dagə]
expedition	ekspedisjon (m)	[ɛkspedi'ʂʉn]

musketeer	musketer (m)	[mʉskə'ter]
cardinal	kardinal (m)	[ka:ɖi'nal]
heraldry	heraldikk (m)	[heral'dik]
heraldic (adj)	heraldisk	[he'raldisk]

189. Leader. Chief. Authorities

king	konge (m)	['kʊŋə]
queen	dronning (m/f)	['drɔniŋ]
royal (adj)	kongelig	['kʊŋəli]
kingdom	kongerike (n)	['kʊŋə,rikə]

| prince | prins (m) | ['prins] |
| princess | prinsesse (m/f) | [prin'sɛsə] |

president	president (m)	[prɛsi'dɛnt]
vice-president	visepresident (m)	['visə prɛsi'dɛnt]
senator	senator (m)	[se'natʊr]

monarch	monark (m)	[mʊ'nark]
ruler (sovereign)	hersker (m)	['hæʂkər]
dictator	diktator (m)	[dik'tatʊr]
tyrant	tyrann (m)	[ty'ran]
magnate	magnat (m)	[maŋ'nat]

director	direktør (m)	[dirɛk'tør]
chief	sjef (m)	['ʂɛf]
manager (director)	forstander (m)	[fɔ'ʂtandər]
boss	boss (m)	['bɔs]
owner	eier (m)	['æjər]

leader	leder (m)	['ledər]
head (~ of delegation)	leder (m)	['ledər]
authorities	myndigheter (m pl)	['mʏndi,hetər]
superiors	overordnede (pl)	['ɔvər,ɔrdnedə]

governor	guvernør (m)	[gʉver'nør]
consul	konsul (m)	['kʊn,sʉl]
diplomat	diplomat (m)	[diplʉ'mat]
mayor	borgermester (m)	[bɔrgər'mɛstər]
sheriff	sheriff (m)	[ʂɛ'rif]

emperor	keiser (m)	['kæjsər]
tsar, czar	tsar (m)	['tsar]
pharaoh	farao (m)	['farɑu]
khan	khan (m)	['kɑn]

190. Road. Way. Directions

road	vei (m)	['væj]
way (direction)	vei (m)	['væj]

highway	motorvei (m)	['mɔtʊr‚væj]
motorway	hovedvei (m)	['hʊvəd‚væj]
trunk road	riksvei (m)	['riks‚væj]

main road	hovedvei (m)	['hʊvəd‚væj]
dirt road	bygdevei (m)	['bʏgdə‚væj]

pathway	sti (m)	['sti]
footpath (troddenpath)	sti (m)	['sti]

Where?	Hvor?	['vʊr]
Where (to)?	Hvorhen?	['vʊrhen]
From where?	Hvorfra?	['vʊrfrɑ]

direction (way)	retning (m/f)	['rɛtniŋ]
to point (~ the way)	å peke	[ɔ 'pekə]

to the left	til venstre	[til 'vɛnstrə]
to the right	til høyre	[til 'højrə]
straight ahead (adv)	rett frem	['rɛt frem]
back (e.g. to turn ~)	tilbake	[til'bɑkə]

bend, curve	kurve (m)	['kʉrvə]
to turn (e.g., ~ left)	å svinge	[ɔ 'sviŋə]
to make a U-turn	å ta en U-sving	[ɔ 'tɑ en 'ʉ:‚sviŋ]

to be visible (mountains, castle, etc.)	å være synlig	[ɔ 'værə 'sʏnli]
to appear (come into view)	å vise seg	[ɔ 'visə sæj]

stop, halt (e.g., during a trip)	stopp (m), hvile (m/f)	['stɔp], ['vilə]
to rest, to pause (vi)	å hvile	[ɔ 'vilə]
rest (pause)	hvile (m/f)	['vilə]

to lose one's way	å gå seg vill	[ɔ 'gɔ sæj 'vil]
to lead to ... (ab. road)	å føre til ...	[ɔ 'førə til ...]
to came out (e.g., on the highway)	å komme ut ...	[ɔ 'kɔmə ʉt ...]
stretch (of the road)	strekning (m)	['strɛkniŋ]

asphalt	asfalt (m)	['ɑs‚fɑlt]
kerb	fortauskant (m)	['fɔ:taʊs‚kɑnt]
ditch	veigrøft (m/f)	['væj‚grœft]
manhole	kum (m), kumlokk (n)	['kʉm], ['kʉm‚lɔk]
roadside (shoulder)	veikant (m)	['væj‚kɑnt]
pit, pothole	grop (m/f)	['grʊp]

to go (on foot)	å gå	[ɔ 'gɔ]
to overtake (vt)	å passere	[ɔ pɑ'serə]
step (footstep)	skritt (n)	['skrit]

on foot (adv)	til fots	[til 'fʊts]
to block (road)	å sperre	[ɔ 'spɛrə]
boom gate	bom (m)	['bʊm]
dead end	blindgate (m/f)	['blin,gatə]

191. Breaking the law. Criminals. Part 1

bandit	banditt (m)	[ban'dit]
crime	forbrytelse (m)	[fɔr'brytəlsə]
criminal (person)	forbryter (m)	[fɔr'brytər]

| thief | tyv (m) | ['tyv] |
| to steal (vi, vt) | å stjele | [ɔ 'stjelə] |

to kidnap (vt)	å kidnappe	[ɔ 'kid,nɛpə]
kidnapping	kidnapping (m)	['kid,nɛpiŋ]
kidnapper	kidnapper (m)	['kid,nɛpər]

| ransom | løsepenger (m pl) | ['løsə,pɛŋər] |
| to demand ransom | å kreve løsepenger | [ɔ 'krevə 'løsə,pɛŋər] |

to rob (vt)	å rane	[ɔ 'ranə]
robbery	ran (n)	['ran]
robber	raner (m)	['ranər]

to extort (vt)	å presse ut	[ɔ 'prɛsə ʉt]
extortionist	utpresser (m)	['ʉt,prɛsər]
extortion	utpressing (m/f)	['ʉt,prɛsiŋ]

to murder, to kill	å myrde	[ɔ 'my:ɖə]
murder	mord (n)	['mʊr]
murderer	morder (m)	['mʊrdər]

gunshot	skudd (n)	['skʉd]
to fire (~ a shot)	å skyte av	[ɔ 'ʂytə ɑ:]
to shoot to death	å skyte ned	[ɔ 'ʂytə ne]
to shoot (vi)	å skyte	[ɔ 'ʂytə]
shooting	skyting, skytning (m/f)	['ʂytiŋ], ['ʂytniŋ]

incident (fight, etc.)	hendelse (m)	['hɛndəlsə]
fight, brawl	slagsmål (n)	['slaks,mol]
Help!	Hjelp!	['jɛlp]
victim	offer (n)	['ɔfər]

to damage (vt)	å skade	[ɔ 'skadə]
damage	skade (m)	['skadə]
dead body, corpse	lik (n)	['lik]
grave (~ crime)	alvorlig	[al'vo:ļi]

to attack (vt)	å anfalle	[ɔ 'an,falə]
to beat (to hit)	å slå	[ɔ 'ʂlɔ]
to beat up	å klå opp	[ɔ 'klɔ ɔp]
to take (rob of sth)	å berøve	[ɔ be'røvə]
to stab to death	å stikke i hjel	[ɔ 'stikə i 'jel]

| to maim (vt) | å lemleste | [ɔ 'lem,lestə] |
| to wound (vt) | å såre | [ɔ 'sɔːrə] |

blackmail	utpressing (m/f)	['ʉt,prɛsiŋ]
to blackmail (vt)	å utpresse	[ɔ 'ʉt,prɛsə]
blackmailer	utpresser (m)	['ʉt,prɛsər]

protection racket	utpressing (m/f)	['ʉt,prɛsiŋ]
racketeer	utpresser (m)	['ʉt,prɛsər]
gangster	gangster (m)	['gɛŋstər]
mafia	mafia (m)	['mɑfiɑ]

pickpocket	lommetyv (m)	['lʉmə,tyv]
burglar	innbruddstyv (m)	['inbrʉds,tyv]
smuggling	smugling (m/f)	['smʉgliŋ]
smuggler	smugler (m)	['smʉglər]

forgery	forfalskning (m/f)	[fɔr'fɑlskniŋ]
to forge (counterfeit)	å forfalske	[ɔ fɔr'fɑlskə]
fake (forged)	falsk	['fɑlsk]

192. Breaking the law. Criminals. Part 2

rape	voldtekt (m)	['vɔl,tɛkt]
to rape (vt)	å voldta	[ɔ 'vɔl,tɑ]
rapist	voldtektsmann (m)	['vɔl,tɛkts mɑn]
maniac	maniker (m)	['mɑnikər]

prostitute (fem.)	prostituert (m)	[prʊstitʉ'eːt]
prostitution	prostitusjon (m)	[prʊstitʉ'ʂʉn]
pimp	hallik (m)	['hɑlik]

| drug addict | narkoman (m) | [nɑrkʊ'mɑn] |
| drug dealer | narkolanger (m) | ['nɑrkɔ,lɑŋər] |

to blow up (bomb)	å sprenge	[ɔ 'sprɛŋə]
explosion	eksplosjon (m)	[ɛksplʊ'ʂʉn]
to set fire	å sette fyr	[ɔ 'sɛtə ,fyr]
arsonist	brannstifter (m)	['brɑn,stiftər]

terrorism	terrorisme (m)	[tɛrʊ'rismə]
terrorist	terrorist (m)	[tɛrʊ'rist]
hostage	gissel (m)	['jisəl]

to swindle (deceive)	å bedra	[ɔ be'drɑ]
swindle, deception	bedrag (n)	[be'drɑg]
swindler	bedrager, svindler (m)	[be'drɑgər], ['svindlər]

to bribe (vt)	å bestikke	[ɔ be'stikə]
bribery	bestikkelse (m)	[be'stikəlsə]
bribe	bestikkelse (m)	[be'stikəlsə]

| poison | gift (m/f) | ['jift] |
| to poison (vt) | å forgifte | [ɔ fɔr'jiftə] |

to poison oneself	å forgifte seg selv	[ɔ forˈjiftə sæj sɛl]
suicide (act)	selvmord (n)	[ˈsɛlˌmʊr]
suicide (person)	selvmorder (m)	[ˈsɛlˌmʊrdər]

to threaten (vt)	å true	[ɔ ˈtrʉə]
threat	trussel (m)	[ˈtrʉsəl]
to make an attempt	å begå mordforsøk	[ɔ beˈgɔ ˈmʊrdfɔˌsøk]
attempt (attack)	mordforsøk (n)	[ˈmʊrdfɔˌsøk]

| to steal (a car) | å stjele | [ɔ ˈstjelə] |
| to hijack (a plane) | å kapre | [ɔ ˈkaprə] |

| revenge | hevn (m) | [ˈhɛvn] |
| to avenge (get revenge) | å hevne | [ɔ ˈhɛvnə] |

to torture (vt)	å torturere	[ɔ tɔːtʉˈrerə]
torture	tortur (m)	[tɔːˈtʉr]
to torment (vt)	å plage	[ɔ ˈplagə]

pirate	pirat, sjørøver (m)	[ˈpiˈrat], [ˈʂøˌrøvər]
hooligan	bølle (m)	[ˈbølə]
armed (adj)	bevæpnet	[beˈvæpnet]
violence	vold (m)	[ˈvɔl]
illegal (unlawful)	illegal	[ˈileˌgal]

| spying (espionage) | spionasje (m) | [spiʉˈnaʂə] |
| to spy (vi) | å spionere | [ɔ spiʉˈnerə] |

193. Police. Law. Part 1

| justice | justis (m), rettspleie (m/f) | [ˈjʉˈstis], [ˈrɛtsˌplæje] |
| court (see you in ~) | rettssal (m) | [ˈrɛtsˌsal] |

judge	dommer (m)	[ˈdɔmər]
jurors	lagrettemedlemmer (n pl)	[ˈlagˌrɛtə medleˈmer]
jury trial	lagrette, juryordning (m)	[ˈlagˌrɛtə], [ˈjʉriˌɔrdniŋ]
to judge, to try (vt)	å dømme	[ɔ ˈdœmə]

lawyer, barrister	advokat (m)	[advʉˈkat]
defendant	anklaget (m)	[ˈanˌklaget]
dock	anklagebenk (m)	[anˈklagəˌbɛnk]

| charge | anklage (m) | [ˈanˌklagə] |
| accused | anklagede (m) | [ˈanˌklagedə] |

| sentence | dom (m) | [ˈdɔm] |
| to sentence (vt) | å dømme | [ɔ ˈdœmə] |

guilty (culprit)	skyldige (m)	[ˈʂyldiə]
to punish (vt)	å straffe	[ɔ ˈstrafə]
punishment	straff, avstraffelse (m)	[ˈstraf], [ˈafˌstrafəlsə]

| fine (penalty) | bot (m/f) | [ˈbʊt] |
| life imprisonment | livsvarig fengsel (n) | [ˈlifsˌvari ˈfɛŋsəl] |

death penalty	dødsstraff (m/f)	['død̩strɑf]
electric chair	elektrisk stol (m)	[ɛ'lektrisk ̩stʊl]
gallows	galge (m)	['gɑlgə]
to execute (vt)	å henrette	[ɔ 'hɛn̩rɛtə]
execution	henrettelse (m)	['hɛn̩rɛtəlsə]
prison	fengsel (n)	['fɛŋsəl]
cell	celle (m)	['sɛlə]
escort (convoy)	eskorte (m)	[ɛs'kɔːtə]
prison officer	fangevokter (m)	['fɑŋə̩vɔktər]
prisoner	fange (m)	['fɑŋə]
handcuffs	håndjern (n pl)	['hɔn̩jæːn̩]
to handcuff (vt)	å sette håndjern	[ɔ 'sɛtə 'hɔn̩jæːn̩]
prison break	flykt (m/f)	['flʏkt]
to break out (vi)	å flykte, å rømme	[ɔ 'flʏktə], [ɔ 'rœmə]
to disappear (vi)	å forsvinne	[ɔ fɔ'ʂvinə]
to release (from prison)	å løslate	[ɔ 'løs̩lɑtə]
amnesty	amnesti (m)	[ɑmnɛ'sti]
police	politi (n)	[pʊli'ti]
police officer	politi (m)	[pʊli'ti]
police station	politistasjon (m)	[pʊli'ti̩stɑ'ʂʊn]
truncheon	gummikølle (m/f)	['gʉmi̩kølə]
megaphone (loudhailer)	megafon (m)	[megɑ'fʉn]
patrol car	patruljebil (m)	[pɑ'trʉljə̩bil]
siren	sirene (m/f)	[si'renə]
to turn on the siren	å slå på sirenen	[ɔ 'ʂlɔ pɔ si'renən]
siren call	sirene hyl (n)	[si'renə ̩hyl]
crime scene	åsted (n)	['ɔsted]
witness	vitne (n)	['vitnə]
freedom	frihet (m)	['fri̩het]
accomplice	medskyldig (m)	['mɛ̩sʏldi]
to flee (vi)	å flykte	[ɔ 'flʏktə]
trace (to leave a ~)	spor (n)	['spʊr]

194. Police. Law. Part 2

search (investigation)	ettersøking (m/f)	['ɛtə̩søkiŋ]
to look for ...	å søke etter ...	[ɔ 'søkə ̩ɛtər ...]
suspicion	mistanke (m)	['mis̩tɑnkə]
suspicious (e.g., ~ vehicle)	mistenkelig	[mis'tɛnkəli]
to stop (cause to halt)	å stoppe	[ɔ 'stɔpə]
to detain (keep in custody)	å anholde	[ɔ 'ɑn̩holə]
case (lawsuit)	sak (m/f)	['sɑk]
investigation	etterforskning (m/f)	['ɛtər̩fɔʂkniŋ]
detective	detektiv (m)	[detɛk'tiv]
investigator	etterforsker (m)	['ɛtər̩fɔʂkər]

hypothesis	versjon (m)	[væ'ʂʊn]
motive	motiv (n)	[mʊ'tiv]
interrogation	forhør (n)	[fɔr'hør]
to interrogate (vt)	å forhøre	[ɔ fɔr'hørə]
to question	å avhøre	[ɔ 'avˌhørə]
(~ neighbors, etc.)		
check (identity ~)	sjekking (m/f)	['ʂɛkiŋ]

round-up (raid)	rassia, razzia (m)	['rasia]
search (~ warrant)	ransakelse (m)	['ranˌsakəlsə]
chase (pursuit)	jakt (m/f)	['jakt]
to pursue, to chase	å forfølge	[ɔ fɔr'følə]
to track (a criminal)	å spore	[ɔ 'spʊrə]

arrest	arrest (m)	[a'rɛst]
to arrest (sb)	å arrestere	[ɔ arɛ'sterə]
to catch (thief, etc.)	å fange	[ɔ 'faŋə]
capture	pågripelse (m)	['pɔˌgripəlsə]

document	dokument (n)	[dɔkʉ'mɛnt]
proof (evidence)	bevis (n)	[be'vis]
to prove (vt)	å bevise	[ɔ be'visə]
footprint	fotspor (n)	['fʉtˌspʊr]
fingerprints	fingeravtrykk (n pl)	['fiŋərˌavtrʏk]
piece of evidence	bevis (n)	[be'vis]

alibi	alibi (n)	['alibi]
innocent (not guilty)	uskyldig	[ʉ'ʂyldi]
injustice	urettferdighet (m)	['ʉrɛtfærdiˌhet]
unjust, unfair (adj)	urettferdig	['ʉrɛtˌfærdi]

criminal (adj)	kriminell	[krimi'nɛl]
to confiscate (vt)	å konfiskere	[ɔ kʉnfi'skerə]
drug (illegal substance)	narkotika (m)	[nar'kɔtika]
weapon, gun	våpen (n)	['vɔpən]
to disarm (vt)	å avvæpne	[ɔ 'avˌvæpnə]
to order (command)	å befale	[ɔ be'falə]
to disappear (vi)	å forsvinne	[ɔ fɔ'ʂvinə]

law	lov (m)	['lɔv]
legal, lawful (adj)	lovlig	['lɔvli]
illegal, illicit (adj)	ulovlig	[ʉ'lɔvli]

responsibility (blame)	ansvar (n)	['anˌsvar]
responsible (adj)	ansvarlig	[ans'vaːˌli]

NATURE

The Earth. Part 1

space	rommet, kosmos (n)	['rʊmə], ['kɔsmɔs]
space (as adj)	rom-	['rʊm-]
outer space	ytre rom (n)	['ytrə ˌrʊm]
world	verden (m)	['værdən]
universe	univers (n)	[ʉni'væʂ]
galaxy	galakse (m)	[ga'lɑksə]
star	stjerne (m/f)	['stjæːŋə]
constellation	stjernebilde (n)	['stjæːŋəˌbildə]
planet	planet (m)	[plɑ'net]
satellite	satellitt (m)	[sɑtɛ'lit]
meteorite	meteoritt (m)	[meteʉ'rit]
comet	komet (m)	[kʊ'met]
asteroid	asteroide (n)	[ɑsterʉ'idə]
orbit	bane (m)	['bɑnə]
to revolve	å rotere	[ɔ rɔ'terə]
(~ around the Earth)		
atmosphere	atmosfære (m)	[ɑtmʊ'sfærə]
the Sun	Solen	['sʊlən]
solar system	solsystem (n)	['sʊl sY'stem]
solar eclipse	solformørkelse (m)	['sʊl fɔr'mœrkəlsə]
the Earth	Jorden	['juːrən]
the Moon	Månen	['moːnən]
Mars	Mars	['mɑʂ]
Venus	Venus	['venʉs]
Jupiter	Jupiter	['jʉpitər]
Saturn	Saturn	['sɑˌtuːŋ]
Mercury	Merkur	[mær'kʉr]
Uranus	Uranus	[ʉ'rɑnʉs]
Neptune	Neptun	[nɛp'tʉn]
Pluto	Pluto	['plʉtʊ]
Milky Way	Melkeveien	['mɛlkəˌvæjən]
Great Bear (Ursa Major)	den Store Bjørn	['dən 'stʊrə ˌbjœːɳ]
North Star	Nordstjernen, Polaris	['nuːrˌstjæːŋən], [pɔ'laris]
Martian	marsbeboer (m)	['mɑʂˌbebʉer]

extraterrestrial (n)	utenomjordisk vesen (n)	['ʉtenɔmˌjuːrdisk 'vesən]
alien	romvesen (n)	['rʊmˌvesən]
flying saucer	flygende tallerken (m)	['flygene tɑ'lærkən]

spaceship	romskip (n)	['rʊmˌşip]
space station	romstasjon (m)	['rʊmˌstɑ'şʊn]
blast-off	start (m), oppskyting (m/f)	['stɑːt], ['ɔpˌşytiŋ]

engine	motor (m)	['mɔtʊr]
nozzle	dyse (m)	['dysə]
fuel	brensel (n), drivstoff (n)	['brɛnsəl], ['drifˌstɔf]

cockpit, flight deck	cockpit (m), flydekk (n)	['kɔkpit], ['flyˌdɛk]
aerial	antenne (m)	[ɑn'tɛnə]
porthole	koøye (n)	['kʊˌøjə]
solar panel	solbatteri (n)	['sʊl batɛ'ri]
spacesuit	romdrakt (m/f)	['rʊmˌdrɑkt]

| weightlessness | vektløshet (m/f) | ['vɛktløsˌhet] |
| oxygen | oksygen (n) | ['ɔksy'gen] |

| docking (in space) | dokking (m/f) | ['dɔkiŋ] |
| to dock (vi, vt) | å dokke | [ɔ 'dɔkə] |

observatory	observatorium (n)	[ɔbsərvɑ'tʊrium]
telescope	teleskop (n)	[tele'skʊp]
to observe (vt)	å observere	[ɔ ɔbsɛr'verə]
to explore (vt)	å utforske	[ɔ 'ʉtˌføşkə]

196. The Earth

the Earth	Jorden	['juːrən]
the globe (the Earth)	jordklode (m)	['juːrˌklɔdə]
planet	planet (m)	[plɑ'net]

atmosphere	atmosfære (m)	[ɑtmʊ'sfærə]
geography	geografi (m)	[geʊgrɑ'fi]
nature	natur (m)	[nɑ'tʉr]

globe (table ~)	globus (m)	['glɔbʉs]
map	kart (n)	['kɑːt]
atlas	atlas (n)	['ɑtlɑs]

Europe	Europa	[ɛʉ'rʊpɑ]
Asia	Asia	['ɑsiɑ]
Africa	Afrika	['ɑfrikɑ]
Australia	Australia	[aʊ'straliɑ]

America	Amerika	[ɑ'merikɑ]
North America	Nord-Amerika	['nʊːr ɑ'merikɑ]
South America	Sør-Amerika	['sør ɑ'merikɑ]

| Antarctica | Antarktis | [ɑn'tɑrktis] |
| the Arctic | Arktis | ['ɑrktis] |

197. Cardinal directions

north	nord (n)	['nuːr]
to the north	mot nord	[muʉt 'nuːr]
in the north	i nord	[i 'nuːr]
northern (adj)	nordlig	['nuːrli]
south	syd, sør	['syd], ['sør]
to the south	mot sør	[muʉt 'sør]
in the south	i sør	[i 'sør]
southern (adj)	sydlig, sørlig	['sydli], ['søːʲi]
west	vest (m)	['vɛst]
to the west	mot vest	[muʉt 'vɛst]
in the west	i vest	[i 'vɛst]
western (adj)	vestlig, vest-	['vɛstli]
east	øst (m)	['øst]
to the east	mot øst	[muʉt 'øst]
in the east	i øst	[i 'øst]
eastern (adj)	østlig	['østli]

198. Sea. Ocean

sea	hav (n)	['hɑv]
ocean	verdenshav (n)	[værdəns'hɑv]
gulf (bay)	bukt (m/f)	['bʉkt]
straits	sund (n)	['sʉn]
land (solid ground)	fastland (n)	['fast,lɑn]
continent (mainland)	fastland, kontinent (n)	['fast,lɑn], [kʉnti'nɛnt]
island	øy (m/f)	['øj]
peninsula	halvøy (m/f)	['hɑl,øːj]
archipelago	skjærgård (m), arkipelag (n)	['şær,gɔr], [ɑrkipe'lɑg]
bay, cove	bukt (m/f)	['bʉkt]
harbour	havn (m/f)	['hɑvn]
lagoon	lagune (m)	[lɑ'gʉnə]
cape	nes (n), kapp (n)	['nes], ['kɑp]
atoll	atoll (m)	[ɑ'tɔl]
reef	rev (n)	['rev]
coral	korall (m)	[kʉ'rɑl]
coral reef	korallrev (n)	[kʉ'rɑl,rɛv]
deep (adj)	dyp	['dyp]
depth (deep water)	dybde (m)	['dʏbdə]
abyss	avgrunn (m)	['ɑv,grʉn]
trench (e.g. Mariana ~)	dyphavsgrop (m/f)	['dyphɑfs,grɔp]
current (Ocean ~)	strøm (m)	['strøm]
to surround (bathe)	å omgi	[ɔ 'ɔm,ji]
shore	kyst (m)	['çyst]

coast	kyst (m)	['çyst]
flow (flood tide)	flo (m/f)	['fluː]
ebb (ebb tide)	ebbe (m), fjære (m/f)	['ɛbə], ['fjæːrə]
shoal	sandbanke (m)	['san‚baŋkə]
bottom (~ of the sea)	bunn (m)	['bʉn]

wave	bølge (m)	['bølgə]
crest (~ of a wave)	bølgekam (m)	['bølgə‚kam]
spume (sea foam)	skum (n)	['skʉm]

storm (sea storm)	storm (m)	['stɔrm]
hurricane	orkan (m)	[ɔr'kan]
tsunami	tsunami (m)	[tsʉ'nami]
calm (dead ~)	stille (m/f)	['stilə]
quiet, calm (adj)	stille	['stilə]

| pole | pol (m) | ['pʉl] |
| polar (adj) | pol-, polar | ['pʉl-], [pʉ'lɑr] |

latitude	bredde, latitude (m)	['brɛdə], ['lɑti‚tʉdə]
longitude	lengde (m/f)	['leŋdə]
parallel	breddegrad (m)	['brɛdə‚grɑd]
equator	ekvator (m)	[ɛ'kvɑtʉr]

sky	himmel (m)	['himəl]
horizon	horisont (m)	[hʉri'sɔnt]
air	luft (f)	['lʉft]

lighthouse	fyr (n)	['fyr]
to dive (vi)	å dykke	[ɔ 'dʏkə]
to sink (ab. boat)	å synke	[ɔ 'sʏnkə]
treasure	skatter (m pl)	['skatər]

199. Seas & Oceans names

Atlantic Ocean	Atlanterhavet	[at'lantər‚have]
Indian Ocean	Indiahavet	['india‚have]
Pacific Ocean	Stillehavet	['stilə‚have]
Arctic Ocean	Polhavet	['pɔl‚have]

Black Sea	Svartehavet	['svɑːʈə‚have]
Red Sea	Rødehavet	['rødə‚have]
Yellow Sea	Gulehavet	['gʉlə‚have]
White Sea	Kvitsjøen, Hvitehavet	['kvit‚søːn], ['vit‚have]

Caspian Sea	Kaspihavet	['kaspi‚have]
Dead Sea	Dødehavet	['dødə'have]
Mediterranean Sea	Middelhavet	['midəl‚have]

| Aegean Sea | Egeerhavet | [ɛ'geːər‚have] |
| Adriatic Sea | Adriahavet | ['adria‚have] |

| Arabian Sea | Arabiahavet | [a'rabia‚have] |
| Sea of Japan | Japanhavet | ['japan‚have] |

| Bering Sea | Beringhavet | ['beriŋ,have] |
| South China Sea | Sør-Kina-havet | ['sør,çina 'have] |

Coral Sea	Korallhavet	[ku'ral,have]
Tasman Sea	Tasmanhavet	[tas'man,have]
Caribbean Sea	Karibhavet	[ka'rib,have]

| Barents Sea | Barentshavet | ['barɛns,have] |
| Kara Sea | Karahavet | ['kara,have] |

North Sea	Nordsjøen	['nuːr,sø:n]
Baltic Sea	Østersjøen	['østə,sø:n]
Norwegian Sea	Norskehavet	['nɔşkə,have]

200. Mountains

mountain	fjell (n)	['fjɛl]
mountain range	fjellkjede (m)	['fjɛl,çɛ:də]
mountain ridge	fjellrygg (m)	['fjɛl,rʏg]

summit, top	topp (m)	['tɔp]
peak	tind (m)	['tin]
foot (~ of the mountain)	fot (m)	['fut]
slope (mountainside)	skråning (m)	['skrɔniŋ]

volcano	vulkan (m)	[vʉl'kan]
active volcano	virksom vulkan (m)	['virksɔm vʉl'kan]
dormant volcano	utslukt vulkan (m)	['ʉt,şlʉkt vʉl'kan]

eruption	utbrudd (n)	['ʉt,brʉd]
crater	krater (n)	['kratər]
magma	magma (m/n)	['magma]
lava	lava (m)	['lava]
molten (~ lava)	glødende	['glødenə]

canyon	canyon (m)	['kanjən]
gorge	gjel (n), kløft (m)	['jel], ['klœft]
crevice	renne (m/f)	['rɛnə]
abyss (chasm)	avgrunn (m)	['av,grʉn]

pass, col	pass (n)	['pas]
plateau	platå (n)	[pla'to]
cliff	klippe (m)	['klipə]
hill	ås (m)	['ɔs]

glacier	bre, jøkel (m)	['bre], ['jøkəl]
waterfall	foss (m)	['fɔs]
geyser	geysir (m)	['gɛjsir]
lake	innsjø (m)	['in'şø]

plain	slette (m/f)	['şletə]
landscape	landskap (n)	['lan,skap]
echo	ekko (n)	['ɛkʉ]
alpinist	alpinist (m)	[alpi'nist]

rock climber	fjellklatrer (m)	['fjɛlˌklatrər]
to conquer (in climbing)	å erobre	[ɔ ɛ'rʊbrə]
climb (an easy ~)	bestigning (m/f)	[be'stigniŋ]

201. Mountains names

The Alps	Alpene	['alpenə]
Mont Blanc	Mont Blanc	[ˌmɔn'blan]
The Pyrenees	Pyreneene	[pyre'ne:ənə]

The Carpathians	Karpatene	[kar'patenə]
The Ural Mountains	Uralfjellene	[ʉ'ral ˌfjɛlenə]
The Caucasus Mountains	Kaukasus	['kaʉkasʉs]
Mount Elbrus	Elbrus	[ɛl'brʉs]

The Altai Mountains	Altaj	[al'taj]
The Tian Shan	Tien Shan	[ti'enˌsan]
The Pamirs	Pamir	[pa'mir]
The Himalayas	Himalaya	[hima'laja]
Mount Everest	Everest	['ɛve'rɛst]

| The Andes | Andes | ['andəs] |
| Mount Kilimanjaro | Kilimanjaro | [kiliman'dʂarʉ] |

202. Rivers

river	elv (m/f)	['ɛlv]
spring (natural source)	kilde (m)	['çildə]
riverbed (river channel)	elveleie (n)	['ɛlveˌlæje]
basin (river valley)	flodbasseng (n)	['flʉd baˌseŋ]
to flow into …	å munne ut …	[ɔ 'mʉnə ʉt …]

| tributary | bielv (m/f) | ['biˌelv] |
| bank (river ~) | bredd (m) | ['brɛd] |

current (stream)	strøm (m)	['strøm]
downstream (adv)	medstrøms	['meˌstrøms]
upstream (adv)	motstrøms	['mʊtˌstrøms]

inundation	oversvømmelse (m)	['ɔvəˌsvœməlsə]
flooding	flom (m)	['flɔm]
to overflow (vi)	å overflø	[ɔ 'ɔvərˌflø]
to flood (vt)	å oversvømme	[ɔ 'ɔveˌsvœmə]

| shallow (shoal) | grunne (m/f) | ['grʉnə] |
| rapids | stryk (m/n) | ['stryk] |

dam	demning (m)	['dɛmniŋ]
canal	kanal (m)	[ka'nal]
reservoir (artificial lake)	reservoar (n)	[resɛrvʉ'ar]
sluice, lock	sluse (m)	['ʂlʉsə]
water body (pond, etc.)	vannmasse (m)	['vanˌmasə]

swamp (marshland)	myr, sump (m)	['myr], ['sʉmp]
bog, marsh	hengemyr (m)	['hɛŋeˌmyr]
whirlpool	virvel (m)	['virvəl]

stream (brook)	bekk (m)	['bɛk]
drinking (ab. water)	drikke-	['drikə-]
fresh (~ water)	fersk-	['fæʂk-]

ice	is (m)	['is]
to freeze over (ab. river, etc.)	å fryse til	[ɔ 'frysə til]

203. Rivers names

Seine	Seine	['sɛːn]
Loire	Loire	[lu'aːr]

Thames	Themsen	['tɛmsən]
Rhine	Rhinen	['riːnən]
Danube	Donau	['dɔnaʊ]

Volga	Volga	['vɔlga]
Don	Don	['dɔn]
Lena	Lena	['lena]

Yellow River	Huang He	[ˌhwɑn'hɛ]
Yangtze	Yangtze	['jaŋtse]
Mekong	Mekong	[me'kɔŋ]
Ganges	Ganges	['gaŋes]

Nile River	Nilen	['nilən]
Congo River	Kongo	['kɔngʊ]
Okavango River	Okavango	[ʊka'vangʊ]
Zambezi River	Zambezi	[sam'besi]
Limpopo River	Limpopo	[limpɔ'pɔ]
Mississippi River	Mississippi	['misi'sipi]

204. Forest

forest, wood	skog (m)	['skʊg]
forest (as adj)	skog-	['skʊg-]

thick forest	tett skog (n)	['tɛt ˌskʊg]
grove	lund (m)	['lʉn]
forest clearing	glenne (m/f)	['glenə]

thicket	krattskog (m)	['krɑtˌskʊg]
scrubland	kratt (n)	['krɑt]

footpath (troddenpath)	sti (m)	['sti]
gully	ravine (m)	[rɑ'vinə]
tree	tre (n)	['trɛ]
leaf	blad (n)	['blɑ]

leaves (foliage)	løv (n)	['løv]
fall of leaves	løvfall (n)	['løv̩fɑl]
to fall (ab. leaves)	å falle	[ɔ 'fɑlə]
top (of the tree)	tretopp (m)	['trɛ̩tɔp]

branch	kvist, gren (m)	['kvist], ['gren]
bough	gren, grein (m/f)	['gren], ['græjn]
bud (on shrub, tree)	knopp (m)	['knɔp]
needle (of the pine tree)	nål (m/f)	['nɔl]
fir cone	kongle (m/f)	['kuŋlə]

tree hollow	trehull (n)	['trɛ̩hʉl]
nest	reir (n)	['ræjr]
burrow (animal hole)	hule (m/f)	['hʉlə]

trunk	stamme (m)	['stɑmə]
root	rot (m/f)	['rʉt]
bark	bark (m)	['bɑrk]
moss	mose (m)	['mʉsə]

to uproot (remove trees or tree stumps)	å rykke opp med roten	[ɔ 'rʏkə ɔp me 'rutən]
to chop down	å felle	[ɔ 'fɛlə]
to deforest (vt)	å hogge ned	[ɔ 'hɔgə 'ne]
tree stump	stubbe (m)	['stʉbə]

campfire	bål (n)	['bɔl]
forest fire	skogbrann (m)	['skʉg̩brɑn]
to extinguish (vt)	å slokke	[ɔ 'ʂløkə]

forest ranger	skogvokter (m)	['skʉg̩vɔktər]
protection	vern (n), beskyttelse (m)	['væ:ɳ], ['be'ʂytəlsə]
to protect (~ nature)	å beskytte	[ɔ be'ʂytə]
poacher	tyvskytter (m)	['tyf̩ʂytər]
steel trap	saks (m/f)	['sɑks]

| to gather, to pick (vt) | å plukke | [ɔ 'plʉkə] |
| to lose one's way | å gå seg vill | [ɔ 'gɔ sæj 'vil] |

205. Natural resources

natural resources	naturressurser (m pl)	[nɑ'tʉr rɛ'sʉʂər]
minerals	mineraler (n pl)	[minə'rɑlər]
deposits	forekomster (m pl)	['forə̩kɔmstər]
field (e.g. oilfield)	felt (m)	['fɛlt]

to mine (extract)	å utvinne	[ɔ 'ʉt̩vinə]
mining (extraction)	utvinning (m/f)	['ʉt̩viniŋ]
ore	malm (m)	['mɑlm]
mine (e.g. for coal)	gruve (m/f)	['grʉvə]
shaft (mine ~)	gruvesjakt (m/f)	['grʉvə̩ʂɑkt]
miner	gruvearbeider (m)	['grʉvə'ɑr̩bæjdər]
gas (natural ~)	gass (m)	['gɑs]
gas pipeline	gassledning (m)	['gɑs̩ledniŋ]

oil (petroleum)	olje (m)	['ɔljə]
oil pipeline	oljeledning (m)	['ɔljə‚ledniŋ]
oil well	oljebrønn (m)	['ɔljə‚brœn]
derrick (tower)	boretårn (n)	['boːrə‚tɔːn]
tanker	tankskip (n)	['tɑnk‚ʂip]
sand	sand (m)	['sɑn]
limestone	kalkstein (m)	['kɑlk‚stæjn]
gravel	grus (m)	['grʉs]
peat	torv (m/f)	['tɔrv]
clay	leir (n)	['læjr]
coal	kull (n)	['kʉl]
iron (ore)	jern (n)	['jæːɳ]
gold	gull (n)	['gʉl]
silver	sølv (n)	['søl]
nickel	nikkel (m)	['nikəl]
copper	kobber (n)	['kɔbər]
zinc	sink (m/n)	['sink]
manganese	mangan (m/n)	[mɑ'ŋɑn]
mercury	kvikksølv (n)	['kvik‚søl]
lead	bly (n)	['bly]
mineral	mineral (n)	[mine'rɑl]
crystal	krystall (m/n)	[kry'stɑl]
marble	marmor (m/n)	['mɑrmʉr]
uranium	uran (m/n)	[ʉ'rɑn]

The Earth. Part 2

weather	vær (n)	['væɾ]
weather forecast	værvarsel (n)	['væɾˌvɑʂəl]
temperature	temperatur (m)	[tɛmpəɾɑ'tʉɾ]
thermometer	termometer (n)	[tɛɾmʉ'me:təɾ]
barometer	barometer (n)	[bɑɾʉ'meːtəɾ]

humid (adj)	fuktig	['fʉkti]
humidity	fuktighet (m)	['fʉktiˌhet]
heat (extreme ~)	hete (m)	['he:tə]
hot (torrid)	het	['het]
it's hot	det er hett	[de ær 'het]

it's warm	det er varmt	[de ær 'vɑrmt]
warm (moderately hot)	varm	['vɑrm]

it's cold	det er kaldt	[de ær 'kɑlt]
cold (adj)	kald	['kɑl]

sun	sol (m/f)	['sʉl]
to shine (vi)	å skinne	[ɔ 'ʂinə]
sunny (day)	solrik	['sʉlˌrik]
to come up (vi)	å gå opp	[ɔ 'gɔ ɔp]
to set (vi)	å gå ned	[ɔ 'gɔ ne]

cloud	sky (m)	['ʂy]
cloudy (adj)	skyet	['ʂy:ət]
rain cloud	regnsky (m/f)	['ræjnˌʂy]
somber (gloomy)	mørk	['mœrk]

rain	regn (n)	['ræjn]
it's raining	det regner	[de 'ræjnəɾ]

rainy (~ day, weather)	regnværs-	['ræjnˌvæʂ-]
to drizzle (vi)	å småregne	[ɔ 'smo:ræjnə]

pouring rain	piskende regn (n)	['piskenə ˌræjn]
downpour	styrtregn (n)	['styːʈˌræjn]
heavy (e.g. ~ rain)	kraftig, sterk	['krɑfti], ['stærk]

puddle	vannpytt (m)	['vɑnˌpʏt]
to get wet (in rain)	å bli våt	[ɔ 'bli 'vɔt]

fog (mist)	tåke (m/f)	['to:kə]
foggy	tåke	['to:kə]
snow	snø (m)	['snø]
it's snowing	det snør	[de 'snør]

207. Severe weather. Natural disasters

thunderstorm	tordenvær (n)	['tʊrdən‚vær]
lightning (~ strike)	lyn (n)	['lyn]
to flash (vi)	å glimte	[ɔ 'glimtə]
thunder	torden (m)	['tʊrdən]
to thunder (vi)	å tordne	[ɔ 'tʊrdnə]
it's thundering	det tordner	[de 'tʊrdnər]
hail	hagle (m/f)	['hɑglə]
it's hailing	det hagler	[de 'hɑglər]
to flood (vt)	å oversvømme	[ɔ 'ɔve‚svœmə]
flood, inundation	oversvømmelse (m)	['ɔve‚svœməlsə]
earthquake	jordskjelv (n)	['ju:r‚sɛlv]
tremor, shoke	skjelv (n)	['sɛlv]
epicentre	episenter (n)	[ɛpi'sɛntər]
eruption	utbrudd (n)	['ʉt‚brʉd]
lava	lava (m)	['lɑvɑ]
twister	skypumpe (m/f)	['sy‚pʉmpə]
tornado	tornado (m)	[tʊ:'nɑdʉ]
typhoon	tyfon (m)	[ty'fʊn]
hurricane	orkan (m)	[ɔr'kɑn]
storm	storm (m)	['stɔrm]
tsunami	tsunami (m)	[tsʉ'nɑmi]
cyclone	syklon (m)	[sy'klun]
bad weather	uvær (n)	['ʉ:‚vær]
fire (accident)	brann (m)	['brɑn]
disaster	katastrofe (m)	[kɑtɑ'strɔfə]
meteorite	meteoritt (m)	[meteʉ'rit]
avalanche	lavine (m)	[lɑ'vinə]
snowslide	snøskred, snøras (n)	['snø‚skred], ['snørɑs]
blizzard	snøstorm (m)	['snø‚stɔrm]
snowstorm	snøstorm (m)	['snø‚stɔrm]

208. Noises. Sounds

silence (quiet)	stillhet (m/f)	['stil‚het]
sound	lyd (m)	['lyd]
noise	støy (m)	['støj]
to make noise	å støye	[ɔ 'støjə]
noisy (adj)	støyende	['støjənə]
loudly (to speak, etc.)	høylytt	['højlʏt]
loud (voice, etc.)	høy	['høj]
constant (e.g., ~ noise)	konstant	[kʊn'stɑnt]

188

cry, shout (n)	skrik (n)	['skrik]
to cry, to shout (vi)	å skrike	[ɔ 'skrikə]
whisper	hvisking (m/f)	['viskiŋ]
to whisper (vi, vt)	å hviske	[ɔ 'viskə]

| barking (dog's ~) | gjøing (m/f) | ['jøːiŋ] |
| to bark (vi) | å gjø | [ɔ 'jø] |

groan (of pain, etc.)	stønn (n)	['stœn]
to groan (vi)	å stønne	[ɔ 'stœnə]
cough	hoste (m)	['hʊstə]
to cough (vi)	å hoste	[ɔ 'hʊstə]

whistle	plystring (m/f)	['plʏstriŋ]
to whistle (vi)	å plystre	[ɔ 'plʏstrə]
knock (at the door)	knakk (m/n)	['knɑk]
to knock (on the door)	å knakke	[ɔ 'knɑkə]

| to crack (vi) | å knake | [ɔ 'knɑkə] |
| crack (cracking sound) | knak (n) | ['knɑk] |

siren	sirene (m/f)	[si'renə]
whistle (factory ~, etc.)	fløyte (m/f)	['fløjtə]
to whistle (ab. train)	å tute	[ɔ 'tʉtə]
honk (car horn sound)	tut (n)	['tʉt]
to honk (vi)	å tute	[ɔ 'tʉtə]

209. Winter

winter (n)	vinter (m)	['vintər]
winter (as adj)	vinter-	['vintər-]
in winter	om vinteren	[ɔm 'vinterən]

snow	snø (m)	['snø]
it's snowing	det snør	[de 'snør]
snowfall	snøfall (n)	['snø‚fal]
snowdrift	snødrive (m/f)	['snø‚drivə]

snowflake	snøfnugg (n)	['snø‚fnʉg]
snowball	snøball (m)	['snø‚bal]
snowman	snømann (m)	['snø‚man]
icicle	istapp (m)	['is‚tap]

December	desember (m)	[de'sɛmbər]
January	januar (m)	['janʉ‚ar]
February	februar (m)	['febrʉ‚ar]

| frost (severe ~, freezing cold) | frost (m/f) | ['frɔst] |
| frosty (weather, air) | frost | ['frɔst] |

below zero (adv)	under null	['ʉnər nʉl]
first frost	lett frost (m)	['let 'frɔst]
hoarfrost	rimfrost (m)	['rim‚frɔst]
cold (cold weather)	kulde (m/f)	['kʉlə]

189

it's cold	det er kaldt	[de ær 'kɑlt]
fur coat	pels (m), pelskåpe (m/f)	['pɛls], ['pɛls,ko:pǝ]
mittens	votter (m pl)	['vɔtǝr]

to fall ill	å bli syk	[ɔ 'bli 'syk]
cold (illness)	forkjølelse (m)	[fɔr'çœlǝlsǝ]
to catch a cold	å forkjøle seg	[ɔ fɔr'çœlǝ sæj]

ice	is (m)	['is]
black ice	islag (n)	['is,lɑg]
to freeze over (ab. river, etc.)	å fryse til	[ɔ 'frysǝ til]
ice floe	isflak (n)	['is,flɑk]

skis	ski (m/f pl)	['şi]
skier	skigåer (m)	['şi,goǝr]
to ski (vi)	å gå på ski	[ɔ 'gɔ pɔ 'şi]
to skate (vi)	å gå på skøyter	[ɔ 'gɔ pɔ 'şøjtǝr]

Fauna

predator	**rovdyr** (n)	['rɔvˌdyr]
tiger	**tiger** (m)	['tigər]
lion	**løve** (m/f)	['løve]
wolf	**ulv** (m)	['ʉlv]
fox	**rev** (m)	['rev]
jaguar	**jaguar** (m)	[jagʉ'ar]
leopard	**leopard** (m)	[leʉ'pard]
cheetah	**gepard** (m)	[ge'pard]
black panther	**panter** (m)	['pantər]
puma	**puma** (m)	['pʉma]
snow leopard	**snøleopard** (m)	['snø leʉ'pard]
lynx	**gaupe** (m/f)	['gaʉpə]
coyote	**coyote, prærieulv** (m)	[kɔ'jotə], ['præriˌʉlv]
jackal	**sjakal** (m)	[ʂa'kal]
hyena	**hyene** (m)	[hy'enə]

animal	**dyr** (n)	['dyr]
beast (animal)	**best, udyr** (n)	['bɛst], ['ʉˌdyr]
squirrel	**ekorn** (n)	['ɛkʉːɳ]
hedgehog	**pinnsvin** (n)	['pinˌsvin]
hare	**hare** (m)	['harə]
rabbit	**kanin** (m)	[ka'nin]
badger	**grevling** (m)	['grɛvliŋ]
raccoon	**vaskebjørn** (m)	['vaskəˌbjœːɳ]
hamster	**hamster** (m)	['hamstər]
marmot	**murmeldyr** (n)	['mʉrməlˌdyr]
mole	**muldvarp** (m)	['mʉlˌvarp]
mouse	**mus** (m/f)	['mʉs]
rat	**rotte** (m/f)	['rɔtə]
bat	**flaggermus** (m/f)	['flagərˌmʉs]
ermine	**røyskatt** (m)	['røjskat]
sable	**sobel** (m)	['sʉbəl]
marten	**mår** (m)	['mɔr]
weasel	**snømus** (m/f)	['snøˌmʉs]
mink	**mink** (m)	['mink]

beaver	bever (m)	['bevər]
otter	oter (m)	['ʊtər]
horse	hest (m)	['hɛst]
moose	elg (m)	['ɛlg]
deer	hjort (m)	['jɔːt]
camel	kamel (m)	[ka'mel]
bison	bison (m)	['bisɔn]
wisent	urokse (m)	['ʉrˌʊksə]
buffalo	bøffel (m)	['bøfəl]
zebra	sebra (m)	['sebra]
antelope	antilope (m)	[anti'lʊpə]
roe deer	rådyr (n)	['rɔˌdyr]
fallow deer	dåhjort, dådyr (n)	['dɔˌjɔːt], ['dɔˌdyr]
chamois	gemse (m)	['gɛmsə]
wild boar	villsvin (n)	['vilˌsvin]
whale	hval (m)	['val]
seal	sel (m)	['sel]
walrus	hvalross (m)	['valˌrɔs]
fur seal	pelssel (m)	['pɛlsˌsel]
dolphin	delfin (m)	[dɛl'fin]
bear	bjørn (m)	['bjœːn̩]
polar bear	isbjørn (m)	['isˌbjœːn̩]
panda	panda (m)	['panda]
monkey	ape (m/f)	['ape]
chimpanzee	sjimpanse (m)	[ʂim'pansə]
orangutan	orangutang (m)	[ʊ'raŋgʉˌtaŋ]
gorilla	gorilla (m)	[gɔ'rila]
macaque	makak (m)	[ma'kak]
gibbon	gibbon (m)	['gibʊn]
elephant	elefant (m)	[ɛle'fant]
rhinoceros	neshorn (n)	['nesˌhuːn̩]
giraffe	sjiraff (m)	[ʂi'raf]
hippopotamus	flodhest (m)	['flʊdˌhɛst]
kangaroo	kenguru (m)	['kɛŋgʉrʉ]
koala (bear)	koala (m)	[kʊ'ala]
mongoose	mangust, mungo (m)	[maŋ'gʉst], ['mʉŋgu]
chinchilla	chinchilla (m)	[ʂin'ʂila]
skunk	skunk (m)	['skunk]
porcupine	hulepinnsvin (n)	['hʉləˌpinsvin]

212. Domestic animals

cat	katt (m)	['kat]
tomcat	hannkatt (m)	['hanˌkat]
dog	hund (m)	['hʉn]

horse	hest (m)	['hɛst]
stallion (male horse)	hingst (m)	['hiŋst]
mare	hoppe, merr (m/f)	['hɔpə], ['mɛr]

cow	ku (f)	['kʉ]
bull	tyr (m)	['tyr]
ox	okse (m)	['ɔksə]

sheep (ewe)	sau (m)	['saʉ]
ram	vær, saubukk (m)	['vær], ['saʉ,bʉk]
goat	geit (m/f)	['jæjt]
billy goat, he-goat	geitebukk (m)	['jæjtə,bʉk]

| donkey | esel (n) | ['ɛsəl] |
| mule | muldyr (n) | ['mʉl,dyr] |

pig	svin (n)	['svin]
piglet	gris (m)	['gris]
rabbit	kanin (m)	[ka'nin]

| hen (chicken) | høne (m/f) | ['hønə] |
| cock | hane (m) | ['hanə] |

duck	and (m/f)	['an]
drake	andrik (m)	['andrik]
goose	gås (m/f)	['gɔs]

| tom turkey, gobbler | kalkunhane (m) | [kal'kʉn,hanə] |
| turkey (hen) | kalkunhøne (m/f) | [kal'kʉn,hønə] |

domestic animals	husdyr (n pl)	['hʉs,dyr]
tame (e.g. ~ hamster)	tam	['tam]
to tame (vt)	å temme	[ɔ 'tɛmə]
to breed (vt)	å avle, å oppdrette	[ɔ 'avlə], [ɔ 'ɔp,drɛtə]

farm	farm, gård (m)	['farm], ['gɔ:r]
poultry	fjærfe (n)	['fjær,fɛ]
cattle	kveg (n)	['kvɛg]
herd (cattle)	flokk, bøling (m)	['flɔk], ['bøliŋ]

stable	stall (m)	['stal]
pigsty	grisehus (n)	['grisə,hʉs]
cowshed	kufjøs (m/n)	['kʉ,fjøs]
rabbit hutch	kaninbur (n)	[ka'nin,bʉr]
hen house	hønsehus (n)	['hønsə,hʉs]

213. Dogs. Dog breeds

dog	hund (m)	['hʉn]
sheepdog	fårehund (m)	['fo:rə,hʉn]
German shepherd	schäferhund (m)	['ʂɛfær,hʉn]
poodle	puddel (m)	['pʉdəl]
dachshund	dachshund (m)	['daʂ,hʉn]
bulldog	bulldogg (m)	['bʉl,dɔg]

boxer	bokser (m)	['bɔksər]
mastiff	mastiff (m)	[mɑs'tif]
Rottweiler	rottweiler (m)	['rɔt͵væjlər]
Doberman	dobermann (m)	['dɔbermɑn]

basset	basset (m)	['basɛt]
bobtail	bobtail (m)	['bɔbtɛjl]
Dalmatian	dalmatiner (m)	[dɑlmɑ'tinər]
cocker spaniel	cocker spaniel (m)	['kɔker ͵spɑniəl]

| Newfoundland | newfoundlandshund (m) | [njʉ'fɑwnd͵lənds 'hʉn] |
| Saint Bernard | sankt bernhardshund (m) | [͵sɑnkt 'bɛːɳɑds͵hʉn] |

husky	husky (m)	['hɑski]
Chow Chow	chihuahua (m)	[t͡ʂi'vɑvɑ]
spitz	spisshund (m)	['spis͵hʉn]
pug	mops (m)	['mɔps]

214. Sounds made by animals

barking (n)	gjøing (m/f)	['jøːiŋ]
to bark (vi)	å gjø	[ɔ 'jø]
to miaow (vi)	å mjaue	[ɔ 'mjaʊe]
to purr (vi)	å spinne	[ɔ 'spinə]

to moo (vi)	å raute	[ɔ 'raʊtə]
to bellow (bull)	å belje, å brøle	[ɔ 'belje], [ɔ 'brøle]
to growl (vi)	å knurre	[ɔ 'knʉrə]

howl (n)	hyl (n)	['hyl]
to howl (vi)	å hyle	[ɔ 'hylə]
to whine (vi)	å klynke	[ɔ 'klʏnkə]

to bleat (sheep)	å breke	[ɔ 'brekə]
to oink, to grunt (pig)	å grynte	[ɔ 'grʏntə]
to squeal (vi)	å hvine	[ɔ 'vinə]

to croak (vi)	å kvekke	[ɔ 'kvɛkə]
to buzz (insect)	å surre	[ɔ 'sʉrə]
to chirp (crickets, grasshopper)	å gnisse	[ɔ 'gnisə]

215. Young animals

cub	unge (m)	['ʉŋə]
kitten	kattunge (m)	['kɑt͵ʉŋə]
baby mouse	museunge (m)	['mʉsə͵ʉŋə]
puppy	valp (m)	['vɑlp]

leveret	hareunge (m)	['hɑrə͵ʉŋə]
baby rabbit	kaninunge (m)	[kɑ'nin͵ʉŋə]
wolf cub	ulvunge (m)	['ʉlv͵ʉŋə]

fox cub	revevalp (m)	['revə,valp]
bear cub	bjørnunge (m)	['bjœ:ɲ,ʉŋə]
lion cub	løveunge (m)	['løvə,ʉŋə]
tiger cub	tigerunge (m)	['tigər,ʉŋə]
elephant calf	elefantunge (m)	[ɛle'fant,ʉŋə]
piglet	gris (m)	['gris]
calf (young cow, bull)	kalv (m)	['kalv]
kid (young goat)	kje (n), geitekilling (m)	['çe], ['jæjtə,çiliŋ]
lamb	lam (n)	['lam]
fawn (young deer)	hjortekalv (m)	['jɔ:ṭə,kalv]
young camel	kamelunge (m)	[ka'mel,ʉŋə]
snakelet (baby snake)	slangeyngel (m)	['ṣlaŋə,yŋəl]
froglet (baby frog)	froskeunge (m)	['frɔskə,ʉŋə]
baby bird	fugleunge (m)	['fʉlə,ʉŋə]
chick (of chicken)	kylling (m)	['çyliŋ]
duckling	andunge (m)	['an,ʉŋə]

216. Birds

bird	fugl (m)	['fʉl]
pigeon	due (m/f)	['dʉə]
sparrow	spurv (m)	['spʉrv]
tit (great tit)	kjøttmeis (m/f)	['çœt,mæjs]
magpie	skjære (m/f)	['ṣærə]
raven	ravn (m)	['ravn]
crow	kråke (m)	['kro:kə]
jackdaw	kaie (m/f)	['kajə]
rook	kornkråke (m/f)	['kʉ:ɲ,kro:kə]
duck	and (m/f)	['an]
goose	gås (m/f)	['gɔs]
pheasant	fasan (m)	[fa'san]
eagle	ørn (m/f)	['œ:ɳ]
hawk	hauk (m)	['haʊk]
falcon	falk (m)	['falk]
vulture	gribb (m)	['grib]
condor (Andean ~)	kondor (m)	[kʊn'dʊr]
swan	svane (m/f)	['svanə]
crane	trane (m/f)	['tranə]
stork	stork (m)	['stɔrk]
parrot	papegøye (m)	[pape'gøjə]
hummingbird	kolibri (m)	[kʊ'libri]
peacock	påfugl (m)	['pɔ,fʉl]
ostrich	struts (m)	['strʉts]
heron	hegre (m)	['hæjrə]

| flamingo | flamingo (m) | [fla'mingʊ] |
| pelican | pelikan (m) | [peli'kan] |

| nightingale | nattergal (m) | ['natər‚gal] |
| swallow | svale (m/f) | ['svalə] |

thrush	trost (m)	['trʊst]
song thrush	måltrost (m)	['moːl‚trʊst]
blackbird	svarttrost (m)	['svaː‚trʊst]

swift	tårnseiler (m), tårnsvale (m/f)	['tɔːn‚sæjlə], ['tɔːn‚svalə]
lark	lerke (m/f)	['lærkə]
quail	vaktel (m)	['vaktəl]

woodpecker	hakkespett (m)	['hakə‚spɛt]
cuckoo	gjøk, gauk (m)	['jøk], ['gaʊk]
owl	ugle (m/f)	['ʉglə]
eagle owl	hubro (m)	['hʉbrʊ]
wood grouse	storfugl (m)	['stʊr‚fʉl]
black grouse	orrfugl (m)	['ɔr‚fʉl]
partridge	rapphøne (m/f)	['rap‚hønə]

starling	stær (m)	['stær]
canary	kanarifugl (m)	[ka'nari‚fʉl]
hazel grouse	jerpe (m/f)	['jærpə]
chaffinch	bokfink (m)	['bʊk‚fink]
bullfinch	dompap (m)	['dʊmpap]

seagull	måke (m/f)	['moːkə]
albatross	albatross (m)	['alba‚trɔs]
penguin	pingvin (m)	[piŋ'vin]

217. Birds. Singing and sounds

to sing (vi)	å synge	[ɔ 'sʏŋə]
to call (animal, bird)	å skrike	[ɔ 'skrikə]
to crow (cock)	å gale	[ɔ 'galə]
cock-a-doodle-doo	kykeliky	[kykəli'kyː]

to cluck (hen)	å kakle	[ɔ 'kaklə]
to caw (crow call)	å krae	[ɔ 'kraə]
to quack (duck call)	å snadre, å rappe	[ɔ 'snadrə], [ɔ 'rapə]
to cheep (vi)	å pipe	[ɔ 'pipə]
to chirp, to twitter	å kvitre	[ɔ 'kvitrə]

218. Fish. Marine animals

bream	brasme (m/f)	['brasmə]
carp	karpe (m)	['karpə]
perch	åbor (m)	['obɔr]
catfish	malle (m)	['malə]
pike	gjedde (m/f)	['jɛdə]

salmon	laks (m)	['lɑks]
sturgeon	stør (m)	['stør]

herring	sild (m/f)	['sil]
Atlantic salmon	atlanterhavslaks (m)	[ɑt'lɑntərhɑfs͵lɑks]
mackerel	makrell (m)	[mɑ'krɛl]
flatfish	rødspette (m/f)	['rø͵spɛtə]

zander, pike perch	gjørs (m)	['jø:ʂ]
cod	torsk (m)	['tɔʂk]
tuna	tunfisk (m)	['tʉn͵fisk]
trout	ørret (m)	['øret]

eel	ål (m)	['ɔl]
electric ray	elektrisk rokke (m/f)	[ɛ'lektrisk ͵rɔkə]
moray eel	murene (m)	[mʉ'rɛnə]
piranha	piraja (m)	[pi'rɑjɑ]

shark	hai (m)	['hɑj]
dolphin	delfin (m)	[dɛl'fin]
whale	hval (m)	['vɑl]

crab	krabbe (m)	['krɑbə]
jellyfish	manet (m/f), meduse (m)	['mɑnet], [me'dʉsə]
octopus	blekksprut (m)	['blek͵sprʉt]

starfish	sjøstjerne (m/f)	['ʂø͵stjæ:ɳə]
sea urchin	sjøpinnsvin (n)	['ʂø:'pin͵svin]
seahorse	sjøhest (m)	['ʂø͵hɛst]

oyster	østers (m)	['østəʂ]
prawn	reke (m/f)	['rekə]
lobster	hummer (m)	['hʉmər]
spiny lobster	langust (m)	[lɑŋ'gʉst]

219. Amphibians. Reptiles

snake	slange (m)	['ʂlɑŋə]
venomous (snake)	giftig	['jifti]

viper	hoggorm, huggorm (m)	['hʉg͵ɔrm], ['hʉg͵ɔrm]
cobra	kobra (m)	['kʉbrɑ]
python	pyton (m)	['pytɔn]
boa	boaslange (m)	['bɔɑ͵slɑŋə]

grass snake	snok (m)	['snʉk]
rattle snake	klapperslange (m)	['klɑpə͵slɑŋə]
anaconda	anakonda (m)	[ɑnɑ'kɔndɑ]

lizard	øgle (m/f)	['øglə]
iguana	iguan (m)	[igʉ'ɑn]
monitor lizard	varan (n)	[vɑ'rɑn]
salamander	salamander (m)	[sɑlɑ'mɑndər]
chameleon	kameleon (m)	[kɑmələ'ʉn]

scorpion	skorpion (m)	[skɔrpi'ʊn]
turtle	skilpadde (m/f)	['ʂil,padə]
frog	frosk (m)	['frɔsk]
toad	padde (m/f)	['padə]
crocodile	krokodille (m)	[krʊkə'dilə]

220. Insects

insect	insekt (n)	['insɛkt]
butterfly	sommerfugl (m)	['sɔmər,fʉl]
ant	maur (m)	['maʊr]
fly	flue (m/f)	['flʉə]
mosquito	mygg (m)	['mʏg]
beetle	bille (m)	['bilə]

wasp	veps (m)	['vɛps]
bee	bie (m/f)	['biə]
bumblebee	humle (m/f)	['hʉmlə]
gadfly (botfly)	brems (m)	['brɛms]

| spider | edderkopp (m) | ['ɛdər,kɔp] |
| spider's web | edderkoppnett (n) | ['ɛdərkɔp,nɛt] |

dragonfly	øyenstikker (m)	['øjən,stikər]
grasshopper	gresshoppe (m/f)	['grɛs,hɔpə]
moth (night butterfly)	nattsvermer (m)	['nat,sværmər]

cockroach	kakerlakk (m)	[kakə'lak]
tick	flått, midd (m)	['flɔt], ['mid]
flea	loppe (f)	['lɔpə]
midge	knott (m)	['knɔt]

locust	vandgresshoppe (m/f)	['van 'grɛs,hɔpə]
snail	snegl (m)	['snæjl]
cricket	siriss (m)	['si,ris]
firefly	ildflue (m/f), lysbille (m)	['il,flʉə], ['lys,bilə]
ladybird	marihøne (m/f)	['mari,hønə]
cockchafer	oldenborre (f)	['ɔldən,bɔrə]

leech	igle (m/f)	['iglə]
caterpillar	sommerfugllarve (m/f)	['sɔmərfʉl,larvə]
earthworm	meitemark (m)	['mæjtə,mark]
larva	larve (m/f)	['larvə]

221. Animals. Body parts

beak	nebb (n)	['nɛb]
wings	vinger (m pl)	['viŋər]
foot (of the bird)	fot (m)	['fʊt]
feathers (plumage)	fjærdrakt (m/f)	['fjær,drakt]
feather	fjær (m/f)	['fjær]
crest	fjærtopp (m)	['fjæ:tɔp]

gills	gjeller (m/f pl)	['jɛlər]
spawn	rogn (m/f)	['rɔŋn]
larva	larve (m/f)	['lɑrvə]
fin	finne (m)	['finə]
scales (of fish, reptile)	skjell (n)	['ʂɛl]

fang (canine)	hoggtann (m/f)	['hɔg,tan]
paw (e.g. cat's ~)	pote (m)	['pɔːtə]
muzzle (snout)	snute (m/f)	['snʉtə]
mouth (cat's ~)	kjeft (m)	['çɛft]
tail	hale (m)	['hɑlə]
whiskers	værhår (n)	['vær,hɔr]

| hoof | klov, hov (m) | ['klɔv], ['hɔv] |
| horn | horn (n) | ['hʉːŋ] |

carapace	ryggskjold (n)	['rʏg,ʂɔl]
shell (mollusk ~)	skall (n)	['skɑl]
eggshell	eggeskall (n)	['ɛgə,skɑl]

| animal's hair (pelage) | pels (m) | ['pɛls] |
| pelt (hide) | skinn (n) | ['ʂin] |

222. Actions of animals

to fly (vi)	å fly	[ɔ 'fly]
to fly in circles	å kretse	[ɔ 'krɛtsə]
to fly away	å fly bort	[ɔ 'fly ,bʉːt]
to flap (~ the wings)	å flakse	[ɔ 'flɑksə]

to peck (vi)	å pikke	[ɔ 'pikə]
to sit on eggs	å ruge på eggene	[ɔ 'rʉgə pɔ 'ɛgenə]
to hatch out (vi)	å klekkes	[ɔ 'klekəs]
to build a nest	å bygge reir	[ɔ 'bʏgə 'ræir]

to slither, to crawl	å krype	[ɔ 'krypə]
to sting, to bite (insect)	å stikke	[ɔ 'stikə]
to bite (ab. animal)	å bite	[ɔ 'bitə]

to sniff (vt)	å snuse	[ɔ 'snʉsə]
to bark (vi)	å gjø	[ɔ 'jø]
to hiss (snake)	å hvese	[ɔ 'vesə]

| to scare (vt) | å skremme | [ɔ 'skrɛmə] |
| to attack (vt) | å overfalle | [ɔ 'ɔvər,falə] |

to gnaw (bone, etc.)	å gnage	[ɔ 'gnɑgə]
to scratch (with claws)	å klore	[ɔ 'klɔrə]
to hide (vi)	å gjemme seg	[ɔ 'jɛmə sæj]

to play (kittens, etc.)	å leke	[ɔ 'lekə]
to hunt (vi, vt)	å jage	[ɔ 'jagə]
to hibernate (vi)	å ligge i dvale	[ɔ 'ligə i 'dvalə]
to go extinct	å dø ut	[ɔ 'dø ʉt]

223. Animals. Habitats

habitat	habitat (n)	[hɑbi'tɑt]
migration	migrasjon (m)	[migrɑ'ʂʊn]
mountain	fjell (n)	['fjɛl]
reef	rev (n)	['rev]
cliff	klippe (m)	['klipə]
forest	skog (m)	['skʊg]
jungle	jungel (m)	['jʉŋəl]
savanna	savanne (m)	[sɑ'vɑnə]
tundra	tundra (m)	['tʉndrɑ]
steppe	steppe (m)	['stɛpə]
desert	ørken (m)	['œrkən]
oasis	oase (m)	[ʊ'ɑsə]
sea	hav (n)	['hɑv]
lake	innsjø (m)	['in'ʂø]
ocean	verdenshav (n)	[værdəns'hɑv]
swamp (marshland)	myr (m/f)	['myr]
freshwater (adj)	ferskvanns-	['fæʂkˌvɑns-]
pond	dam (m)	['dɑm]
river	elv (m/f)	['ɛlv]
den (bear's ~)	hi (n)	['hi]
nest	reir (n)	['ræjr]
tree hollow	trehull (n)	['trɛˌhʉl]
burrow (animal hole)	hule (m/f)	['hʉlə]
anthill	maurtue (m/f)	['mɑʊːˌtʉə]

224. Animal care

zoo	zoo, dyrepark (m)	['sʊː], [dyrə'pɑrk]
nature reserve	naturreservat (n)	[nɑ'tʉr resɛr'vɑt]
breeder (cattery, kennel, etc.)	oppdretter (m)	['ɔpˌdrɛtər]
open-air cage	voliere (m)	[vɔ'ljer]
cage	bur (n)	['bʉr]
kennel	kennel (m)	['kɛnəl]
dovecot	duehus (n)	['dʉəˌhʉs]
aquarium (fish tank)	akvarium (n)	[ɑ'kvɑrium]
dolphinarium	delfinarium (n)	[dɛlfi'nɑrium]
to breed (animals)	å avle, å oppdrette	[ɔ 'ɑvlə], [ɔ 'ɔpˌdrɛtə]
brood, litter	avkom (n)	['ɑvˌkɔm]
to tame (vt)	å temme	[ɔ 'tɛmə]
to train (animals)	å dressere	[ɔ drɛ'serə]
feed (fodder, etc.)	fôr (n)	['fʊr]
to feed (vt)	å utfore	[ɔ 'ʉtˌfɔrə]

pet shop	dyrebutikk (m)	['dyrəbʉ'tik]
muzzle (for dog)	munnkurv (m)	['mʉnˌkʉrv]
collar (e.g., dog ~)	halsbånd (n)	['halsˌbɔn]
name (of an animal)	navn (n)	['navn]
pedigree (dog's ~)	stamtavle (m/f)	['stamˌtavlə]

225. Animals. Miscellaneous

pack (wolves)	flokk (m)	['flɔk]
flock (birds)	flokk (m)	['flɔk]
shoal, school (fish)	stim (m/n)	['stim]
herd (horses)	flokk (m)	['flɔk]

| male (n) | hann (m) | ['han] |
| female (n) | hunn (m) | ['hʉn] |

hungry (adj)	sulten	['sʉltən]
wild (adj)	vill	['vil]
dangerous (adj)	farlig	['faːⱡi]

226. Horses

| horse | hest (m) | ['hɛst] |
| breed (race) | rase (m) | ['rasə] |

| foal | føll (n) | ['føl] |
| mare | hoppe, merr (m/f) | ['hɔpə], ['mɛr] |

mustang	mustang (m)	['mʉstaŋ]
pony	ponni (m)	['pɔni]
draught horse	kaldblodshest (m)	['kalblʉdsˌhɛst]

| mane | man (m/f) | ['man] |
| tail | hale (m) | ['halə] |

hoof	hov (m)	['hɔv]
horseshoe	hestesko (m)	['hɛstəˌskʉ]
to shoe (vt)	å sko	[ɔ 'skʉː]
blacksmith	smed, hovslager (m)	['sme], ['hɔfsˌlagər]

saddle	sal (m)	['sal]
stirrup	stigbøyle (m)	['stigˌbøjlə]
bridle	bissel (n)	['bisəl]
reins	tømmer (m pl)	['tœmər]
whip (for riding)	pisk (m)	['pisk]

rider	rytter (m)	['rʏtər]
to saddle up (vt)	å sale	[ɔ 'salə]
to mount a horse	å stige opp på hesten	[ɔ 'stiːə ɔp pɔ 'hɛstən]

| gallop | galopp (m) | [ga'lɔp] |
| to gallop (vi) | å galoppere | [ɔ galɔ'perə] |

trot (n)	trav (n)	['trɑv]
at a trot (adv)	i trav	[i 'trɑv]
to go at a trot	å trave	[ɔ 'trɑvə]

| racehorse | veddeløpshest (m) | ['vɛdeˌløps hɛst] |
| horse racing | hesteveddeløp (n) | ['hɛstə 'vedeˌløp] |

stable	stall (m)	['stɑl]
to feed (vt)	å utfore	[ɔ 'ʉtˌforə]
hay	høy (n)	['høj]
to water (animals)	å vanne	[ɔ 'vɑnə]
to wash (horse)	å børste	[ɔ 'bøʂtə]

horse-drawn cart	hestevogn (m/f)	['hɛstəˌvɔŋn]
to graze (vi)	å beite	[ɔ 'bæjtə]
to neigh (vi)	å vrinske, å knegge	[ɔ 'vrinskə], [ɔ 'knɛgə]
to kick (to buck)	å sparke bakut	[ɔ 'spɑrkə 'bɑkˌʉt]

Flora

tree	tre (n)	['trɛ]
deciduous (adj)	løv-	['løv-]
coniferous (adj)	bar-	['bɑr-]
evergreen (adj)	eviggrønt	['ɛvi,grœnt]
apple tree	epletre (n)	['ɛplə,trɛ]
pear tree	pæretre (n)	['pærə,trɛ]
sweet cherry tree	morelltre (n)	[mʊ'rɛl,trɛ]
sour cherry tree	kirsebærtre (n)	['çiʂəbær,trɛ]
plum tree	plommetre (n)	['plʊmə,trɛ]
birch	bjørk (f)	['bjœrk]
oak	eik (f)	['æjk]
linden tree	lind (m/f)	['lin]
aspen	osp (m/f)	['ɔsp]
maple	lønn (m/f)	['lœn]
spruce	gran (m/f)	['grɑn]
pine	furu (m/f)	['fʉrʉ]
larch	lerk (m)	['lærk]
fir tree	edelgran (m/f)	['ɛdəl,grɑn]
cedar	seder (m)	['sedər]
poplar	poppel (m)	['pɔpəl]
rowan	rogn (m/f)	['rɔŋn]
willow	pil (m/f)	['pil]
alder	or, older (m/f)	['ʊr], ['ɔldər]
beech	bøk (m)	['bøk]
elm	alm (m)	['ɑlm]
ash (tree)	ask (m/f)	['ɑsk]
chestnut	kastanjetre (n)	[kɑ'stɑnje,trɛ]
magnolia	magnolia (m)	[mɑŋ'nʉliɑ]
palm tree	palme (m)	['pɑlmə]
cypress	sypress (m)	[sʏ'prɛs]
mangrove	mangrove (m)	[mɑŋ'grʊvə]
baobab	apebrødtre (n)	['ɑpebrø,trɛ]
eucalyptus	eukalyptus (m)	[ɛvkɑ'lyptʉs]
sequoia	sequoia (m)	['sek,vɔjɑ]

bush	busk (m)	['bʉsk]
shrub	busk (m)	['bʉsk]

| grapevine | vinranke (m) | ['vin‚rɑnkə] |
| vineyard | vinmark (m/f) | ['vin‚mɑrk] |

raspberry bush	bringebærbusk (m)	['briŋə‚bær bʉsk]
blackcurrant bush	solbærbusk (m)	['sʉlbær‚bʉsk]
redcurrant bush	ripsbusk (m)	['rips‚bʉsk]
gooseberry bush	stikkelsbærbusk (m)	['stikəlsbær‚bʉsk]

acacia	akasie (m)	[ɑ'kɑsiə]
barberry	berberis (m)	['bærberis]
jasmine	sjasmin (m)	[ʂɑs'min]

juniper	einer (m)	['æjnər]
rosebush	rosenbusk (m)	['rʉsən‚bʉsk]
dog rose	steinnype (m/f)	['stæjn‚nypə]

229. Mushrooms

mushroom	sopp (m)	['sɔp]
edible mushroom	spiselig sopp (m)	['spisəli ‚sɔp]
poisonous mushroom	giftig sopp (m)	['jifti ‚sɔp]
cap	hatt (m)	['hɑt]
stipe	stilk (m)	['stilk]

cep, penny bun	steinsopp (m)	['stæjn‚sɔp]
orange-cap boletus	rødskrubb (m/n)	['rø‚skrʉb]
birch bolete	brunskrubb (m/n)	['brʉn‚skrʉb]
chanterelle	kantarell (m)	[kɑntɑ'rel]
russula	kremle (m/f)	['krɛmlə]

morel	morkel (m)	['mɔrkəl]
fly agaric	fluesopp (m)	['flʉə‚sɔp]
death cap	grønn fluesopp (m)	['grœn 'flʉə‚sɔp]

230. Fruits. Berries

fruit	frukt (m/f)	['frʉkt]
fruits	frukter (m/f pl)	['frʉktər]
apple	eple (n)	['ɛplə]
pear	pære (m/f)	['pærə]
plum	plomme (m/f)	['plʉmə]

strawberry (garden ~)	jordbær (n)	['juːr‚bær]
sour cherry	kirsebær (n)	['çiʂə‚bær]
sweet cherry	morell (m)	[mʉ'rɛl]
grape	drue (m)	['drʉə]

raspberry	bringebær (n)	['briŋə‚bær]
blackcurrant	solbær (n)	['sʉl‚bær]
redcurrant	rips (m)	['rips]
gooseberry	stikkelsbær (n)	['stikəls‚bær]
cranberry	tranebær (n)	['trɑnə‚bær]

orange	appelsin (m)	[apel'sin]
tangerine	mandarin (m)	[manda'rin]
pineapple	ananas (m)	['ananas]
banana	banan (m)	[ba'nan]
date	daddel (m)	['dadəl]

lemon	sitron (m)	[si'trʊn]
apricot	aprikos (m)	[apri'kʊs]
peach	fersken (m)	['fæʂkən]
kiwi	kiwi (m)	['kivi]
grapefruit	grapefrukt (m/f)	['grɛjp,frʉkt]

berry	bær (n)	['bær]
berries	bær (n pl)	['bær]
cowberry	tyttebær (n)	['tʏtə,bær]
wild strawberry	markjordbær (n)	['mark ju:r,bær]
bilberry	blåbær (n)	['blɔ,bær]

231. Flowers. Plants

| flower | blomst (m) | ['blɔmst] |
| bouquet (of flowers) | bukett (m) | [bʉ'kɛt] |

rose (flower)	rose (m/f)	['rʊsə]
tulip	tulipan (m)	[tʉli'pan]
carnation	nellik (m)	['nɛlik]
gladiolus	gladiolus (m)	[gladi'ɔlʉs]

cornflower	kornblomst (m)	['kʊ:ɳ,blɔmst]
harebell	blåklokke (m/f)	['blɔ,klɔkə]
dandelion	løvetann (m/f)	['løvə,tan]
camomile	kamille (m)	[ka'milə]

aloe	aloe (m)	['alʊe]
cactus	kaktus (m)	['kaktʉs]
rubber plant, ficus	gummiplante (m/f)	['gʉmi,plantə]

lily	lilje (m)	['liljə]
geranium	geranium (m)	[ge'ranium]
hyacinth	hyasint (m)	[hia'sint]

mimosa	mimose (m/f)	[mi'mɔsə]
narcissus	narsiss (m)	[na'ʂis]
nasturtium	blomkarse (m)	['blɔm,kaʂə]

orchid	orkidé (m)	[ɔrki'de]
peony	peon, pion (m)	[pe'ʊn], [pi'ʊn]
violet	fiol (m)	[fi'ʊl]

pansy	stemorsblomst (m)	['stemʉʂ,blɔmst]
forget-me-not	forglemmegei (m)	[fɔr'gleməˌjæj]
daisy	tusenfryd (m)	['tʉsən,fryd]
poppy	valmue (m)	['valmʉe]
hemp	hamp (m)	['hamp]

mint	mynte (m/f)	['mʏntə]
lily of the valley	liljekonvall (m)	['liljə kɔn'val]
snowdrop	snøklokke (m/f)	['snøˌklɔkə]

nettle	nesle (m/f)	['nɛslə]
sorrel	syre (m/f)	['syrə]
water lily	nøkkerose (m/f)	['nøkəˌruse]
fern	bregne (m/f)	['brɛjnə]
lichen	lav (m/n)	['lɑv]

conservatory (greenhouse)	drivhus (n)	['drivˌhʉs]
lawn	gressplen (m)	['grɛsˌplen]
flowerbed	blomsterbed (n)	['blɔmstərˌbed]

plant	plante (m/f), vekst (m)	['plantə], ['vɛkst]
grass	gras (n)	['grɑs]
blade of grass	grasstrå (n)	['grɑsˌstrɔ]

leaf	blad (n)	['blɑ]
petal	kronblad (n)	['krɔnˌblɑ]
stem	stilk (m)	['stilk]
tuber	rotknoll (m)	['rʉtˌknɔl]

| young plant (shoot) | spire (m/f) | ['spirə] |
| thorn | torn (m) | ['tʊːn] |

to blossom (vi)	å blomstre	[ɔ 'blɔmstrə]
to fade, to wither	å visne	[ɔ 'visnə]
smell (odour)	lukt (m/f)	['lʉkt]
to cut (flowers)	å skjære av	[ɔ 'ʂæːrə ɑ:]
to pick (a flower)	å plukke	[ɔ 'plʉkə]

232. Cereals, grains

grain	korn (n)	['kʊːn]
cereal crops	cerealer (n pl)	[sere'alər]
ear (of barley, etc.)	aks (n)	['ɑks]

wheat	hvete (m)	['vetə]
rye	rug (m)	['rʉg]
oats	havre (m)	['hɑvrə]

| millet | hirse (m) | ['hiʂə] |
| barley | bygg (m/n) | ['bʏg] |

maize	mais (m)	['mais]
rice	ris (m)	['ris]
buckwheat	bokhvete (m)	['bʊkˌvetə]

pea plant	ert (m/f)	['æːʈ]
kidney bean	bønne (m/f)	['bœnə]
soya	soya (m)	['sɔja]
lentil	linse (m/f)	['linsə]
beans (pulse crops)	bønner (m/f pl)	['bœnər]

233. Vegetables. Greens

| vegetables | grønnsaker (m pl) | ['grœn͵sakər] |
| greens | grønnsaker (m pl) | ['grœn͵sakər] |

tomato	tomat (m)	[tʊ'mat]
cucumber	agurk (m)	[a'gʉrk]
carrot	gulrot (m/f)	['gʉl͵rʊt]
potato	potet (m/f)	[pʊ'tet]
onion	løk (m)	['løk]
garlic	hvitløk (m)	['vit͵løk]

cabbage	kål (m)	['kɔl]
cauliflower	blomkål (m)	['blɔm͵kɔl]
Brussels sprouts	rosenkål (m)	['rʊsən͵kɔl]
broccoli	brokkoli (m)	['brɔkɔli]

beetroot	rødbete (m/f)	['rø͵betə]
aubergine	aubergine (m)	[ɔbɛr'şin]
marrow	squash (m)	['skvɔş]
pumpkin	gresskar (n)	['grɛskar]
turnip	nepe (m/f)	['nepə]

parsley	persille (m/f)	[pæ'şilə]
dill	dill (m)	['dil]
lettuce	salat (m)	[sa'lat]
celery	selleri (m/n)	[sɛle͵ri]
asparagus	asparges (m)	[a'sparşəs]
spinach	spinat (m)	[spi'nat]

pea	erter (m pl)	['æ:ʈər]
beans	bønner (m/f pl)	['bœnər]
maize	mais (m)	['mais]
kidney bean	bønne (m/f)	['bœnə]

pepper	pepper (m)	['pɛpər]
radish	reddik (m)	['rɛdik]
artichoke	artisjokk (m)	[͵aːʈi'şɔk]

REGIONAL GEOGRAPHY

234. Western Europe

Europe	Europa	[ɛʉˈrʊpɑ]
European Union	Den Europeiske Union	[den ɛʉrʊˈpɛiskə ʉniˈɔn]
European (n)	europeer (m)	[ɛʉrʊˈpeər]
European (adj)	europeisk	[ɛʉrʊˈpɛisk]

Austria	Østerrike	[ˈøstəˌrikə]
Austrian (masc.)	østerriker (m)	[ˈøstəˌrikər]
Austrian (fem.)	østerriksk kvinne (m/f)	[ˈøstəˌriksk ˌkvinə]
Austrian (adj)	østerriksk	[ˈøstəˌriksk]

Great Britain	Storbritannia	[ˈstʉr briˌtɑniɑ]
England	England	[ˈɛŋlɑn]
British (masc.)	brite (m)	[ˈbritə]
British (fem.)	brite (m)	[ˈbritə]
English, British (adj)	engelsk, britisk	[ˈɛŋelsk], [ˈbritisk]

Belgium	Belgia	[ˈbɛlgiɑ]
Belgian (masc.)	belgier (m)	[ˈbɛlgiər]
Belgian (fem.)	belgisk kvinne (m/f)	[ˈbɛlgisk ˌkvinə]
Belgian (adj)	belgisk	[ˈbɛlgisk]

Germany	Tyskland	[ˈtʏsklɑn]
German (masc.)	tysker (m)	[ˈtʏskər]
German (fem.)	tysk kvinne (m/f)	[ˈtʏsk ˌkvinə]
German (adj)	tysk	[ˈtʏsk]

Netherlands	Nederland	[ˈnedəˌlɑn]
Holland	Holland	[ˈhɔlɑn]
Dutch (masc.)	hollender (m)	[ˈhɔˌlendər]
Dutch (fem.)	hollandsk kvinne (m/f)	[ˈhɔˌlɑnsk ˌkvinə]
Dutch (adj)	hollandsk	[ˈhɔˌlɑnsk]

Greece	Hellas	[ˈhɛlɑs]
Greek (masc.)	greker (m)	[ˈgrekər]
Greek (fem.)	gresk kvinne (m/f)	[ˈgrɛsk ˌkvinə]
Greek (adj)	gresk	[ˈgrɛsk]

Denmark	Danmark	[ˈdɑnmɑrk]
Dane (masc.)	danske (m)	[ˈdɑnskə]
Dane (fem.)	dansk kvinne (m/f)	[ˈdɑnsk ˌkvinə]
Danish (adj)	dansk	[ˈdɑnsk]

Ireland	Irland	[ˈirlɑn]
Irish (masc.)	irlender, irlending (m)	[ˈirˌlenər], [ˈirˌleniŋ]
Irish (fem.)	irsk kvinne (m/f)	[ˈiːʂk ˌkvinə]
Irish (adj)	irsk	[ˈiːʂk]

Iceland	Island	['islɑn]
Icelander (masc.)	islending (m)	['isˌleniŋ]
Icelander (fem.)	islandsk kvinne (m/f)	['isˌlɑnsk ˌkvinə]
Icelandic (adj)	islandsk	['isˌlɑnsk]

Spain	Spania	['spɑniɑ]
Spaniard (masc.)	spanier (m)	['spɑniər]
Spaniard (fem.)	spansk kvinne (m/f)	['spɑnsk ˌkvinə]
Spanish (adj)	spansk	['spɑnsk]

Italy	Italia	[i'tɑliɑ]
Italian (masc.)	italiener (m)	[itɑ'ljɛnər]
Italian (fem.)	italiensk kvinne (m/f)	[itɑ'ljɛnsk ˌkvinə]
Italian (adj)	italiensk	[itɑ'ljɛnsk]

Cyprus	Kypros	['kʏprʊs]
Cypriot (masc.)	kypriot (m)	[kʏpri'ʊt]
Cypriot (fem.)	kypriotisk kvinne (m/f)	[kʏpri'ʊtisk ˌkvinə]
Cypriot (adj)	kypriotisk	[kʏpri'ʊtisk]

Malta	Malta	['mɑltɑ]
Maltese (masc.)	malteser (m)	[mɑl'tesər]
Maltese (fem.)	maltesisk kvinne (m/f)	[mɑl'tesisk ˌkvinə]
Maltese (adj)	maltesisk	[mɑl'tesisk]

Norway	Norge	['nɔrgə]
Norwegian (masc.)	nordmann (m)	['nʊːrmɑn]
Norwegian (fem.)	norsk kvinne (m/f)	['nɔʂk ˌkvinə]
Norwegian (adj)	norsk	['nɔʂk]

Portugal	Portugal	[pɔːtʉ'gɑl]
Portuguese (masc.)	portugiser (m)	[pɔːtʉ'gisər]
Portuguese (fem.)	portugisisk kvinne (m/f)	[pɔːtʉ'gisisk ˌkvinə]
Portuguese (adj)	portugisisk	[pɔːtʉ'gisisk]

Finland	Finland	['finlɑn]
Finn (masc.)	finne (m)	['finə]
Finn (fem.)	finsk kvinne (m/f)	['finsk ˌkvinə]
Finnish (adj)	finsk	['finsk]

France	Frankrike	['frɑnkrikə]
French (masc.)	franskmann (m)	['frɑnskˌmɑn]
French (fem.)	fransk kvinne (m/f)	['frɑnsk ˌkvinə]
French (adj)	fransk	['frɑnsk]

Sweden	Sverige	['sværiə]
Swede (masc.)	svenske (m)	['svɛnskə]
Swede (fem.)	svensk kvinne (m/f)	['svɛnsk ˌkvinə]
Swedish (adj)	svensk	['svɛnsk]

Switzerland	Sveits	['svæjts]
Swiss (masc.)	sveitser (m)	['svæjtsər]
Swiss (fem.)	sveitsisk kvinne (m/f)	['svæjtsisk ˌkvinə]
Swiss (adj)	sveitsisk	['svæjtsisk]
Scotland	Skottland	['skɔtlɑn]
Scottish (masc.)	skotte (m)	['skɔtə]

| Scottish (fem.) | skotsk kvinne (m/f) | ['skɔtsk ˌkvinə] |
| Scottish (adj) | skotsk | ['skɔtsk] |

Vatican City	Vatikanet	['vɑtiˌkɑnə]
Liechtenstein	Liechtenstein	['lihtɛnʂtæjn]
Luxembourg	Luxembourg	['lʉksɛmˌbʉrg]
Monaco	Monaco	[mʊ'nɑkʊ]

235. Central and Eastern Europe

Albania	Albania	[al'bɑniɑ]
Albanian (masc.)	albaner (m)	[al'bɑnər]
Albanian (fem.)	albansk kvinne (m)	[al'bɑnsk ˌkvinə]
Albanian (adj)	albansk	[al'bɑnsk]

Bulgaria	Bulgaria	[bʉl'gɑriɑ]
Bulgarian (masc.)	bulgarer (m)	[bʉl'gɑrər]
Bulgarian (fem.)	bulgarsk kvinne (m/f)	[bʉl'gɑʂk ˌkvinə]
Bulgarian (adj)	bulgarsk	[bʉl'gɑʂk]

Hungary	Ungarn	['ʉŋɑːɳ]
Hungarian (masc.)	ungarer (m)	['ʉŋɑrər]
Hungarian (fem.)	ungarsk kvinne (m/f)	['ʉŋɑʂk ˌkvinə]
Hungarian (adj)	ungarsk	['ʉŋɑʂk]

Latvia	Latvia	['lɑtviɑ]
Latvian (masc.)	latvier (m)	['lɑtviər]
Latvian (fem.)	latvisk kvinne (m/f)	['lɑtvisk ˌkvinə]
Latvian (adj)	latvisk	['lɑtvisk]

Lithuania	Litauen	['liˌtɑʊən]
Lithuanian (masc.)	litauer (m)	['liˌtɑʊər]
Lithuanian (fem.)	litauisk kvinne (m/f)	['liˌtɑʊisk ˌkvinə]
Lithuanian (adj)	litauisk	['liˌtɑʊisk]

Poland	Polen	['pʊlen]
Pole (masc.)	polakk (m)	[pʊ'lɑk]
Pole (fem.)	polsk kvinne (m/f)	['pʊlsk ˌkvinə]
Polish (adj)	polsk	['pʊlsk]

Romania	Romania	[rʊ'mɑniɑ]
Romanian (masc.)	rumener (m)	[rʉ'menər]
Romanian (fem.)	rumensk kvinne (m/f)	[rʉ'mɛnsk ˌkvinə]
Romanian (adj)	rumensk	[rʉ'mɛnsk]

Serbia	Serbia	['særbiɑ]
Serbian (masc.)	serber (m)	['særbər]
Serbian (fem.)	serbisk kvinne (m/f)	['særbisk ˌkvinə]
Serbian (adj)	serbisk	['særbisk]

Slovakia	Slovakia	[ʂlʊ'vɑkiɑ]
Slovak (masc.)	slovak (m)	[ʂlʊ'vɑk]
Slovak (fem.)	slovakisk kvinne (m/f)	[ʂlʊ'vɑkisk ˌkvinə]
Slovak (adj)	slovakisk	[ʂlʊ'vɑkisk]

Croatia	Kroatia	[kru'atia]
Croatian (masc.)	kroat (m)	[kru'at]
Croatian (fem.)	kroatisk kvinne (m/f)	[kru'atisk ‚kvinə]
Croatian (adj)	kroatisk	[kru'atisk]

Czech Republic	Tsjekkia	['tsɛkija]
Czech (masc.)	tsjekker (m)	['tsɛkər]
Czech (fem.)	tsjekkisk kvinne (m/f)	['tsɛkisk ‚kvinə]
Czech (adj)	tsjekkisk	['tsɛkisk]

Estonia	Estland	['ɛstlɑn]
Estonian (masc.)	estlender (m)	['ɛst‚lendər]
Estonian (fem.)	estisk kvinne (m/f)	['ɛstisk ‚kvinə]
Estonian (adj)	estisk	['ɛstisk]

Bosnia and Herzegovina	Bosnia-Hercegovina	['bɔsnia hersegɔ‚vina]
North Macedonia	Makedonia	[make'dɔnia]
Slovenia	Slovenia	[ṣlu'venia]
Montenegro	Montenegro	['mɔntə‚nɛgru]

236. Former USSR countries

Azerbaijan	Aserbajdsjan	[aserbajd'ṣan]
Azerbaijani (masc.)	aserbajdsjaner (m)	[aserbajd'ṣanər]
Azerbaijani (fem.)	aserbajdsjansk kvinne (m)	[aserbajd'ṣansk ‚kvinə]
Azerbaijani, Azeri (adj)	aserbajdsjansk	[aserbajd'ṣansk]

Armenia	Armenia	[ar'menia]
Armenian (masc.)	armener (m)	[ar'menər]
Armenian (fem.)	armensk kvinne (m)	[ar'mensk ‚kvinə]
Armenian (adj)	armensk	[ar'mensk]

Belarus	Hviterussland	['vitə‚ruslan]
Belarusian (masc.)	hviterusser (m)	['vitə‚rusər]
Belarusian (fem.)	hviterussisk kvinne (m/f)	['vitə‚rusisk ‚kvinə]
Belarusian (adj)	hviterussisk	['vitə‚rusisk]

Georgia	Georgia	[ge'ɔrgia]
Georgian (masc.)	georgier (m)	[ge'ɔrgiər]
Georgian (fem.)	georgisk kvinne (m/f)	[ge'ɔrgisk ‚kvinə]
Georgian (adj)	georgisk	[ge'ɔrgisk]

Kazakhstan	Kasakhstan	[ka'sak‚stan]
Kazakh (masc.)	kasakh (m)	[ka'sak]
Kazakh (fem.)	kasakhisk kvinne (m/f)	[ka'sakisk ‚kvinə]
Kazakh (adj)	kasakhisk	[ka'sakisk]

Kirghizia	Kirgisistan	[kir'gisi‚stan]
Kirghiz (masc.)	kirgiser (m)	[kir'gisər]
Kirghiz (fem.)	kirgisisk kvinne (m/f)	[kir'gisisk ‚kvinə]
Kirghiz (adj)	kirgisisk	[kir'gisisk]

| Moldova, Moldavia | Moldova | [mɔl'dova] |
| Moldavian (masc.) | moldover (m) | [mɔl'dovər] |

Moldavian (fem.)	moldovsk kvinne (m/f)	[mɔl'dɔvsk ˌkvinə]
Moldavian (adj)	moldovsk	[mɔl'dɔvsk]
Russia	Russland	['rʉslɑn]
Russian (masc.)	russer (m)	['rʉsər]
Russian (fem.)	russisk kvinne (m/f)	['rʉsisk ˌkvinə]
Russian (adj)	russisk	['rʉsisk]
Tajikistan	Tadsjikistan	[tɑ'dʂikiˌstɑn]
Tajik (masc.)	tadsjik, tadsjiker (m)	[tɑ'dʂik], [tɑ'dʂikər]
Tajik (fem.)	tadsjikisk kvinne (m/f)	[tɑ'dʂikisk ˌkvinə]
Tajik (adj)	tadsjikisk	[tɑ'dʂikisk]
Turkmenistan	Turkmenistan	[tʉrk'meniˌstɑn]
Turkmen (masc.)	turkmen (m)	[tʉrk'men]
Turkmen (fem.)	turkmensk kvinne (m/f)	[tʉrk'mensk ˌkvinə]
Turkmenian (adj)	turkmensk	[tʉrk'mensk]
Uzbekistan	Usbekistan	[ʉs'bekiˌstɑn]
Uzbek (masc.)	usbek, usbeker (m)	[ʉs'bek], [ʉs'bekər]
Uzbek (fem.)	usbekisk kvinne (m/f)	[ʉs'bekisk ˌkvinə]
Uzbek (adj)	usbekisk	[ʉs'bekisk]
Ukraine	Ukraina	[ʉkrɑ'inɑ]
Ukrainian (masc.)	ukrainer (m)	[ʉkrɑ'inər]
Ukrainian (fem.)	ukrainsk kvinne (m/f)	[ʉkrɑ'insk ˌkvinə]
Ukrainian (adj)	ukrainsk	[ʉkrɑ'insk]

237. Asia

Asia	Asia	['ɑsiɑ]
Asian (adj)	asiatisk	[ɑsi'ɑtisk]
Vietnam	Vietnam	['vjɛtnɑm]
Vietnamese (masc.)	vietnameser (m)	[vjɛtnɑ'mesər]
Vietnamese (fem.)	vietnamesisk kvinne (m/f)	[vjɛtnɑ'mesisk ˌkvinə]
Vietnamese (adj)	vietnamesisk	[vjɛtnɑ'mesisk]
India	India	['indiɑ]
Indian (masc.)	inder (m)	['indər]
Indian (fem.)	indisk kvinne (m/f)	['indisk ˌkvinə]
Indian (adj)	indisk	['indisk]
Israel	Israel	['isrɑel]
Israeli (masc.)	israeler (m)	[isrɑ'elər]
Israeli (fem.)	israelsk kvinne (m/f)	[isrɑ'elsk ˌkvinə]
Israeli (adj)	israelsk	[isrɑ'elsk]
Jew (n)	jøde (m)	['jødə]
Jewess (n)	jødisk kvinne (m/f)	['jødisk ˌkvinə]
Jewish (adj)	jødisk	['jødisk]
China	Kina	['çinɑ]
Chinese (masc.)	kineser (m)	[çi'nesər]

| Chinese (fem.) | kinesisk kvinne (m/f) | [çi'nesisk ˌkvinə] |
| Chinese (adj) | kinesisk | [çi'nesisk] |

Korean (masc.)	koreaner (m)	[kʊre'anər]
Korean (fem.)	koreansk kvinne (m/f)	[kʊre'ansk ˌkvinə]
Korean (adj)	koreansk	[kʊre'ansk]

Lebanon	Libanon	['libanɔn]
Lebanese (masc.)	libaneser (m)	[liba'nesər]
Lebanese (fem.)	libanesisk kvinne (m/f)	[liba'nesisk ˌkvinə]
Lebanese (adj)	libanesisk	[liba'nesisk]

Mongolia	Mongolia	[mʊŋ'gulia]
Mongolian (masc.)	mongol (m)	[mʊŋ'gul]
Mongolian (fem.)	mongolsk kvinne (m/f)	[mʊn'gɔlsk ˌkvinə]
Mongolian (adj)	mongolsk	[mʊn'gɔlsk]

Malaysia	Malaysia	[ma'lajsia]
Malaysian (masc.)	malayer (m)	[ma'lajər]
Malaysian (fem.)	malayisk kvinne (m/f)	[ma'lajisk ˌkvinə]
Malaysian (adj)	malayisk	[ma'lajisk]

Pakistan	Pakistan	['pakiˌstan]
Pakistani (masc.)	pakistaner (m)	[paki'stanər]
Pakistani (fem.)	pakistansk kvinne (m/f)	[paki'stansk ˌkvinə]
Pakistani (adj)	pakistansk	[paki'stansk]

Saudi Arabia	Saudi-Arabia	['saʊdi a'rabia]
Arab (masc.)	araber (m)	[a'rabər]
Arab (fem.)	arabisk kvinne (m)	[a'rabisk ˌkvinə]
Arabic, Arabian (adj)	arabisk	[a'rabisk]

Thailand	Thailand	['tajlan]
Thai (masc.)	thailender (m)	['tajlendər]
Thai (fem.)	thailandsk kvinne (m/f)	['tajlansk ˌkvinə]
Thai (adj)	thailandsk	['tajlansk]

Taiwan	Taiwan	['tajˌvan]
Taiwanese (masc.)	taiwaner (m)	[taj'vanər]
Taiwanese (fem.)	taiwansk kvinne (m/f)	[taj'vansk ˌkvinə]
Taiwanese (adj)	taiwansk	[taj'vansk]

Turkey	Tyrkia	[tyrkia]
Turk (masc.)	tyrker (m)	['tyrkər]
Turk (fem.)	tyrkisk kvinne (m/f)	['tyrkisk ˌkvinə]
Turkish (adj)	tyrkisk	['tyrkisk]

Japan	Japan	['japan]
Japanese (masc.)	japaner (m)	[ja'panər]
Japanese (fem.)	japansk kvinne (m/f)	['japansk ˌkvinə]
Japanese (adj)	japansk	['japansk]

Afghanistan	Afghanistan	[af'ganiˌstan]
Bangladesh	Bangladesh	[bangla'dɛʂ]
Indonesia	Indonesia	[indʊ'nesia]
Jordan	Jordan	['jɔrdan]

Iraq	Irak	['irɑk]
Iran	Iran	['irɑn]
Cambodia	Kambodsja	[kɑm'bɔdʂɑ]
Kuwait	Kuwait	['kʉvɑjt]

Laos	Laos	['lɑɔs]
Myanmar	Myanmar	['mjænmɑ]
Nepal	Nepal	['nepɑl]
United Arab Emirates	Forente Arabiske Emiratene	[fɔ'rentə ɑ'rɑbiskə ɛmi'rɑtenə]

Syria	Syria	['syriɑ]
Palestine	Palestina	[pɑle'stinɑ]
South Korea	Sør-Korea	['sør kʉˌreɑ]
North Korea	Nord-Korea	['nuːr kʉ'rɛɑ]

238. North America

United States of America	Amerikas Forente Stater	[ɑ'merikɑs fɔ'rentə 'stɑtər]
American (masc.)	amerikaner (m)	[ameri'kanər]
American (fem.)	amerikansk kvinne (m)	[ameri'kɑnsk ˌkvinə]
American (adj)	amerikansk	[ameri'kɑnsk]

Canada	Canada	['kɑnɑdɑ]
Canadian (masc.)	kanadier (m)	[kɑ'nɑdiər]
Canadian (fem.)	kanadisk kvinne (m/f)	[kɑ'nɑdisk ˌkvinə]
Canadian (adj)	kanadisk	[kɑ'nɑdisk]

Mexico	Mexico	['mɛksikʉ]
Mexican (masc.)	meksikaner (m)	[mɛksi'kanər]
Mexican (fem.)	meksikansk kvinne (m/f)	[mɛksi'kɑnsk ˌkvinə]
Mexican (adj)	meksikansk	[mɛksi'kɑnsk]

239. Central and South America

Argentina	Argentina	[ɑrgɛn'tinɑ]
Argentinian (masc.)	argentiner (m)	[ɑrgɛn'tinər]
Argentinian (fem.)	argentinsk kvinne (m)	[ɑrgɛn'tinsk ˌkvinə]
Argentinian (adj)	argentinsk	[ɑrgɛn'tinsk]

Brazil	Brasilia	[brɑ'siliɑ]
Brazilian (masc.)	brasilianer (m)	[brɑsili'ɑnər]
Brazilian (fem.)	brasiliansk kvinne (m/f)	[brɑsili'ɑnsk ˌkvinə]
Brazilian (adj)	brasiliansk	[brɑsili'ɑnsk]

Colombia	Colombia	[kɔ'lʊmbiɑ]
Colombian (masc.)	colombianer (m)	[kɔlʊmbi'ɑnər]
Colombian (fem.)	colombiansk kvinne (m/f)	[kɔlʊmbi'ɑnsk ˌkvinə]
Colombian (adj)	colombiansk	[kɔlʊmbi'ɑnsk]

| Cuba | Cuba | ['kʉbɑ] |
| Cuban (masc.) | kubaner (m) | [kʉ'bɑnər] |

| Cuban (fem.) | kubansk kvinne (m/f) | [kʉ'bɑnsk ˌkvinə] |
| Cuban (adj) | kubansk | [kʉ'bɑnsk] |

Chile	Chile	['tʂilə]
Chilean (masc.)	chilener (m)	[tʂi'lenər]
Chilean (fem.)	chilensk kvinne (m/f)	[tʂi'lensk ˌkvinə]
Chilean (adj)	chilensk	[tʂi'lensk]

Bolivia	Bolivia	[bɔ'livia]
Venezuela	Venezuela	[venesʉ'ɛla]
Paraguay	Paraguay	[pɑrɑg'wɑj]
Peru	Peru	[pe'ru:]

Suriname	Surinam	['sʉriˌnɑm]
Uruguay	Uruguay	[ʉrygʉ'ɑj]
Ecuador	Ecuador	[ɛkʉɑ'dɔr]

The Bahamas	Bahamas	[bɑ'hamɑs]
Haiti	Haiti	[ha'iti]
Dominican Republic	Dominikanske Republikken	[dʉmini'kɑnskə repʉ'blikən]
Panama	Panama	['pɑnɑmɑ]
Jamaica	Jamaica	[ʂɑ'mɑjkɑ]

240. Africa

Egypt	Egypt	[ɛ'gypt]
Egyptian (masc.)	egypter (m)	[ɛ'gyptər]
Egyptian (fem.)	egyptisk kvinne (m/f)	[ɛ'gyptisk ˌkvinə]
Egyptian (adj)	egyptisk	[ɛ'gyptisk]

Morocco	Marokko	[mɑ'rɔkʉ]
Moroccan (masc.)	marokkaner (m)	[mɑrɔ'kɑnər]
Moroccan (fem.)	marokkansk kvinne (m/f)	[mɑrɔ'kɑnsk ˌkvinə]
Moroccan (adj)	marokkansk	[mɑrɔ'kɑnsk]

Tunisia	Tunisia	['tʉ'nisia]
Tunisian (masc.)	tuneser (m)	[tʉ'nesər]
Tunisian (fem.)	tunesisk kvinne (m/f)	[tʉ'nesisk ˌkvinə]
Tunisian (adj)	tunesisk	[tʉ'nesisk]

Ghana	Ghana	['gɑnɑ]
Zanzibar	Zanzibar	['sɑnsibɑr]
Kenya	Kenya	['kenyɑ]
Libya	Libya	['libiɑ]
Madagascar	Madagaskar	[mɑdɑ'gɑskɑr]

Namibia	Namibia	[nɑ'mibia]
Senegal	Senegal	[sene'gɑl]
Tanzania	Tanzania	['tɑnsɑˌnia]
South Africa	Republikken Sør-Afrika	[repʉ'bliken 'sørˌafrikɑ]

African (masc.)	afrikaner (m)	[afri'kɑnər]
African (fem.)	afrikansk kvinne (m)	[afri'kɑnsk ˌkvinə]
African (adj)	afrikansk	[afri'kɑnsk]

241. Australia. Oceania

Australia	Australia	[aʊˈstralɪa]
Australian (masc.)	australier (m)	[aʊˈstralɪər]
Australian (fem.)	australsk kvinne (m/f)	[aʊˈstralsk ˌkvinə]
Australian (adj)	australsk	[aʊˈstralsk]
New Zealand	New Zealand	[njʉˈselan]
New Zealander (masc.)	newzealender (m)	[njʉˈselendər]
New Zealander (fem.)	newzealandsk kvinne (m/f)	[njʉˈselansk ˌkvinə]
New Zealand (as adj)	newzealandsk	[njʉˈselansk]
Tasmania	Tasmania	[tasˈmania]
French Polynesia	Fransk Polynesia	[ˈfransk pɔlyˈnesia]

242. Cities

Amsterdam	Amsterdam	[ˈamstɛrˌdam]
Ankara	Ankara	[ˈankara]
Athens	Athen, Aten	[aˈten]
Baghdad	Bagdad	[ˈbagdad]
Bangkok	Bangkok	[ˈbankɔk]
Barcelona	Barcelona	[barsəˈluna]
Beijing	Peking, Beijing	[ˈpekiŋ], [ˈbɛjʒin]
Beirut	Beirut	[ˈbæjˌrʉt]
Berlin	Berlin	[bɛrˈlin]
Mumbai (Bombay)	Bombay	[ˈbombɛj]
Bonn	Bonn	[ˈbɔn]
Bordeaux	Bordeaux	[bɔrˈdɔː]
Bratislava	Bratislava	[bratiˈslava]
Brussels	Brussel	[ˈbrʉsɛl]
Bucharest	Bukarest	[ˈbʉkaˈrɛst]
Budapest	Budapest	[ˈbʉdapɛst]
Cairo	Kairo	[ˈkajrʉ]
Kolkata (Calcutta)	Calcutta	[kalˈkʉta]
Chicago	Chicago	[ʂiˈkagʉ]
Copenhagen	København	[ˈçøbənˌhavn]
Dar-es-Salaam	Dar-es-Salaam	[ˈdaresaˌlam]
Delhi	Delhi	[ˈdɛli]
Dubai	Dubai	[ˈdʉbaj]
Dublin	Dublin	[ˈdøblin]
Düsseldorf	Düsseldorf	[ˈdʉsəlˌdɔrf]
Florence	Firenze	[fiˈrɛnsə]
Frankfurt	Frankfurt	[ˈfrankfʉːt]
Geneva	Genève	[ʂeˈnɛv]
The Hague	Haag	[ˈhag]
Hamburg	Hamburg	[ˈhambʉrg]

Hanoi	Hanoi	['hanɔj]
Havana	Havana	[ha'vana]
Helsinki	Helsinki	['hɛlsinki]
Hiroshima	Hiroshima	[hirʊ'ʂima]
Hong Kong	Hongkong	['hɔn,kɔŋ]
Istanbul	Istanbul	['istanbʉl]
Jerusalem	Jerusalem	[je'rʉsalem]
Kyiv	Kiev	['kiːef]
Kuala Lumpur	Kuala Lumpur	[kʉ'ala 'lʉmpʉr]
Lisbon	Lisboa	['lisbʊa]
London	London	['lɔndɔn]
Los Angeles	Los Angeles	[ˌlɔs'ænʤələs]
Lyons	Lyon	[li'ɔn]
Madrid	Madrid	[ma'drid]
Marseille	Marseille	[mar'sɛj]
Mexico City	Mexico City	['mɛksikʊ 'siti]
Miami	Miami	[ma'jami]
Montreal	Montreal	[mɔntri'ɔl]
Moscow	Moskva	[mɔ'skva]
Munich	München	['mʉnhən]
Nairobi	Nairobi	[naj'rʊbi]
Naples	Napoli	['napʊli]
New York	New York	[njʉ 'jork]
Nice	Nice	['nis]
Oslo	Oslo	['ɔʂlʊ]
Ottawa	Ottawa	['ɔtava]
Paris	Paris	[pa'ris]
Prague	Praha	['praha]
Rio de Janeiro	Rio de Janeiro	['riu de ʂa'næjrʊ]
Rome	Roma	['rʊma]
Saint Petersburg	Sankt Petersburg	[ˌsankt 'petɛʂ,bʉrg]
Seoul	Seoul	[se'uːl]
Shanghai	Shanghai	['ʂaŋhaj]
Singapore	Singapore	['siŋa'por]
Stockholm	Stockholm	['stɔkhɔlm]
Sydney	Sydney	['sidni]
Taipei	Taipei	['tajpæj]
Tokyo	Tokyo	['tɔkiʊ]
Toronto	Toronto	[tɔ'rɔntʊ]
Venice	Venezia	[ve'netsia]
Vienna	Wien	['vin]
Warsaw	Warszawa	[va'ʂava]
Washington	Washington	['vɔʂiŋtən]

243. Politics. Government. Part 1

| politics | politikk (m) | [pʊli'tik] |
| political (adj) | politisk | [pʊ'litisk] |

politician	politiker (m)	[pʊ'litikər]
state (country)	stat (m)	['stɑt]
citizen	statsborger (m)	['stɑʦ͵bɔrgər]
citizenship	statsborgerskap (n)	['stɑʦbɔrgə͵skap]

| national emblem | riksvåpen (n) | ['riks͵vɔpən] |
| national anthem | nasjonalsang (m) | [nɑʂʊ'nɑl͵sɑŋ] |

government	regjering (m/f)	[rɛ'jeriŋ]
head of state	landets leder (m)	['lɑnɛʦ ͵leder]
parliament	parlament (n)	[pɑ:[ɑ'mɛnt]
party	parti (n)	[pɑ:'ʈi]

| capitalism | kapitalisme (n) | [kɑpitɑ'lismə] |
| capitalist (adj) | kapitalistisk | [kɑpitɑ'listisk] |

| socialism | sosialisme (m) | [sʊsiɑ'lismə] |
| socialist (adj) | sosialistisk | [sʊsiɑ'listisk] |

communism	kommunisme (m)	[kʊmʉ'nismə]
communist (adj)	kommunistisk	[kʊmʉ'nistisk]
communist (n)	kommunist (m)	[kʊmʉ'nist]

democracy	demokrati (n)	[demʊkrɑ'ti]
democrat	demokrat (m)	[demʊ'krɑt]
democratic (adj)	demokratisk	[demʊ'krɑtisk]
Democratic party	demokratisk parti (n)	[demʊ'krɑtisk pɑ:'ʈi]

| liberal (n) | liberaler (m) | [libə'rɑlər] |
| Liberal (adj) | liberal | [libə'rɑl] |

| conservative (n) | konservativ (m) | [kʊn'sɛrvɑ͵tiv] |
| conservative (adj) | konservativ | [kʊn'sɛrvɑ͵tiv] |

republic (n)	republikk (m)	[repʉ'blik]
republican (n)	republikaner (m)	[repʉbli'kɑnər]
Republican party	republikanske parti (n)	[repʉbli'kɑnskə pɑ:'ʈi]

elections	valg (n)	['vɑlg]
to elect (vt)	å velge	[ɔ 'vɛlgə]
elector, voter	velger (m)	['vɛlgər]
election campaign	valgkampanje (m)	['vɑlg kɑm'pɑnjə]

voting (n)	avstemning, votering (m)	['ɑf͵stɛmniŋ], ['vɔteriŋ]
to vote (vi)	å stemme	[ɔ 'stɛmə]
suffrage, right to vote	stemmerett (m)	['stɛmə͵rɛt]

candidate	kandidat (m)	[kɑndi'dɑt]
to run for (~ President)	å kandidere	[ɔ kɑndi'derə]
campaign	kampanje (m)	[kɑm'pɑnjə]

| opposition (as adj) | opposisjons- | [ɔpʊsi'ʂʊns-] |
| opposition (n) | opposisjon (m) | [ɔpʊsi'ʂʊn] |

| visit | besøk (n) | [be'søk] |
| official visit | offisielt besøk (n) | [ɔfi'sjɛlt be'søk] |

international (adj)	internasjonal	['intɛ:ŋaʂʉˌnal]
negotiations	forhandlinger (m pl)	[fɔr'hɑndliŋər]
to negotiate (vi)	å forhandle	[ɔ fɔr'hɑndlə]

244. Politics. Government. Part 2

society	samfunn (n)	['sɑmˌfʉn]
constitution	grunnlov (m)	['grʉnˌlɔv]
power (political control)	makt (m)	['mɑkt]
corruption	korrupsjon (m)	[kʉrʉp'ʂʉn]

| law (justice) | lov (m) | ['lɔv] |
| legal (legitimate) | lovlig | ['lɔvli] |

| justice (fairness) | rettferdighet (m) | [rɛt'færdiˌhet] |
| just (fair) | rettferdig | [rɛt'færdi] |

committee	komité (m)	[kʉmi'te]
bill (draft law)	lovforslag (n)	['lɔvˌfɔʂlɑg]
budget	budsjett (n)	[bʉd'ʂɛt]
policy	politikk (m)	[pʉli'tik]
reform	reform (m/f)	[rɛ'fɔrm]
radical (adj)	radikal	[rɑdi'kɑl]

power (strength, force)	kraft (m/f)	['krɑft]
powerful (adj)	mektig	['mɛkti]
supporter	tilhenger (m)	['tilˌhɛŋər]
influence	innflytelse (m)	['inˌflytəlsə]

regime (e.g. military ~)	regime (n)	[rɛ'ʂimə]
conflict	konflikt (m)	[kʉn'flikt]
conspiracy (plot)	sammensvergelse (m)	['sɑmənˌsværgəlsə]
provocation	provokasjon (m)	[prʉvʉkɑ'ʂʉn]

to overthrow (regime, etc.)	å styrte	[ɔ 'sty:ʈə]
overthrow (of a government)	styrting (m/f)	['sty:ʈiŋ]
revolution	revolusjon (m)	[revʉlʉ'ʂʉn]

| coup d'état | statskupp (n) | ['stɑtsˌkʉp] |
| military coup | militærkupp (n) | [mili'tærˌkʉp] |

crisis	krise (m/f)	['krisə]
economic recession	økonomisk nedgang (m)	[økʉ'nɔmisk 'nedˌgɑŋ]
demonstrator (protester)	demonstrant (m)	[demɔn'strɑnt]
demonstration	demonstrasjon (m)	[demɔnstrɑ'ʂʉn]
martial law	krigstilstand (m)	['krigstilˌstɑn]
military base	militærbase (m)	[mili'tærˌbɑsə]

| stability | stabilitet (m) | [stɑbili'tet] |
| stable (adj) | stabil | [stɑ'bil] |

exploitation	utbytting (m/f)	['ʉtˌbytiŋ]
to exploit (workers)	å utbytte	[ɔ 'ʉtˌbytə]
racism	rasisme (m)	[rɑ'sismə]

racist	rasist (m)	[ra'sist]
fascism	fascisme (m)	[fa'ṣismə]
fascist	fascist (m)	[fa'ṣist]

245. Countries. Miscellaneous

foreigner	utlending (m)	['ʉt,leniŋ]
foreign (adj)	utenlandsk	['ʉtən,lansk]
abroad (in a foreign country)	i utlandet	[i 'ʉt,lanə]

emigrant	emigrant (m)	[ɛmi'grant]
emigration	emigrasjon (m)	[ɛmigra'ṣʉn]
to emigrate (vi)	å emigrere	[ɔ ɛmi'grɛrə]

the West	Vesten	['vɛstən]
the East	Østen	['østən]
the Far East	Det fjerne østen	['de 'fjæ:ŋə ,østɛn]
civilization	sivilisasjon (m)	[sivilisa'ṣʉn]
humanity (mankind)	menneskehet (m)	['mɛnəske,het]
the world (earth)	verden (m)	['væɾdən]
peace	fred (m)	['frɛd]
worldwide (adj)	verdens-	['væɾdəns-]

homeland	fedreland (n)	['fædrə,lan]
people (population)	folk (n)	['fɔlk]
population	befolkning (m)	[be'fɔlkniŋ]
people (a lot of ~)	folk (n)	['fɔlk]
nation (people)	nasjon (m)	[na'ṣʉn]
generation	generasjon (m)	[genera'ṣʉn]
territory (area)	territorium (n)	[tɛri'tʉrium]
region	region (m)	[rɛgi'ʉn]
state (part of a country)	delstat (m)	['del,stat]

tradition	tradisjon (m)	[tradi'ṣʉn]
custom (tradition)	skikk, sedvane (m)	['ṣik], ['sɛd,vanə]
ecology	økologi (m)	[økʉlʉ'gi]

Indian (Native American)	indianer (m)	[indi'anər]
Gypsy (masc.)	sigøyner (m)	[si'gøjnər]
Gypsy (fem.)	sigøynerske (m/f)	[si'gøjnəskə]
Gypsy (adj)	sigøynersk	[si'gøjnəṣk]

empire	imperium, keiserrike (n)	['im'perium], ['kæjsə,rike]
colony	koloni (m)	[kʉlu'ni]
slavery	slaveri (n)	[slavɛ'ri]
invasion	invasjon (m)	[inva'ṣʉn]
famine	hungersnød (m/f)	['hʉŋɛṣ,nød]

246. Major religious groups. Confessions

| religion | religion (m) | [religi'ʉn] |
| religious (adj) | religiøs | [reli'gjøs] |

faith, belief	tro (m)	['trʊ]
to believe (in God)	å tro	[ɔ 'trʊ]
believer	troende (m)	['trʊenə]

| atheism | ateisme (m) | [ɑte'ismə] |
| atheist | ateist (m) | [ɑte'ist] |

Christianity	kristendom (m)	['kristən͵dɔm]
Christian (n)	kristen (m)	['kristən]
Christian (adj)	kristelig	['kristəli]

Catholicism	katolisisme (m)	[kɑtʊli'sismə]
Catholic (n)	katolikk (m)	[kɑtʊ'lik]
Catholic (adj)	katolsk	[kɑ'tʊlsk]

Protestantism	protestantisme (m)	[prʊtɛstɑn'tismə]
Protestant Church	den protestantiske kirke	[den prʊtɛ'stɑntiskə ͵çirkə]
Protestant (n)	protestant (m)	[prʊtɛ'stɑnt]

Orthodoxy	ortodoksi (m)	[ɔ:tʊdʊk'si]
Orthodox Church	den ortodokse kirke	[den ɔ:tʊ'dɔksə ͵çirkə]
Orthodox (n)	ortodoks (n)	[ɔ:tʊ'dɔks]

Presbyterianism	presbyterianisme (m)	[prɛsbytæriɑ'nismə]
Presbyterian Church	den presbyterianske kirke	[den prɛsbyteri'ɑnskə ͵çirkə]
Presbyterian (n)	presbyterianer (m)	[prɛsbytæri'ɑnər]

| Lutheranism | lutherdom (m) | [lʉtər'dɔm] |
| Lutheran (n) | lutheraner (m) | [lʉtə'rɑnər] |

| Baptist Church | baptisme (m) | [bɑp'tismə] |
| Baptist (n) | baptist (m) | [bɑp'tist] |

| Anglican Church | den anglikanske kirke | [den ɑŋli'kɑnskə ͵çirkə] |
| Anglican (n) | anglikaner (m) | [ɑŋli'kɑnər] |

| Mormonism | mormonisme (m) | [mɔrmɔ'nismə] |
| Mormon (n) | mormon (m) | [mʊr'mʊn] |

| Judaism | judaisme (m) | ['jʉdɑ͵ismə] |
| Jew (n) | judeer (m) | ['jʉ'deər] |

| Buddhism | buddhisme (m) | [bʉ'dismə] |
| Buddhist (n) | buddhist (m) | [bʉ'dist] |

| Hinduism | hinduisme (m) | [hindʉ'ismə] |
| Hindu (n) | hindu (m) | ['hindʉ] |

Islam	islam	['islɑm]
Muslim (n)	muslim (m)	[mʉ'slim]
Muslim (adj)	muslimsk	[mʉ'slimsk]

Shiah Islam	sjiisme (m)	[ʂi'ismə]
Shiite (n)	sjiitt (m)	[ʂi'it]
Sunni Islam	sunnisme (m)	[sʉ'nismə]
Sunnite (n)	sunnimuslim (m)	['sʉni mʉs͵lim]

247. Religions. Priests

priest	prest (m)	['prɛst]
the Pope	Paven	['pɑvən]
monk, friar	munk (m)	['mʉnk]
nun	nonne (m/f)	['nɔnə]
pastor	pastor (m)	['pɑstʉr]
abbot	abbed (m)	['ɑbed]
vicar (parish priest)	sogneprest (m)	['sɔŋnə‚prɛst]
bishop	biskop (m)	['biskɔp]
cardinal	kardinal (m)	[kɑ:ɖi'nɑl]
preacher	predikant (m)	[prɛdi'kɑnt]
preaching	preken (m)	['prɛkən]
parishioners	menighet (m/f)	['meni‚het]
believer	troende (m)	['trʉenə]
atheist	ateist (m)	[ɑte'ist]

248. Faith. Christianity. Islam

Adam	Adam	['ɑdɑm]
Eve	Eva	['ɛvɑ]
God	Gud (m)	['gʉd]
the Lord	Herren	['hæːrən]
the Almighty	Den Allmektige	[den ɑl'mɛktiə]
sin	synd (m/f)	['sʏn]
to sin (vi)	å synde	[ɔ 'sʏnə]
sinner (masc.)	synder (m)	['sʏnər]
sinner (fem.)	synderinne (m)	['sʏnə‚rinə]
hell	helvete (n)	['hɛlvetə]
paradise	paradis (n)	['pɑrɑ‚dis]
Jesus	Jesus	['jesʉs]
Jesus Christ	Jesus Kristus	['jesʉs ‚kristʉs]
the Holy Spirit	Den Hellige Ånd	[dən 'hɛliə ‚on]
the Saviour	Frelseren	['frelserən]
the Virgin Mary	Jomfru Maria	['jɔmfrʉ mɑ‚riɑ]
the Devil	Djevel (m)	['djevəl]
devil's (adj)	djevelsk	['djevəlsk]
Satan	Satan	['sɑtɑn]
satanic (adj)	satanisk	[sɑ'tɑnisk]
angel	engel (m)	['ɛŋəl]
guardian angel	skytsengel (m)	['sʏts‚ɛŋəl]
angelic (adj)	engle-	['ɛŋlə-]

apostle	apostel (m)	[a'postəl]
archangel	erkeengel (m)	['ærkə‚æŋəl]
the Antichrist	Antikrist	['anti‚krist]

Church	kirken (m)	['çirkən]
Bible	bibel (m)	['bibəl]
biblical (adj)	bibelsk	['bibəlsk]

Old Testament	Det Gamle Testamente	[de 'gamlə tɛsta'mentə]
New Testament	Det Nye Testamente	[de 'nye tɛsta'mentə]
Gospel	evangelium (n)	[ɛvan'gelium]
Holy Scripture	Den Hellige Skrift	[dən 'hɛliə ‚skrift]
Heaven	Himmerike (n)	['himə‚rikə]

Commandment	bud (n)	['bʉd]
prophet	profet (m)	[prʊ'fet]
prophecy	profeti (m)	[prʊfe'ti]

Allah	Allah	['ala]
Mohammed	Muhammed	[mʉ'hamed]
the Koran	Koranen	[kʊ'ranən]

mosque	moské (m)	[mʊ'ske]
mullah	mulla (m)	['mʉla]
prayer	bønn (m)	['bœn]
to pray (vi, vt)	å be	[ɔ 'be]

pilgrimage	pilegrimsreise (m/f)	['piləgrims‚ræjsə]
pilgrim	pilegrim (m)	['piləgrim]
Mecca	Mekka	['mɛka]

church	kirke (m/f)	['çirkə]
temple	tempel (n)	['tɛmpəl]
cathedral	katedral (m)	[kate'dral]
Gothic (adj)	gotisk	['gotisk]
synagogue	synagoge (m)	[syna'gʊgə]
mosque	moské (m)	[mʊ'ske]

chapel	kapell (n)	[ka'pɛl]
abbey	abbedi (n)	['abedi]
convent	kloster (n)	['klɔstər]
monastery	kloster (n)	['klɔstər]

bell (church ~s)	klokke (m/f)	['klɔkə]
bell tower	klokketårn (n)	['klɔkə‚to:ŋ]
to ring (ab. bells)	å ringe	[ɔ 'riŋə]

cross	kors (n)	['kɔ:ʂ]
cupola (roof)	kuppel (m)	['kʉpəl]
icon	ikon (m/n)	[i'kʊn]

soul	sjel (m)	['ʂɛl]
fate (destiny)	skjebne (m)	['ʂɛbnə]
evil (n)	ondskap (n)	['ʊn‚skap]
good (n)	godhet (n)	['gʊ‚het]
vampire	vampyr (m)	[vam'pyr]

witch (evil ~)	heks (m)	['hɛks]
demon	demon (m)	[de'mʊn]
spirit	ånd (m)	['ɔn]
redemption (giving us ~)	forløsning (m/f)	[fɔː'løsniŋ]
to redeem (vt)	å sone	[ɔ 'sʊnə]
church service	gudstjeneste (m)	['gʉts‚tjenɛstə]
to say mass	å holde gudstjeneste	[ɔ 'hɔldə 'gʉts‚tjenɛstə]
confession	skriftemål (n)	['skriftə‚mol]
to confess (vi)	å skrifte	[ɔ 'skriftə]
saint (n)	helgen (m)	['hɛlgən]
sacred (holy)	hellig	['hɛli]
holy water	vievann (n)	['viə‚vɑn]
ritual (n)	ritual (n)	[ritʉ'ɑl]
ritual (adj)	rituell	[ritʉ'ɛl]
sacrifice	ofring (m/f)	['ɔfriŋ]
superstition	overtro (m)	['ɔvə‚trʊ]
superstitious (adj)	overtroisk	['ɔvə‚trʊisk]
afterlife	livet etter dette	['livə ‚ɛtər 'dɛtə]
eternal life	det evige liv	[de ‚eviə 'liv]

MISCELLANEOUS

249. Various useful words

English	Norwegian	Pronunciation
background (green ~)	**bakgrunn** (m)	['bɑk‚grʉn]
balance (of the situation)	**balanse** (m)	[bɑ'lɑnsə]
barrier (obstacle)	**hinder** (n)	['hindər]
base (basis)	**basis** (n)	['bɑsis]
beginning	**begynnelse** (m)	[be'jinəlsə]
category	**kategori** (m)	[kɑtegʉ'ri]
cause (reason)	**årsak** (m/f)	['oː‚sɑk]
choice	**valg** (n)	['vɑlg]
coincidence	**sammenfall** (n)	['sɑmən‚fɑl]
comfortable (~ chair)	**bekvem**	[be'kvem]
comparison	**sammenlikning** (m)	['sɑmən‚likniŋ]
compensation	**kompensasjon** (m)	[kʉmpɛnsɑ'ʂʉn]
degree (extent, amount)	**grad** (m)	['grɑd]
development	**utvikling** (m/f)	['ʉt‚vikliŋ]
difference	**skilnad, forskjell** (m)	['ʂilnɑd], ['foːʂɛl]
effect (e.g. of drugs)	**effekt** (m)	[ɛ'fɛkt]
effort (exertion)	**anstrengelse** (m)	['ɑn‚strɛŋəlsə]
element	**element** (n)	[ɛle'mɛnt]
end (finish)	**slutt** (m)	['ʂlʉt]
example (illustration)	**eksempel** (n)	[ɛk'sɛmpəl]
fact	**faktum** (n)	['fɑktum]
frequent (adj)	**hyppig**	['hʏpi]
growth (development)	**vekst** (m)	['vɛkst]
help	**hjelp** (m)	['jɛlp]
ideal	**ideal** (n)	[ide'ɑl]
kind (sort, type)	**slags** (n)	['ʂlɑks]
labyrinth	**labyrint** (m)	[lɑby'rint]
mistake, error	**feil** (m)	['fæjl]
moment	**moment** (n)	[mɔ'mɛnt]
object (thing)	**objekt** (n)	[ɔb'jɛkt]
obstacle	**hindring** (m/f)	['hindriŋ]
original (original copy)	**original** (m)	[ɔrigi'nɑl]
part (~ of sth)	**del** (m)	['del]
particle, small part	**partikel** (m)	[pɑː'ʈikəl]
pause (break)	**pause** (m)	['pausə]
position	**posisjon** (m)	[pɔsi'ʂʉn]
principle	**prinsipp** (n)	[prin'sip]
problem	**problem** (n)	[prʉ'blem]
process	**prosess** (m)	[prʉ'sɛs]

progress	fremskritt (n)	['frɛm‚skrit]
property (quality)	egenskap (m)	['ɛgən‚skɑp]
reaction	reaksjon (m)	[rɛɑk'ʂʉn]
risk	risiko (m)	['risikʉ]

secret	hemmelighet (m/f)	['hɛməli‚het]
series	serie (m)	['seriə]
shape (outer form)	form (m/f)	['fɔrm]
situation	situasjon (m)	[situɑ'ʂʉn]
solution	løsning (m)	['løsniŋ]

standard (adj)	standard-	['stɑn‚dɑr-]
standard (level of quality)	standard (m)	['stɑn‚dɑr]
stop (pause)	stopp (m), hvile (m/f)	['stɔp], ['vilə]
style	stil (m)	['stil]

system	system (n)	[sɣ'stem]
table (chart)	tabell (m)	[tɑ'bɛl]
tempo, rate	tempo (n)	['tɛmpʉ]
term (word, expression)	term (m)	['tɛrm]
thing (object, item)	ting (m)	['tiŋ]

truth (e.g. moment of ~)	sannhet (m)	['sɑn‚het]
turn (please wait your ~)	tur (m)	['tʉr]
type (sort, kind)	type (m)	['typə]
urgent (adj)	omgående	['ɔm‚gɔ:nə]
urgently	omgående	['ɔm‚gɔ:nə]

utility (usefulness)	nytte (m/f)	['nɣtə]
variant (alternative)	variant (m)	[vɑri'ɑnt]
way (means, method)	måte (m)	['mo:tə]
zone	sone (m/f)	['sʉnə]

250. Modifiers. Adjectives. Part 1

additional (adj)	ytterligere	['ytə‚ʟiərə]
ancient (~ civilization)	oldtidens, antikkens	['ɔl‚tidəns], [ɑn'tikəns]
artificial (adj)	kunstig	['kʉnsti]
back, rear (adj)	bak-	['bɑk-]
bad (adj)	dårlig	['do:ʟi]

beautiful (~ palace)	vakker	['vɑkər]
beautiful (person)	vakker	['vɑkər]
big (in size)	stor	['stʉr]
bitter (taste)	bitter	['bitər]
blind (sightless)	blind	['blin]

calm, quiet (adj)	rolig	['rʉli]
careless (negligent)	slurvet	['ʂlʉrvət]
caring (~ father)	omsorgsfull	['ɔm‚sɔrgsfʉl]
central (adj)	sentral	[sɛn'trɑl]

| cheap (low-priced) | billig | ['bili] |
| cheerful (adj) | glad, munter | ['glɑ], ['mʉntər] |

children's (adj)	barne-	['bɑ:ŋə-]
civil (~ law)	sivil	[si'vil]
clandestine (secret)	hemmelig	['hɛməli]

clean (free from dirt)	ren	['ren]
clear (explanation, etc.)	klar	['klɑr]
clever (intelligent)	klok	['klʊk]
close (near in space)	nær	['nær]
closed (adj)	stengt	['stɛŋt]

cloudless (sky)	skyfri	['ʂy‚fri]
cold (drink, weather)	kald	['kɑl]
compatible (adj)	forenelig	[fo'renli]
contented (satisfied)	nøgd, tilfreds	['nøgd], [til'frɛds]
continuous (uninterrupted)	uavbrutt	[ʉ:'av‚brʉt]

cool (weather)	kjølig	['çœli]
dangerous (adj)	farlig	['fɑ:ḷi]
dark (room)	mørk	['mœrk]
dead (not alive)	død	['dø]
dense (fog, smoke)	tykk	['tʏk]

destitute (extremely poor)	utfattig	['ʉt‚fɑti]
different (not the same)	ulike	['ʉlikə]
difficult (decision)	svær	['svær]
difficult (problem, task)	komplisert	[kʊmpli'sɛ:t̪]
dim, faint (light)	svak	['svak]

dirty (not clean)	skitten	['ʂitən]
distant (in space)	fjern	['fjæ:ṇ]
dry (clothes, etc.)	tørr	['tœr]
easy (not difficult)	lett	['let]

empty (glass, room)	tom	['tɔm]
even (e.g. ~ surface)	jevn	['jɛvn]
exact (amount)	presis, eksakt	[prɛ'sis], [ɛk'sakt]
excellent (adj)	utmerket	['ʉt‚mærkət]
excessive (adj)	overdreven	['ɔvə‚dreven]

expensive (adj)	dyr	['dyr]
exterior (adj)	ytre	['ytrə]
far (the ~ East)	fjern	['fjæ:ṇ]
fast (quick)	hastig	['hɑsti]
fatty (food)	fet	['fet]

fertile (land, soil)	fruktbar	['frʉkt‚bɑr]
flat (~ panel display)	flat	['flɑt]
foreign (adj)	utenlandsk	['ʉtən‚lɑnsk]
fragile (china, glass)	skjør	['ʂør]

free (at no cost)	gratis	['grɑtis]
free (unrestricted)	fri	['fri]
fresh (~ water)	fersk-	['fæʂk-]
fresh (e.g. ~ bread)	fersk	['fæʂk]
frozen (food)	frossen, dypfryst	['frɔsən], ['dyp‚frʏst]
full (completely filled)	full	['fʉl]

gloomy (house, forecast)	mørk	['mœrk]
good (book, etc.)	bra	['brɑ]
good, kind (kindhearted)	god	['gʊ]
grateful (adj)	takknemlig	[tɑk'nɛmli]

happy (adj)	lykkelig	['lʏkəli]
hard (not soft)	hard	['hɑr]
heavy (in weight)	tung	['tʉŋ]
hostile (adj)	fiendtlig	['fjɛntli]
hot (adj)	het, varm	['het], ['vɑrm]

huge (adj)	enorm	[ɛ'nɔrm]
humid (adj)	fuktig	['fʉkti]
hungry (adj)	sulten	['sʉltən]
ill (sick, unwell)	syk	['syk]
immobile (adj)	ubevegelig, urørlig	[ʉbe'vɛgli], [ʉ'rø:[i]

important (adj)	viktig	['vikti]
impossible (adj)	umulig	[ʉ'mʉli]
incomprehensible	uforståelig	[ʉfɔ'ʂtɔəli]
indispensable (adj)	nødvendig	['nød‚vɛndi]
inexperienced (adj)	uerfaren	[ʉer'fɑrən]

insignificant (adj)	ubetydelig	[ʉbe'tydəli]
interior (adj)	indre	['indrə]
joint (~ decision)	felles	['fɛləs]
last (e.g. ~ week)	forrige	['fɔriə]

last (final)	sist	['sist]
left (e.g. ~ side)	venstre	['vɛnstrə]
legal (legitimate)	lovlig	['lɔvli]
light (in weight)	lett	['let]
light (pale color)	lys	['lys]

limited (adj)	begrenset	[be'grɛnsət]
liquid (fluid)	flytende	['flytnə]
long (e.g. ~ hair)	lang	['lɑŋ]
loud (voice, etc.)	høy	['høj]
low (voice)	lav	['lɑv]

251. Modifiers. Adjectives. Part 2

main (principal)	hoved-	['hɔvəd-]
matt, matte	matt	['mɑt]
meticulous (job)	nøyaktig	['nøjakti]
mysterious (adj)	mystisk	['mʏstisk]
narrow (street, etc.)	smal	['smɑl]

native (~ country)	hjem-	['jɛm-]
nearby (adj)	nær	['nær]
needed (necessary)	nødvendig	['nød‚vɛndi]
negative (~ response)	negativ	['negɑ‚tiv]
neighbouring (adj)	nabo-	['nɑbʉ-]
nervous (adj)	nervøs	[nær'vøs]

new (adj)	ny	['ny]
next (e.g. ~ week)	neste	['nɛstə]
nice (agreeable)	snill	['snil]

pleasant (voice)	trivelig, behagelig	['trivli], [be'hagli]
normal (adj)	normal	[nɔr'mal]
not big (adj)	liten, ikke stor	['litən], [ˌikə 'stʊr]
not difficult (adj)	lett	['let]

obligatory (adj)	obligatorisk	[ɔbliga'tʊrisk]
old (house)	gammel	['gaməl]
open (adj)	åpen	['ɔpən]
opposite (adj)	motsatt	['mʊtˌsat]
ordinary (usual)	vanlig	['vanli]

original (unusual)	original	[ɔrigi'nal]
past (recent)	forrige	['fɔriə]
permanent (adj)	fast, permanent	['fast], ['pɛrmaˌnɛnt]
personal (adj)	personlig	[pæ'sʊnli]
polite (adj)	høflig	['høfli]

poor (not rich)	fattig	['fati]
possible (adj)	mulig	['mʉli]
present (current)	nåværende	['nɔˌværenə]
previous (adj)	foregående	['fɔrəˌgo:ŋə]
principal (main)	hoved-, prinsipal	['hɔvəd-], ['prinsiˌpal]

private (~ jet)	privat	[pri'vat]
probable (adj)	sannsynlig	[san'synli]
prolonged (e.g. ~ applause)	langvarig	['laŋˌvari]
public (open to all)	offentlig	['ɔfentli]

punctual (person)	punktlig	['pʉnktli]
quiet (tranquil)	rolig	['rʉli]
rare (adj)	sjelden	['ʂɛlən]
raw (uncooked)	rå	['rɔ]

right (not left)	høyre	['højrə]
right, correct (adj)	riktig	['rikti]
ripe (fruit)	moden	['mʊdən]
risky (adj)	risikabel	[risi'kabəl]
sad (~ look)	trist	['trist]

sad (depressing)	sørgmodig	[sør'mʊdi]
safe (not dangerous)	sikker	['sikər]
salty (food)	salt	['salt]
satisfied (customer)	fornøyd, tilfreds	[fɔr'nøjd], [til'frɛds]

second hand (adj)	brukt, secondhand	['brʉkt], ['sekɔnˌhɛŋ]
shallow (water)	grunn	['grʉn]
sharp (blade, etc.)	skarp	['skarp]
short (in length)	kort	['kʊːt]

short, short-lived (adj)	kortvarig	['kʊːtˌvari]
short-sighted (adj)	nærsynt	['næˌsynt]
significant (notable)	betydelig	[be'tydəli]

| similar (adj) | lik | ['lik] |
| simple (easy) | enkel | ['ɛnkəl] |

skinny	benete, mager	['benetə], ['magər]
small (in size)	liten	['litən]
smooth (surface)	glatt	['glat]
soft (~ toys)	bløt	['bløt]
solid (~ wall)	solid, holdbar	[su'lid], ['hɔl,bɑr]

sour (flavour, taste)	sur	['sʉr]
spacious (house, etc.)	rommelig	['rʊmeli]
special (adj)	spesial	[spesi'ɑl]
straight (line, road)	rett	['rɛt]
strong (person)	sterk	['stærk]

stupid (foolish)	dum	['dʉm]
suitable (e.g. ~ for drinking)	egnet	['æjnət]
sunny (day)	solrik	['sʉl,rik]
superb, perfect (adj)	utmerket	['ʉt,mærkət]
swarthy (dark-skinned)	mørkhudet	['mœrk,hʉdət]

sweet (sugary)	søt	['søt]
tanned (adj)	solbrent	['sʉl,brɛnt]
tasty (delicious)	lekker	['lekər]
tender (affectionate)	øm	['øm]

the highest (adj)	høyest	['højɛst]
the most important	viktigste	['viktigstə]
the nearest	nærmeste	['nærmɛstə]
the same, equal (adj)	samme, lik	['samə], ['lik]

thick (e.g. ~ fog)	tykk	['tʏk]
thick (wall, slice)	tykk	['tʏk]
thin (person)	slank, tynn	['s̩lɑnk], ['tʏn]
tight (~ shoes)	trange	['trɑŋə]
tired (exhausted)	trett	['trɛt]

tiring (adj)	trøttende	['trœtɛnə]
transparent (adj)	transparent	['trɑnspɑ,rɑŋ]
unclear (adj)	uklar	['ʉ,klɑr]
unique (exceptional)	unik	[ʉ'nik]
various (adj)	forskjellig	[fɔ'ʂɛli]

warm (moderately hot)	varm	['vɑrm]
wet (e.g. ~ clothes)	våt	['vɔt]
whole (entire, complete)	hel	['hel]
wide (e.g. ~ road)	bred	['bre]
young (adj)	ung	['ʉŋ]

MAIN 500 VERBS

to accompany (vt)	å følge	[ɔ 'fø!ə]
to accuse (vt)	å anklage	[ɔ 'anˌklɑgə]
to acknowledge (admit)	å erkjenne	[ɔ ær'çɛnə]
to act (take action)	å handle	[ɔ 'handlə]
to add (supplement)	å tilføye	[ɔ 'tilˌføjə]
to address (speak to)	å tiltale	[ɔ 'tilˌtɑlə]
to admire (vi)	å beundre	[ɔ be'ʉndrə]
to advertise (vt)	å reklamere	[ɔ rɛklɑ'merə]
to advise (vt)	å råde	[ɔ ' roːdə]
to affirm (assert)	å påstå	[ɔ 'pɔˌstɔ]
to agree (say yes)	å samtykke	[ɔ 'samˌtʏkə]
to aim (to point a weapon)	å sikte på ...	[ɔ 'siktə pɔ ...]
to allow (sb to do sth)	å tillate	[ɔ 'tiˌlɑtə]
to amputate (vt)	å amputere	[ɔ ampʉ'terə]
to answer (vi, vt)	å svare	[ɔ 'svɑrə]
to apologize (vi)	å unnskylde seg	[ɔ 'ʉnˌsylə sæj]
to appear (come into view)	å dukke opp	[ɔ 'dʉkə ɔp]
to applaud (vi, vt)	å applaudere	[ɔ aplɑʊ'derə]
to appoint (assign)	å utnevne	[ɔ 'ʉtˌnɛvnə]
to approach (come closer)	å nærme seg	[ɔ 'nærmə sæj]
to arrive (ab. train)	å ankomme	[ɔ 'anˌkɔmə]
to ask (~ sb to do sth)	å be	[ɔ 'be]
to aspire to ...	å aspirere	[ɔ aspi'rerə]
to assist (help)	å assistere	[ɔ asi'sterə]
to attack (mil.)	å angripe	[ɔ 'anˌgripə]
to attain (objectives)	å oppnå	[ɔ 'ɔpnɔ]
to avenge (get revenge)	å hevne	[ɔ 'hɛvnə]
to avoid (danger, task)	å unngå	[ɔ 'ʉnˌgɔ]
to award (give a medal to)	å belønne	[ɔ be'lœnə]
to battle (vi)	å kjempe	[ɔ 'çɛmpə]
to be (vi)	å være	[ɔ 'værə]
to be a cause of ...	å forårsake	[ɔ forɔ:'ʂakə]
to be afraid	å frykte	[ɔ 'frʏktə]
to be angry (with ...)	å være vred på ...	[ɔ 'værə vred pɔ ...]
to be at war	å være i krig	[ɔ 'værə i ˌkrig]
to be based (on ...)	å være basert på ...	[ɔ 'værə bɑ'sɛːt pɔ ...]
to be bored	å kjede seg	[ɔ 'çedə sæj]

to be convinced	å være overbevist	[ɔ 'væːrə 'ɔvərbeˌvist]
to be enough	å være nok	[ɔ 'væːrə ˌnɔk]
to be envious	å misunne	[ɔ 'misˌʉnə]
to be indignant	å bli indignert	[ɔ 'bli indi'gnɛːt]
to be interested in ...	å interessere seg	[ɔ intəre'serə sæj]

to be lost in thought	å gruble	[ɔ 'grʉblə]
to be lying (~ on the table)	å ligge	[ɔ 'ligə]
to be needed	å være behøv	[ɔ 'væːrə bə'høv]
to be perplexed (puzzled)	å være forvirret	[ɔ 'væːrə for'virət]

to be preserved	å bevares	[ɔ be'vɑrəs]
to be required	å være nødvendig	[ɔ 'væːrə 'nødˌvɛndi]
to be surprised	å bli forundret	[ɔ 'bli fo'rʉndrət]
to be worried	å bekymre seg	[ɔ be'çymrə sæj]

to beat (to hit)	å slå	[ɔ 'ʂlɔ]
to become (e.g. ~ old)	å bli	[ɔ 'bli]
to behave (vi)	å oppføre seg	[ɔ 'ɔpˌførə sæj]
to believe (think)	å tro	[ɔ 'trʉ]

to belong to ...	å tilhøre ...	[ɔ 'tilˌhørə ...]
to berth (moor)	å fortøye	[ɔ fɔ:'tøjə]
to blind (other drivers)	å blende	[ɔ 'blenə]
to blow (wind)	å blåse	[ɔ 'blo:sə]

to blush (vi)	å rødme	[ɔ 'rødmə]
to boast (vi)	å prale	[ɔ 'pralə]
to borrow (money)	å låne	[ɔ 'lo:nə]
to break (branch, toy, etc.)	å bryte	[ɔ 'brytə]

to breathe (vi)	å ånde	[ɔ 'ɔndə]
to bring (sth)	å bringe	[ɔ 'briŋə]
to burn (paper, logs)	å brenne	[ɔ 'brɛnə]
to buy (purchase)	å kjøpe	[ɔ 'çœ:pə]

to call (~ for help)	å tilkalle	[ɔ 'tilˌkalə]
to call (yell for sb)	å kalle	[ɔ 'kalə]
to calm down (vt)	å berolige	[ɔ be'rʉliə]
can (v aux)	å kunne	[ɔ 'kʉnə]

to cancel (call off)	å avlyse, å annullere	[ɔ 'avˌlysə], [ɔ anʉ'lerə]
to cast off (of a boat or ship)	å kaste loss	[ɔ 'kastə lɔs]
to catch (e.g. ~ a ball)	å fange	[ɔ 'faŋə]
to change (~ one's opinion)	å endre	[ɔ 'ɛndrə]
to change (exchange)	å veksle	[ɔ 'vɛkslə]

to charm (vt)	å sjarmere	[ɔ 'ʂarˌmerə]
to choose (select)	å velge	[ɔ 'vɛlgə]
to chop off (with an axe)	å hugge av	[ɔ 'hʉgə a:]
to clean (e.g. kettle from scale)	å rengjøre	[ɔ rɛn'jørə]

to clean (shoes, etc.)	å rense	[ɔ 'rɛnsə]
to clean up (tidy)	å rydde	[ɔ 'rydə]
to close (vt)	å lukke	[ɔ 'lʉkə]

to comb one's hair	å kamme	[ɔ 'kɑmə]
to come down (the stairs)	å gå ned	[ɔ 'gɔ ne]
to come out (book)	å komme ut	[ɔ 'kɔmə ʉt]
to compare (vt)	å sammenlikne	[ɔ 'sɑmənˌlikne]
to compensate (vt)	å kompensere	[ɔ kʉmpen'serə]

to compete (vi)	å konkurrere	[ɔ kʉnkʉ'rerə]
to compile (~ a list)	å sammenstille	[ɔ 'sɑmənˌstilə]
to complain (vi, vt)	å klage	[ɔ 'klɑgə]
to complicate (vt)	å komplisere	[ɔ kʉmpli'serə]

to compose (music, etc.)	å komponere	[ɔ kʉmpʉ'nerə]
to compromise (reputation)	å kompromittere	[ɔ kʉmprʉmi'terə]
to concentrate (vi)	å konsentrere seg	[ɔ kʉnsen'trerə sæj]
to confess (criminal)	å tilstå	[ɔ 'tilˌstɔ]

to confuse (mix up)	å forveksle	[ɔ fɔr'vɛkʂlə]
to congratulate (vt)	å gratulere	[ɔ grɑtʉ'lerə]
to consult (doctor, expert)	å konsultere	[ɔ kʉnsʉl'terə]
to continue (~ to do sth)	å fortsette	[ɔ 'fortˌsɛtə]

to control (vt)	å kontrollere	[ɔ kʉntrɔ'lerə]
to convince (vt)	å overbevise	[ɔ 'ɔvərbeˌvisə]
to cooperate (vi)	å samarbeide	[ɔ 'sɑmarˌbæjdə]
to coordinate (vt)	å koordinere	[ɔ kɔːɖi'nerə]

to correct (an error)	å rette	[ɔ 'rɛtə]
to cost (vt)	å koste	[ɔ 'kɔstə]
to count (money, etc.)	å telle	[ɔ 'tɛlə]
to count on ...	å regne med ...	[ɔ 'rɛjnə me ...]

to crack (ceiling, wall)	å sprekke	[ɔ 'sprɛkə]
to create (vt)	å opprette	[ɔ 'ɔpˌrɛtə]
to crush, to squash (~ a bug)	å knuse	[ɔ 'knʉsə]
to cry (weep)	å gråte	[ɔ 'groːtə]
to cut off (with a knife)	å skjære av	[ɔ 'ʂæːrə ɑː]

253. Verbs D-G

to dare (~ to do sth)	å våge	[ɔ 'voːgə]
to date from ...	å datere seg	[ɔ dɑ'terə sæj]
to deceive (vi, vt)	å fuske	[ɔ 'fʉskə]
to decide (~ to do sth)	å beslutte	[ɔ be'ʂlʉtə]

to decorate (tree, street)	å pryde	[ɔ 'prydə]
to dedicate (book, etc.)	å tilegne	[ɔ 'tilˌegnə]
to defend (a country, etc.)	å forsvare	[ɔ fɔ'ʂvarə]
to defend oneself	å forsvare seg	[ɔ fɔ'ʂvarə sæj]

to demand (request firmly)	å kreve	[ɔ 'krevə]
to denounce (vt)	å angi	[ɔ 'anˌji]
to deny (vt)	å fornekte	[ɔ fɔː'ŋɛktə]
to depend on ...	å avhenge av ...	[ɔ 'avˌheŋə ɑː ...]
to deprive (vt)	å berøve	[ɔ be'røvə]

to deserve (vt)	å fortjene	[ɔ fo'tjenə]
to design (machine, etc.)	å prosjektere	[ɔ pruʂɛk'terə]
to desire (want, wish)	å ønske	[ɔ 'ønskə]
to despise (vt)	å forakte	[ɔ fo'raktə]

to destroy (documents, etc.)	å ødelegge	[ɔ 'ødə,legə]
to differ (from sth)	å skille seg fra ...	[ɔ 'ʂilə sæej fra ...]
to dig (tunnel, etc.)	å grave	[ɔ 'gravə]
to direct (point the way)	å vise vei	[ɔ 'visə væj]

to disappear (vi)	å forsvinne	[ɔ fo'ʂvinə]
to discover (new land, etc.)	å oppdage	[ɔ 'ɔp,dagə]
to discuss (vt)	å diskutere	[ɔ disku'terə]
to distribute (leaflets, etc.)	å dele ut	[ɔ 'delə ʉt]

to disturb (vt)	å forstyrre	[ɔ fo'ʂtyrə]
to dive (vi)	å dykke	[ɔ 'dykə]
to divide (math)	å dividere	[ɔ divi'derə]
to do (vt)	å gjøre	[ɔ 'jørə]

to do the laundry	å vaske	[ɔ 'vaskə]
to double (increase)	å fordoble	[ɔ for'doblə]
to doubt (have doubts)	å tvile	[ɔ 'tvilə]
to draw a conclusion	å konkludere	[ɔ kʉnklʉ'derə]

to dream (daydream)	å drømme	[ɔ 'drœmə]
to dream (in sleep)	å drømme	[ɔ 'drœmə]
to drink (vi, vt)	å drikke	[ɔ 'drikə]
to drive a car	å kjøre bil	[ɔ 'çœːrə ,bil]
to drive away (scare away)	å jage bort	[ɔ 'jagə 'bʉːt]

to drop (let fall)	å tappe	[ɔ 'tapə]
to drown (ab. person)	å drukne	[ɔ 'drʉknə]
to dry (clothes, hair)	å tørke	[ɔ 'tœrkə]
to eat (vi, vt)	å spise	[ɔ 'spisə]

to eavesdrop (vi)	å tyvlytte	[ɔ 'tyv,lytə]
to emit (diffuse - odor, etc.)	å spre, å sprede	[ɔ 'sprej], [ɔ 'spredə]
to enjoy oneself	å more seg	[ɔ 'mʉrə sæj]
to enter (on the list)	å skrive inn	[ɔ 'skrivə in]

to enter (room, house, etc.)	å komme inn	[ɔ 'kɔmə in]
to entertain (amuse)	å underholde	[ɔ 'ʉnər,holə]
to equip (fit out)	å utstyre	[ɔ 'ʉt,styrə]
to examine (proposal)	å undersøke	[ɔ 'ʉnə,ʂøkə]

to exchange (sth)	å utveksle	[ɔ 'ʉt,vɛkslə]
to excuse (forgive)	å unnskylde	[ɔ 'ʉn,sylə]
to exist (vi)	å eksistere	[ɔ ɛksi'sterə]
to expect (anticipate)	å forvente	[ɔ for'vɛntə]

to expect (foresee)	å forutse	[ɔ 'forʉt,sə]
to expel (from school, etc.)	å uteslutte	[ɔ 'ʉtə,slʉtə]
to explain (vt)	å forklare	[ɔ for'klarə]
to express (vt)	å uttrykke	[ɔ 'ʉt,rykə]
to extinguish (a fire)	å slokke	[ɔ 'ʂløkə]

to fall in love (with ...)	å forelske seg i ...	[ɔ fɔ'rɛlskə sæj i ...]
to fancy (vt)	å like	[ɔ 'likə]
to feed (provide food)	å mate	[ɔ 'matə]

to fight (against the enemy)	å kjempe	[ɔ 'çɛmpə]
to fight (vi)	å slåss	[ɔ 'ṣlɔs]
to fill (glass, bottle)	å fylle	[ɔ 'fʏlə]
to find (~ lost items)	å finne	[ɔ 'finə]

to finish (vt)	å slutte	[ɔ 'ṣlʉtə]
to fish (angle)	å fiske	[ɔ 'fiskə]
to fit (ab. dress, etc.)	å passe	[ɔ 'pasə]
to flatter (vt)	å smigre	[ɔ 'smigrə]

to fly (bird, plane)	å fly	[ɔ 'fly]
to follow ... (come after)	å følge etter ...	[ɔ 'følə 'ɛtər ...]
to forbid (vt)	å forby	[ɔ fɔr'by]
to force (compel)	å tvinge	[ɔ 'tviŋə]

to forget (vi, vt)	å glemme	[ɔ 'glemə]
to forgive (pardon)	å tilgi	[ɔ 'tilˌji]
to form (constitute)	å danne, å forme	[ɔ 'danə], [ɔ 'fɔrmə]
to get dirty (vi)	å skitne seg til	[ɔ 'ṣitnə sæj til]

to get infected (with ...)	å bli smittet	[ɔ 'bli 'smitət]
to get irritated	å bli irritert	[ɔ 'bli iri'tɛːt]
to get married	å gifte seg	[ɔ 'jiftə sæj]
to get rid of ...	å bli kvitt ...	[ɔ 'bli 'kvit ...]

to get tired	å bli trett	[ɔ 'bli 'trɛt]
to get up (arise from bed)	å stå opp	[ɔ 'stɔː ɔp]
to give (vt)	å gi	[ɔ 'ji]
to give a bath (to bath)	å bade	[ɔ 'badə]

to give a hug, to hug (vt)	å omfavne	[ɔ 'ɔmˌfavnə]
to give in (yield to)	å gi etter	[ɔ 'ji 'ɛtər]
to glimpse (vt)	å bemerke	[ɔ be'mærkə]
to go (by car, etc.)	å kjøre	[ɔ 'çœːrə]

to go (on foot)	å gå	[ɔ 'gɔ]
to go for a swim	å bade	[ɔ 'badə]
to go out (for dinner, etc.)	å gå ut	[ɔ 'gɔ ʉt]
to go to bed (go to sleep)	å gå til sengs	[ɔ 'gɔ til 'sɛŋs]

to greet (vt)	å hilse	[ɔ 'hilsə]
to grow (plants)	å avle	[ɔ 'avlə]
to guarantee (vt)	å garantere	[ɔ garan'terə]
to guess (the answer)	å gjette	[ɔ 'jɛtə]

254. Verbs H-M

to hand out (distribute)	å dele ut	[ɔ 'delə ʉt]
to hang (curtains, etc.)	å henge	[ɔ 'hɛŋə]
to have (vt)	å ha	[ɔ 'ha]

| to have a bath | å vaske seg | [ɔ 'vɑskə sæj] |
| to have a try | å forsøke | [ɔ fɔ'søkə] |

to have breakfast	å spise frokost	[ɔ 'spisə ˌfrʉkɔst]
to have dinner	å spise middag	[ɔ 'spisə 'miˌdɑ]
to have lunch	å spise lunsj	[ɔ 'spisə ˌlʉnʂ]
to head (group, etc.)	å lede	[ɔ 'ledə]
to hear (vt)	å høre	[ɔ 'hørə]

to heat (vt)	å varme	[ɔ 'vɑrmə]
to help (vt)	å hjelpe	[ɔ 'jɛlpə]
to hide (vt)	å gjemme	[ɔ 'jɛmə]
to hire (e.g. ~ a boat)	å leie	[ɔ 'læjə]
to hire (staff)	å ansette	[ɔ 'anˌsɛtə]

to hope (vi, vt)	å håpe	[ɔ 'hoːpə]
to hunt (for food, sport)	å jage	[ɔ 'jagə]
to hurry (vi)	å skynde seg	[ɔ 'ʂynə sæj]
to imagine (to picture)	å forestille seg	[ɔ 'fɔrəˌstilə sæj]
to imitate (vt)	å imitere	[ɔ imi'terə]

to implore (vt)	å bønnefalle	[ɔ 'bœnəˌfalə]
to import (vt)	å importere	[ɔ impɔ:'terə]
to increase (vi)	å øke	[ɔ 'økə]
to increase (vt)	å øke	[ɔ 'økə]
to infect (vt)	å smitte	[ɔ 'smitə]

to influence (vt)	å påvirke	[ɔ 'poˌvirkə]
to inform (e.g. ~ the police about ...)	å meddele	[ɔ 'mɛdˌdelə]
to inform (vt)	å informere	[ɔ infɔr'merə]
to inherit (vt)	å arve	[ɔ 'arvə]
to inquire (about ...)	å få vite	[ɔ 'fɔ 'vitə]

to insert (put in)	å sette inn	[ɔ 'sɛtə in]
to insinuate (imply)	å insinuere	[ɔ insinʉ'erə]
to insist (vi, vt)	å insistere	[ɔ insi'sterə]
to inspire (vt)	å inspirere	[ɔ inspi'rerə]
to instruct (teach)	å instruere	[ɔ instrʉ'erə]

to insult (offend)	å fornærme	[ɔ fɔ:'ŋærmə]
to interest (vt)	å interessere	[ɔ intərə'serə]
to intervene (vi)	å intervenere	[ɔ intərve'nerə]
to introduce (sb to sb)	å presentere	[ɔ presen'terə]

to invent (machine, etc.)	å oppfinne	[ɔ 'ɔpˌfinə]
to invite (vt)	å innby, å invitere	[ɔ 'inby], [ɔ invi'terə]
to iron (clothes)	å stryke	[ɔ 'strykə]
to irritate (annoy)	å irritere	[ɔ iri'terə]
to isolate (vt)	å isolere	[ɔ isʉ'lerə]

to join (political party, etc.)	å tilslutte seg ...	[ɔ 'tilˌslʉtə sæj ...]
to joke (be kidding)	å spøke	[ɔ 'spøkə]
to keep (old letters, etc.)	å beholde	[ɔ be'hɔlə]
to keep silent, to hush	å tie	[ɔ 'tie]
to kill (vt)	å døde, å myrde	[ɔ 'dødə], [ɔ 'mʏːdə]

to knock (on the door)	å knakke	[ɔ 'knakə]
to know (sb)	å kjenne	[ɔ 'çɛnə]
to know (sth)	å vite	[ɔ 'vitə]
to laugh (vi)	å le, å skratte	[ɔ 'le], [ɔ 'skratə]
to launch (start up)	å starte	[ɔ 'sta:tə]
to leave (~ for Mexico)	å afrejse	[ɔ 'af͵ræjsə]
to leave (forget sth)	å glemme	[ɔ 'glemə]
to leave (spouse)	å forlate, å etterlate	[ɔ fɔ'latə], [ɔ ɛtə'latə]
to liberate (city, etc.)	å befri	[ɔ be'fri]
to lie (~ on the floor)	å ligge	[ɔ 'ligə]
to lie (tell untruth)	å lyve	[ɔ 'lyvə]
to light (campfire, etc.)	å tenne	[ɔ 'tɛnə]
to light up (illuminate)	å belyse	[ɔ be'lysə]
to limit (vt)	å begrense	[ɔ be'grɛnsə]
to listen (vi)	å lye, å lytte	[ɔ 'lye], [ɔ 'lʏtə]
to live (~ in France)	å bo	[ɔ 'bʊ]
to live (exist)	å leve	[ɔ 'levə]
to load (gun)	å lade	[ɔ 'ladə]
to load (vehicle, etc.)	å laste	[ɔ 'lastə]
to look (I'm just ~ing)	å se	[ɔ 'se]
to look for ... (search)	å søke ...	[ɔ 'søkə ...]
to look like (resemble)	å ligne, å likne	[ɔ 'linə], [ɔ 'liknə]
to lose (umbrella, etc.)	å miste	[ɔ 'mistə]
to love (e.g. ~ dancing)	å elske	[ɔ 'ɛlskə]
to love (sb)	å elske	[ɔ 'ɛlskə]
to lower (blind, head)	å heise ned	[ɔ 'hæjsə ne]
to make (~ dinner)	å lage	[ɔ 'lagə]
to make a mistake	å gjøre feil	[ɔ 'jørə ͵fæjl]
to make angry	å gjøre sint	[ɔ 'jørə ͵sint]
to make easier	å lette	[ɔ 'letə]
to make multiple copies	å kopiere	[ɔ kʊ'pjerə]
to make the acquaintance	å stifte bekjentskap med ...	[ɔ 'stiftə be'çɛn͵skap me ...]
to make use (of ...)	å anvende	[ɔ 'an͵vɛnə]
to manage, to run	å styre, å lede	[ɔ 'styrə], [ɔ 'ledə]
to mark (make a mark)	å markere	[ɔ mar'kerə]
to mean (signify)	å bety	[ɔ 'bety]
to memorize (vt)	å memorere	[ɔ memʊ'rerə]
to mention (talk about)	å omtale, å nevne	[ɔ 'ɔm͵talə], [ɔ 'nɛvnə]
to miss (school, etc.)	å skulke	[ɔ 'skʉlkə]
to mix (combine, blend)	å blande	[ɔ 'blanə]
to mock (make fun of)	å håne	[ɔ 'ho:nə]
to move (to shift)	å flytte	[ɔ 'flʏtə]
to multiply (math)	å multiplisere	[ɔ mʉltipli'serə]
must (v aux)	å måtte	[ɔ 'mo:tə]

255. Verbs N-R

to name, to call (vt)	å kalle	[ɔ 'kalə]
to negotiate (vi)	å forhandle	[ɔ fɔr'handlə]
to note (write down)	å notere	[ɔ nʉ'terə]
to notice (see)	å bemerke	[ɔ be'mærkə]
to obey (vi, vt)	å underordne seg	[ɔ 'ʉnər‚ɔrdnə sæj]
to object (vi, vt)	å innvende	[ɔ 'in‚vɛnə]
to observe (see)	å observere	[ɔ ɔbsɛr'verə]
to offend (vt)	å fornærme	[ɔ fɔ:'ŋærmə]
to omit (word, phrase)	å utelate	[ɔ 'ʉtə‚latə]
to open (vt)	å åpne	[ɔ 'ɔpnə]
to order (in restaurant)	å bestille	[ɔ be'stilə]
to order (mil.)	å beordre	[ɔ be'ɔrdrə]
to organize (concert, party)	å arrangere	[ɔ araŋ'ʂerə]
to overestimate (vt)	å overvurdere	[ɔ 'ɔvərvʉ:‚derə]
to own (possess)	å besidde, å eie	[ɔ bɛ'sidə], [ɔ 'æjə]
to participate (vi)	å delta	[ɔ 'dɛlta]
to pass through (by car, etc.)	å passere	[ɔ pa'serə]
to pay (vi, vt)	å betale	[ɔ be'talə]
to peep, to spy on	å kikke	[ɔ 'çikə]
to penetrate (vt)	å trenge inn	[ɔ 'trɛŋə in]
to permit (vt)	å tillate	[ɔ 'ti‚latə]
to pick (flowers)	å plukke	[ɔ 'plʉkə]
to place (put, set)	å plassere	[ɔ pla'serə]
to plan (~ to do sth)	å planlegge	[ɔ 'plan‚legə]
to play (actor)	å spille	[ɔ 'spilə]
to play (children)	å leke	[ɔ 'lekə]
to point (~ the way)	å peke	[ɔ 'pekə]
to pour (liquid)	å helle opp	[ɔ 'hɛlə ɔp]
to pray (vi, vt)	å be	[ɔ 'be]
to prefer (vt)	å foretrekke	[ɔ 'fɔrə‚trɛkə]
to prepare (~ a plan)	å forberede	[ɔ 'fɔrbə‚redə]
to present (sb to sb)	å presentere	[ɔ presen'terə]
to preserve (peace, life)	å bevare	[ɔ be'varə]
to prevail (vt)	å dominere	[ɔ dʉmi'nerə]
to progress (move forward)	å gå framover	[ɔ 'gɔ ‚fram'ɔvər]
to promise (vt)	å love	[ɔ 'lɔvə]
to pronounce (vt)	å uttale	[ɔ 'ʉt‚talə]
to propose (vt)	å foreslå	[ɔ 'fɔrə‚ʂlɔ]
to protect (e.g. ~ nature)	å beskytte	[ɔ be'ʂytə]
to protest (vi)	å protestere	[ɔ prʉte'sterə]
to prove (vt)	å bevise	[ɔ be'visə]
to provoke (vt)	å provosere	[ɔ prʉvu'serə]
to pull (~ the rope)	å trekke	[ɔ 'trɛkə]
to punish (vt)	å straffe	[ɔ 'strafə]

to push (~ the door)	å skubbe, å støte	[ɔ 'skɵbə], [ɔ 'støtə]
to put away (vt)	å stue unna	[ɔ 'stɵə 'ɵna]
to put in order	å bringe orden	[ɔ 'briŋə 'ɔrdən]
to put, to place	å legge	[ɔ 'legə]

to quote (cite)	å sitere	[ɔ si'terə]
to reach (arrive at)	å nå	[ɔ 'nɔː]
to read (vi, vt)	å lese	[ɔ 'lesə]
to realize (a dream)	å realisere	[ɔ reali'serə]
to recognize (identify sb)	å gjenkjenne	[ɔ 'jen̩çɛnə]

to recommend (vt)	å anbefale	[ɔ 'anbe̩falə]
to recover (~ from flu)	å bli frisk	[ɔ 'bli 'frisk]
to redo (do again)	å gjøre om	[ɔ 'jørə ɔm]
to reduce (speed, etc.)	å minske	[ɔ 'minskə]

to refuse (~ sb)	å avslå	[ɔ 'af̩slɔ]
to regret (be sorry)	å beklage	[ɔ be'klagə]
to reinforce (vt)	å styrke	[ɔ 'styrkə]
to remember (Do you ~ me?)	å huske	[ɔ 'hɵskə]

to remember (I can't ~ her name)	å huske	[ɔ 'hɵskə]
to remind of ...	å påminne	[ɔ 'po̩minə]
to remove (~ a stain)	å fjerne	[ɔ 'fjæːŋə]
to remove (~ an obstacle)	å fjerne	[ɔ 'fjæːŋə]

to rent (sth from sb)	å leie	[ɔ 'læjə]
to repair (mend)	å reparere	[ɔ repa'rerə]
to repeat (say again)	å gjenta	[ɔ 'jɛnta]
to report (make a report)	å rapportere	[ɔ rapɔː'ʈerə]

to reproach (vt)	å bebreide	[ɔ be'bræjdə]
to reserve, to book	å reservere	[ɔ resɛr'verə]
to restrain (hold back)	å avholde	[ɔ 'av̩hɔlə]
to return (come back)	å komme tilbake	[ɔ 'kɔmə til'bakə]

to risk, to take a risk	å risikere	[ɔ risi'kerə]
to rub out (erase)	å viske ut	[ɔ 'viskə ɵt]
to run (move fast)	å løpe	[ɔ 'løpə]
to rush (hurry sb)	å skynde	[ɔ 'ʂynə]

256. Verbs S-W

to satisfy (please)	å tilfredsstille	[ɔ 'tilfrɛds̩stilə]
to save (rescue)	å redde	[ɔ 'rɛdə]
to say (~ thank you)	å si	[ɔ 'si]
to scold (vt)	å skjelle	[ɔ 'ʂɛːlə]

to scratch (with claws)	å klore	[ɔ 'klɔrə]
to select (to pick)	å velge ut	[ɔ 'vɛlgə ɵt]
to sell (goods)	å selge	[ɔ 'sɛlə]
to send (a letter)	å sende	[ɔ 'sɛnə]
to send back (vt)	å sende tilbake	[ɔ 'sɛnə til'bakə]

to sense (~ danger)	å kjenne	[ɔ 'çɛnə]
to sentence (vt)	å dømme	[ɔ 'dœmə]
to serve (in restaurant)	å betjene	[ɔ be'tjenə]
to settle (a conflict)	å løse	[ɔ 'løsə]
to shake (vt)	å riste	[ɔ 'ristə]
to shave (vi)	å barbere seg	[ɔ bɑr'berə sæj]
to shine (gleam)	å skinne	[ɔ 'ʂinə]
to shiver (with cold)	å skjelve	[ɔ 'ʂɛlvə]
to shoot (vi)	å skyte	[ɔ 'ʂytə]
to shout (vi)	å skrike	[ɔ 'skrikə]
to show (to display)	å vise	[ɔ 'visə]
to shudder (vi)	å gyse	[ɔ 'jisə]
to sigh (vi)	å sukke	[ɔ 'sʉkə]
to sign (document)	å underskrive	[ɔ 'ʉnəˌskrivə]
to signify (mean)	å bety	[ɔ 'bety]
to simplify (vt)	å forenkle	[ɔ fɔ'rɛnklə]
to sin (vi)	å synde	[ɔ 'sʏnə]
to sit (be sitting)	å sitte	[ɔ 'sitə]
to sit down (vi)	å sette seg	[ɔ 'sɛtə sæj]
to smell (emit an odor)	å lukte	[ɔ 'lʉktə]
to smell (inhale the odor)	å lukte	[ɔ 'lʉktə]
to smile (vi)	å smile	[ɔ 'smilə]
to snap (vi, ab. rope)	å gå i stykker	[ɔ 'gɔ i 'stʏkər]
to solve (problem)	å løse	[ɔ 'løsə]
to sow (seed, crop)	å så	[ɔ 'sɔ]
to spill (liquid)	å spille	[ɔ 'spilə]
to spill out, scatter (flour, etc.)	å bli spilt	[ɔ 'bli 'spilt]
to spit (vi)	å spytte	[ɔ 'spʏtə]
to stand (toothache, cold)	å tåle	[ɔ 'to:lə]
to start (begin)	å begynne	[ɔ be'jinə]
to steal (money, etc.)	å stjele	[ɔ 'stjelə]
to stop (for pause, etc.)	å stoppe	[ɔ 'stɔpə]
to stop (please ~ calling me)	å slutte	[ɔ 'ʂlʉtə]
to stop talking	å slutte å snakke	[ɔ 'ʂlʉtə ɔ 'snakə]
to stroke (caress)	å stryke	[ɔ 'strykə]
to study (vt)	å studere	[ɔ stʉ'derə]
to suffer (feel pain)	å lide	[ɔ 'lidə]
to support (cause, idea)	å støtte	[ɔ 'stœtə]
to suppose (assume)	å anta, å formode	[ɔ 'anˌtɑ], [ɔ fɔr'mʉdə]
to surface (ab. submarine)	å dykke opp	[ɔ 'dʏkə ɔp]
to surprise (amaze)	å forundre	[ɔ fɔ'rʉndrə]
to suspect (vt)	å mistenke	[ɔ 'misˌtɛnkə]
to swim (vi)	å svømme	[ɔ 'svœmə]
to take (get hold of)	å ta	[ɔ 'tɑ]
to take a rest	å hvile	[ɔ 'vilə]

to take away (e.g. about waiter)	å fjerne	[ɔ 'fjæːŋə]
to take off (aeroplane)	å løfte	[ɔ 'lœftə]
to take off (painting, curtains, etc.)	å ta ned	[ɔ 'tɑ ne]
to take pictures	å fotografere	[ɔ fotɔgrɑ'ferə]
to talk to ...	å tale med ...	[ɔ 'tɑlə me ...]
to teach (give lessons)	å undervise	[ɔ 'ʉnər‚visə]
to tear off, to rip off (vt)	å rive av	[ɔ 'rivə ɑː]
to tell (story, joke)	å fortelle	[ɔ fɔː'tɛlə]
to thank (vt)	å takke	[ɔ 'tɑkə]
to think (believe)	å tro	[ɔ 'trʊ]
to think (vi, vt)	å tenke	[ɔ 'tɛnkə]
to threaten (vt)	å true	[ɔ 'trʉə]
to throw (stone, etc.)	å kaste	[ɔ 'kɑstə]
to tie to ...	å binde fast	[ɔ 'binə 'fɑst]
to tie up (prisoner)	å binde	[ɔ 'binə]
to tire (make tired)	å trette	[ɔ 'trɛtə]
to touch (one's arm, etc.)	å røre	[ɔ 'rørə]
to tower (over ...)	å rage over	[ɔ 'rɑgə 'ɔvər]
to train (animals)	å dressere	[ɔ drɛ'serə]
to train (sb)	å trene	[ɔ 'trenə]
to train (vi)	å trene	[ɔ 'trenə]
to transform (vt)	å transformere	[ɔ trɑnsfɔr'merə]
to translate (vt)	å oversette	[ɔ 'ɔvə‚sɛtə]
to treat (illness)	å behandle	[ɔ be'hɑndlə]
to trust (vt)	å stole på	[ɔ 'stʉlə pɔ]
to try (attempt)	å prøve	[ɔ 'prøvə]
to turn (e.g., ~ left)	å svinge	[ɔ 'sviŋə]
to turn away (vi)	å vende seg bort	[ɔ 'vɛnə sæj bʊːt]
to turn off (the light)	å slokke	[ɔ 'ʂløkə]
to turn on (computer, etc.)	å slå på	[ɔ 'ʂlɔ pɔ]
to turn over (stone, etc.)	å vende	[ɔ 'vɛnə]
to underestimate (vt)	å undervurdere	[ɔ 'ʉnərvʉː‚derə]
to underline (vt)	å understreke	[ɔ 'ʉnə‚strekə]
to understand (vt)	å forstå	[ɔ fɔ'ʂtɔ]
to undertake (vt)	å foreta	[ɔ 'fɔrə‚tɑ]
to unite (vt)	å forene	[ɔ fɔ'renə]
to untie (vt)	å løse opp	[ɔ 'løsə ɔp]
to use (phrase, word)	å anvende	[ɔ 'ɑn‚vɛnə]
to vaccinate (vt)	å vaksinere	[ɔ vɑksi'nerə]
to vote (vi)	å stemme	[ɔ 'stɛmə]
to wait (vt)	å vente	[ɔ 'vɛntə]
to wake (sb)	å vekke	[ɔ 'vɛkə]
to want (wish, desire)	å ville	[ɔ 'vilə]
to warn (of a danger)	å advare	[ɔ 'ɑd‚vɑrə]

to wash (clean)	å vaske	[ɔ 'vɑskə]
to water (plants)	å vanne	[ɔ 'vɑnə]
to wave (the hand)	å vinke	[ɔ 'vinkə]
to weigh (have weight)	å veie	[ɔ 'væjə]
to work (vi)	å arbeide	[ɔ 'ɑrˌbæjdə]
to worry (make anxious)	å bekymre, å uroe	[ɔ be'çymrə], [ɔ 'ʉːrʊə]
to worry (vi)	å uroe seg	[ɔ 'ʉːrʊə sæj]
to wrap (parcel, etc.)	å pakke inn	[ɔ 'pɑkə in]
to wrestle (sport)	å bryte	[ɔ 'brytə]
to write (vt)	å skrive	[ɔ 'skrivə]
to write down	å skrive ned	[ɔ 'skrivə ne]